MW00488523

the RESCUER

The RESCUER

FIRST EDITION

Copyright 2022 Rich Ulrich

Library of Congress Control Number: 2022933726

Hardcover ISBN: 978-1-7369334-9-7

Paperback ISBN: 978-1-7369334-7-3

eBook ISBN: 978-1-7369334-8-0

Book designed by Mark Karis

Printed in the United States of America

the RESCUER

fixing himself for a better us

RICH ULRICH, MHA

SHENANDOAH
PRESS

"The Rescuer: Fixing Himself for a Better Us" is my gift to you three wonderful children. A pathway on how to live for others. You are my greatest gift! It is an honor to be your father. I love you.

CONTENTS

FOREWORD

BY RON DEPOMPA
CHIEF OF POLICE (RET.), GLENDALE CALIFORNIA

Rich joined our department in 1989. I came to know him in the mid-nineties when he began taking administration of justice classes at Glendale Community College (GCC). I was a captain and guest lecturer for adjunct faculty. Shortly after that time, I joined the faculty at GCC. After Rich became a certified Drug Recognition Expert (DRE), I had him substitute for my drug class. My students highly praised Rich's teaching. Rich joined our department's teaching core for our Drug Abuse Recognition (DAR) program. Under the tutelage of Officer Lorenz, Rich became a certified instructor with the California Department of Justice and the International Association of Chiefs of Police DRE programs.

Rich taught throughout the state of California, nationwide police agencies, parole and pardon bureaus, drug courts, US military, Department of Defense, Homeland Security, Health and Human Services, addiction specialists, became a testing officer for the National Highway Traffic Safety Administration (NHTSA), the US Coast Guard (impaired boating sobriety testing), and for private corporations. He eventually became a board member for a pharmaceutical manufacturer that developed anti-microbials. He worked with the ministry of the Congo and Dr. Oketch in West Africa during the Ebola crisis in 2014. He and Doctor Chapman, MD, developed a testing protocol for patients in the Ebola Treatment Units (ETU's) in Liberia and Sierra Leone with Biocence administration.

Despite all of his involved projects, he never neglected his duties with our department. Rich's heart to serve and inspire others lead him into many of the aforementioned areas. Rich was always looking for ways to improve our training and the development of our personnel. Over his tenure with us, he trained thirty-six officers, and many became our current leaders of our agency today.

After Rich retired, he decided to go back to college where he obtained a degree in criminal justice to place a capstone on his career. He then was accepted into USC Sole Price School of Public Policy where he graduated with his master's degree in health administration. I was honored to write his recommendation to the selection board. Rich graduated the program with honors.

Rich faced some severe atrocities growing up and in his adult life. Despite this, he never wavered, served in the military, and became a man of high integrity. Over the many years I have had the pleasure of knowing Rich, he has always demonstrated a thirst for knowledge and a desire to excel. However, this drive has always been focused on the goal of helping and lifting others up. Rich is one of the most humble, selfless professionals I have ever worked with. Throughout his life's journey he has experienced many lessons and gained much wisdom and is now excited to share his insights with others.

Rich's book is nothing short of inspiring to those who have faced tragedy, disappointment and hopelessness and are looking for ways to overcome and find a pathway to success. *The Rescuer: Fixing Himself for a Better Us* is written by someone who lives what he believes. This book will change your life!

Rich and police chief Ron DePompa (*left*), at Rich's retirement, December 2013 (Author's collection)

PREFACE

"What to do when we find ourselves at that crossroads where the subject of retirement becomes impossible to ignore. You will learn about how to clarify your mastery and replant it in a new garden, so that it can be harvested for many years to come."

—CHIP CONLEY

RE-INVENTING MYSELF

Here I was in my fifties, a single parent, forced to retire, no college degree, no home, poor family relations, and suffering from intense physical and emotional pain. Where do I start? How do I begin?

Chip Conley, in his book, *Wisdom at Work: The Making of a Modern Elder*, speaks about change and re-invention as a costume that we may need to change into at some point in our lives:

> Sometimes we get a shock to the system that wakes us up and tells us it's time to evolve. For some, that can be a health scare that reminds us our time is precious. For others, it can be the end of a marriage, losing our job, or the approach of a milestone birthday. Yet in the absence of alarm clock events like these, it can be hard to muster the courage and motivation to shed a costume that has historically fit us so perfectly. If you're feeling like you're easing into the winter of your life but want to remember what it's like to be in midsummer, you

might consider seeking out an internship as a low-risk way to try on a new costume or identity.[1]

I took on several internships during my adventure of fixing myself while attending colleges, completing two degrees, and volunteering with the administration of a hospital. I had worn the costume of *rescuer* most of my life. I knew that in order to be successful in this change, I would need a new costume or costumes. I realized that some of these costumes would be ones I had never worn before and some that I had temporarily worn in the past. Forgiveness and servitude appeared to be my starting point costumes. On my journey, I realized that these two costumes earned me the greatest respect from others and were keys that opened up the doors of opportunity for an amazing life (see chapter 9, Forgiveness). It is my hope that after reading my life's journey, you will realize that I am no better than anyone else and that I made mistakes just like you. We all do. I failed at things, and I excelled at things—but I am far from perfect. I hope you will ask yourself the same question I did: "Where do I go from here?"

MARY RUTH CHAPIN

Grandmothers can have a special place in a child's life. For me, it was my Gram, Mary Ruth Chapin. Gram was from the town of Ottumwa, Iowa. She became her high school class president and even wrote her Ottumwa High School song.

Shortly after graduating from high school, Gram took a job at the US Treasury Department where she met her husband, who was a bank examiner. She told me about attending Washington Senator baseball games. She loved when the Yankees came to town for games so she could watch Babe Ruth, Lou Gehrig, and Joe Di Maggio play at Griffith Stadium.

Gram eventually moved to Southern California after my uncle's health required him to be in warmer climate. My mother was born

---

1 Chip Conley, *Wisdom at Work: The Making of a Modern Elder* (New York: Crown Publishing Group, 2018),

in Inglewood, California, and the family eventually settled in El Sereno, California.

My sister and I spent many weekends at Gram's El Sereno home. We enjoyed cooking meals with Gram and playing in her backyard and in plastic pools we had set up in different places in her backyard. I loved waking up for the milkman, who delivered the butter, eggs, milk, and ice cream to her house. Gram taught me how to dance the waltz as we

Rich and Gram in El Monte, CA 1963 (Author's collection)

listened to her album collection from the 1930-40s. We listened to Old-Time Radio stories as we sat around the radio in the dining room. You would have to use your imagination as you listened to these amazing storytellers. I set up my play train on her dining room table. We ate our meals on TV trays or card tables. When our parents came to get us, we didn't want to leave. When my father was murdered, Gram gave up her career and retired early to help my mother raise my sister and me. Gram prayed for us every day when we left our home. This became an everyday ritual. I remember she told me that when she prayed for me, she felt as though my life was spared in order to help others in the future. I clung to that belief my entire life.

When I told her that I wanted to enlist into the Air Force and they denied my enlistment for medical reasons (childhood asthma), she prayed for me. She told me that I would be accepted. It was not long afterward that an Air Force commercial came on the television. She knew I was going to make it into the military. During my entire military service, Gram sent me letters of encouragement every week. She never forgot. I shared these letters with other military members who had no family. Gram was with me in spirit and truth throughout my journey. I included her in the preface of my life's voyage because she laid the foundation of who I became in life and the principles and morals for which I lived. I know that *fixing myself for a better us* would be an anthem she would have believed for me. So, Gram, here's the answer to your prayers: My life and its *journey of courage,* a way to thank you for sacrificing your personal life and career to help me and our family in crisis.

MOVE! THE TRAIN IS COMING!

Officer Trudeau and I were dispatched to Sonora Avenue and the railroad tracks to check the well-being of a driver whose car was seen driving on the railroad tracks. When we arrived on scene, we saw that the driver was trying to free the vehicle from the rails but was unsuccessful. We each were driving a patrol car and pulled onto the ballast (the rocks the rails are situated upon) near the tracks. We stopped just short of the stuck car and called out to the driver who exited the vehicle. The man had to hold on to the driver's door to stand. As we got closer to the male, we could smell the alcohol emitting from him. We tried to escort him away from the tracks, but he wanted to fight with us. The three of us were struggling to stay balanced on the loose gravel around the tracks. Officer Trudeau requested police dispatch notify the railroad authority to stop all rail traffic in both directions until we could remove his vehicle from the tracks.

As soon as he made the request, we heard the sound of a train horn in the distance. Our police cars were too close to the rails. We had to get them away from the tracks but were busy trying to control the intoxicated man. The man kept swinging at us with his closed fists while we were trying to grab his arms to try and control him so he could be safely detained. We eventually were able to handcuff him on the ground. As all three of us were down, I could see the lights of the approaching train coming toward us. We brought the man to his feet. With great difficulty we were able to move him off the tracks and over to where I could handcuff him to a chain-link fence. We ran to our police cars, which were going to be struck by the train if we left them there. The train showed no signs of slowing down and now was sounding its horn. I hopped into my patrol car and started the engine.

Officer Trudeau's car was in front of mine, and he accelerated too fast. His left rear tire began to spin as he lost traction. He was not going anywhere. I kept looking in my rear-view mirror and saw the train approaching and becoming larger in my rear and side views. I was sure I was going to be killed by the train. I remember thinking to myself, "this is it for me. I saw my children's faces as someone was telling them how their father perished in a train wreck trying to save a man's life. How did I ever become a rescuer?" I asked myself. Just then officer Trudeau's rear tires caught traction, and he was able to turn right and escape. I followed closely behind. I may have even rammed his bumper in the process as the train passed quickly by me and into the suspect's car, which was torn into pieces as the train slowly came to a stop.

Train slams into car
Glendale police Officer James Trudeau and ain conductor B.N. Black check over a car that was hit by the train at San Fernando Road and Sonora Avenue in Glendale late Sunday. The driver of the car, Svetoslav Dragomirov Jivkou, 20, of Burbank was arrested on suspicion of drunk driving after police found him sitting his car, which was stuck on the railroad track, about 10 p.m.

Gene Blevine/Special to the Daily Ne

Article of train incident with officers Trudeau and Ulrich (Courtesy of the *Daily News*, photo by Gene Blevine)

1

MY CHILDHOOD

"Children are likely to live up to what you believe in them."
— LADY BIRD JOHNSON

THE BABY BOOMER
In 1962 the economy of the United States was stable. A gallon of gas cost 28 cents and the average cost of a new home was $12,550.00. John F. Kennedy was President of the United States and Marine Lt. Col. John Glenn was piloting NASA's Mercury Friendship 7 in the first successful orbit of the earth. My parents were at Huntington Memorial Hospital, Pasadena, California, awaiting my arrival and wondering if I would be born during this significant event. They settled for the next morning, February 21, 1962, at 2:30 a.m.

My parents struggled financially at the beginning of their marriage, even with both of them working. Because of my paternal grandfather's harsh criticism of my father, he was determined to become successful by the time he reached his thirtieth birthday. He was approaching millionaire status by then. He owned and operated Ulrich Insurance Services, Inc. with three offices: Los Angeles, San Francisco and San

Diego. He had apartments in each of these cities. I traveled with my father on many of his business trips. It was there that I developed my love for adventure. I became an expert in knowing my way around these towns and developed a decent sense of direction as a result. I loved flying except for the cigarette smoke inside the passenger cabin. I can still recall the stewardesses coming down the isles saying, "Cigars, cigarettes. Coffee, tea, or bullion."

New parents, February 1962 (Photo by Mary Chapin)

Life was good for our family, and we traveled everywhere and anywhere we wanted. My parents loved to camp, and we spent many weekends camping at El Capitan in Santa Barbara, California, in our trailer and eventually our class A motor home.

Most of my childhood years were spent living in Southern California. My mother stayed at home with my sister, Beverly, and me. My father and I had a close relationship and did many father-and-son things together, such as Indian Guides, YMCA, and sports.

My parents hosted parties on a regular basis. My father belonged to the Playboy Diners Club, which afforded him the opportunity to meet many famous people. I remember one time we went to Las Vegas and stayed at the Flamingo Hotel and Casino. My father introduced me to a man who owned the casino. I wonder now if it might have been Jimmy Hoffa.

"The Mohawks" YMCA Indian Guides. Mr. Persinger and his son Jon (*right*), my father and me. (Photo by Dolores Ulrich)

THE SPIRIT OF CHRISTMAS

Life was good for my sister and me. I remember Christmastime at our home. My father would have us write down our Christmas lists and address them to Santa Claus. I must have put down at least twenty things. I could not decide which gift meant the most to me, so I wrote them all down. My mother would bake cookies for Santa and my sister, and I would make sure there was a plate of them with milk waiting for Santa when he arrived at our home. My father went to so much trouble and expense to convince my sister and me of the jolly fat man's existence. One time we were eating at one of the local pizza restaurants when I heard Santa's sleigh bells. My father had previously excused himself to the bathroom and moments later, I heard the jingle jangling sounds of sleigh bells outside the restaurant window. I learned later that my father had snuck out the back of the restaurant and crouched down below the window by our table, so he could shake the bells. My mother was no slouch in the story-telling department either. She would play right along with the scripted scene. She would say, "Well, it sounds like Santa is in the neighborhood." Of course, I could not eat a thing. That was probably not the best thing to say just before we ate. I pulled on my mother's purse and insisted that we go home before Santa came to the house.

We hopped into my father's blue '65 Ford Mustang and sped toward our home in the hills of Glendale. The trip home took too long for a young boy who knew in his infinite wisdom there was no way to beat Santa's jet-fast sleigh. When we arrived home, Dad's car came to a screeching halt in the garage. If you know anything about '65 Mustangs, you have to wait for the occupants in front of you to exit before you can move the front seat forward and out of your way.

As soon as my mother removed herself from the car, I was gone. In a flash I ran into our spacious living room. To my relief, there were just the precious few presents under the tree that were there before we left for dinner. My sister arrived shortly after me, and we concluded together that we needed to fix Santa's snack and place it on one of the tables near the fireplace so Saint Nick would not miss our generosity.

After completing the snack task, our mother checked to make sure everything was in order for Santa. She then yelled, "Okay. Off to bed. Remember, Santa's in the neighborhood!" About that time, I heard the sleigh bells outside near the front yard.

I looked at my sister and excitingly said, "Hurry. Let's go." The two of us ran up the flight of stairs as fast as we could and jumped into our beds. My heart was racing as I lay there in silence. My mother came into my room and said, "You better close your eyes. The elves will be looking into your bedroom window to see if you are sleeping. Santa will not come until you are fast asleep." With those marching orders, I closed my eyes as tight as I could and somehow fell asleep despite all the excitement.

In 1969 Christmas day came at last. It must have been 6:00 a.m. when I jumped out of bed and ran downstairs. I reached the bottom of the stairs and rounded the corner to the left. "Wow!" was my only expression. I thought about *The Wizard of Oz* when Dorothy opens the door to the Land of Oz and everything was in beautiful Technicolor.

That is what I saw that Christmas day. There were presents covering the living room floor. The room was filled with gifts. That was the last Christmas I had with my father.

THE LOSS OF OUR PATRIARCH, MY FATHER

It was March 27, 1970, the day before my sister's sixth birthday. Our parents had made plans to take us to Knotts Berry Farm for the day to celebrate. My father had picked out a new bicycle for my sister and left if at the shop before he had departed for San Diego a few days prior. The goal was to go to the bicycle shop on our way to Knotts. My mother offered to pick up the bicycle early to save him time, but he insisted that he wanted to do it together. My sister and I were excited to take a trip and kept asking our mother "when is Daddy coming home?" My mother had received a call very late the night before from my dad's business partner telling her he had fallen off the back of the boat when they went fishing and members of the Sheriff's Department had been searching for him but were unable to locate him. Our neighbors were aware that my mother was awaiting any news and came over to offer support. They planned a party for my sister as a distraction, but it seemed like something wasn't right. After waiting all day for some hopeful news, our mother realized he was lost and she took my sister and I by the hand and led us upstairs into her bedroom.

We knew something was very wrong when she said that she wanted to talk with us in her room. "I have something very serious to tell you. Your father was out in the ocean on a fishing trip, and he fell off the boat and drowned." I sat on the bed and cried. My sister began asking questions in rapid succession that sped up after each question.

"Where in the ocean is he? What happened to him? When is he coming back?" She finally stopped questioning and began screaming over and over, "The fish are eating my daddy!! The fish are eating my daddy!!"

"We will see him in heaven again," was the comfort my mother offered us.

After this difficult pill was eventually consumed, I had the horrible feeling that I was now an outcast, different than my friends who still had fathers. I knew that my life was about to change forever.

Glendale Man Lost Off Boat

Coast Guard cutters and Navy patrol boats are searching today off San Diego's Point Loma for a Glendale man last seen fishing from his rented cabin cruiser Friday night.

The Coast Guard said the missing man, Richard J. Ulrich Jr., 22, rented a cabin cruiser

with a friend, Sherm, at was at the told authorities he was at the wheel while Ulrich was trolling at the stern. When J looked back, he said Ulrich had disappeared. He said he marked the area with life preservers and returned to a dock to report the incident.

The boats and a helicopter searched through the night and others have joined their efforts. Ulrich is an insurance agent who lives at 951 Pebbleshire Road with his wife, Dolores, and two children — Richard, 8, and Beverly, 6.

The family moved to Glendale four years ago from San Marino.

RICHARD ULRICH JR.

Glendale News-Press, March 28, 1970

The following Christmas my mother had to explain that Santa was based on a person called Saint Nicholas and was formed to give people hope. Santa Clause represented the spirit of giving. I had an idea that his visits were created by my parents but had so much fun, I kept the belief in my heart. My sister eventually figured out Santa's identity.

My mother was a stay-at-home mom until she started nursing school. She had completed her LVN program and was planning to complete the RN program. In addition to schooling, she handled the accounting and payroll in my father's insurance company. I can only imagine the fear that would try and take residence in her heart. It was the following week after learning of my father's drowning that several of my schoolmates had apparently heard what had happened to my dad from other kids in the neighborhood. They kept staring at me on the bus while on our way to school and whispering to one another. No one said hello to me. They ignored me like I had the plague. Finally, I saw my neighbor Jon at school, and he greeted me with, "I heard what happened. My mom told me. I'm sorry." I remember going to the school bathroom and crying. I felt so rejected and alone. I eventually went to class. Rumors had spread like an infection because even the teachers knew. I was late for home period (first class), and the teacher said nothing about my tardiness but just welcomed me to the class.

ELEMENTARY LIFE

In school I would act out as a way of dealing with my lack of self-esteem and pain. I would blow spit wads from straws onto the cafeteria walls. I would also launch food from plastic spoons onto to the same walls with no concern that someone had to eventually clean it up. Those catapulted edible projectiles found their way to the bullies. I really hated bullies and made sure to target them with everything and anything I could launch their way.

We had a football team at Verdugo Woodlands Elementary School. I loved football and made the team despite my asthma. I remember playing another school at Glendale High School's Moyse Field. I was so happy to be a part of a team. I almost caught an interception in the game. It was the first time I did not feel like an outcast. I remember how I felt as I put on the uniform and placed the helmet on my head. I think we won the game! It was a great day for me. I was able to forget that I was different from all the other boys who still had fathers.

One day shortly after my father's death, I awoke in severe pain and unable to move. My doctor ordered an ambulance that transported me to the hospital. It was later determined that I had come down with transient synovitis of the hip. It was so bad that I had to be transported by ambulance to the hospital. Transient synovitis of the hip (TS) is a relatively common disorder in children three to eight years of age with an average annual incidence of 0.2% in the general population. TS is usually confirmed by ruling out other severe causes of symptoms in the hip such as septic arthritis, osteomyelitis, Legg-Perthes' disease, juvenile idiopathic arthritis, fractures and tumors.[1] I remember my mother speaking to

---

1   Asche, S.S., van Rijn, R.M., Bessems, J.H. et al. "What is the clinical course of transient synovitis in children: a systematic review of the literature?" *Chiropr Man Therap* 21, 39 (2013), 21, 39, http://doi.org/10.1186/2045-709X-21-39.

someone on the phone prior to my ambulance transport to the hospital. She explained that she did not have any money to pay for my medical treatment. I was taken to Glendale Adventist Hospital emergency and eventually admitted. I can still remember eating the red Jell-O and looking out the windows at the mountains of Glendale, California. I remember my uncle Carl coming to visit me. I learned later my mother had to be dishonest and say we had insurance in order to get me admitted. I also learned that my uncle Carl paid for my entire medical treatments and hospital bill. (see *Forgiveness* chapter to explain hardship).

Keeping up with the Joneses was not very easy for my mother. She had to work multiple jobs; it was a daunting task. Making house payments and covering other expenses was a challenge. My mother had thirty-two pending lawsuits against her as a corporate officer of the business when it was taken over by the IRS simply due to a bounced check because of the bank accounts being closed. She had lost her savings, and the IRS had already seized all of the family and business assets. It was time for her to rent out our home to make ends meet. Leaving our family home and moving was not easy for any of us.

THE HOOD

We packed up our things and moved in with my grandmother (Mary Ruth Chapin, a.k.a. Gram) in El Sereno, California. Unfortunately, my mother was not aware that this town was slowly being taken over by the Eighteenth Street gang who lived in and around Gram's house.

Eighteenth Street gang is a predominately Hispanic and Central American gang also known as Calle 18, Barrio 18 and Mara 18. It has strong ties to the Mexican mafia and recruits members from El Salvador (where MS-13 originated). Eighteenth Street gang has also been referred to as the Children's Army because they recruit from elementary and middle schools in El Sereno and other East Los Angeles Schools.

Living in El Sereno was not easy since the majority of my schoolmates at Sierra Park Elementary School spoke Spanish. They could say things about me, and I would have no idea what they were saying. I was teased on the playground because I was one of the few white kids at the school.

One day I walked to Gee's, a local neighborhood market, to pick up some ice cream on the way home. About half-way back to Gram's house, I was confronted by three high school boys wearing blue bandanas, flannel shirts, and jeans. They surrounded me on the sidewalk and started making hand signals that I did not understand at the time but now know to be gang signs. They kept asking me, "Who do you run with?" I told them I did not understand what they meant. They shouted, "niño blanco estúpido" (stupid white boy) several times and tried hitting me with a three-foot metal chain. I was standing in front of a chain linked fence, which worked to my advantage. The chain caught the top of the fence that surrounded a neighbor's yard. The kid who swung it at me was forced to move in my direction as the chain shortened and he tried to free it. I used the opportunity to kick him in the crotch. This caused a good distraction, and I was able to run with the other two chasing me. I was about five blocks away from Gram's and was able to outrun them. I made it to Gram's gate, ran into the front yard, and to the front porch area just as the two gang members arrived at the front gate and stopped. They shouted something in Spanish and ran away.

Gram asked me what happened, and I told her the story. My mom was at work and not able to help me. Gram walked out front with her gat, a rubberized stick she carried to protect her from stray dogs when she walked her dog Happy in the neighborhood. She and I watched as the boys walked over to her gardener's home. The boys hung out there until they saw Gram walking over there at a rapid pace. The boys fled as Gram approached. Gram met with her gardener and told him of the encounter. Apparently, the boys were friends with her gardener's son. Gram told him what had happened to me, and he assured Gram that this behavior toward me would stop immediately.

After Gram's trip to her gardener's home, all attacks and harassment by the gang members in the neighborhood ended. Apparently, the gardener's son was a leader in the Eighteenth Street gang. The boys who tried to assault me went to their leaders' home to brag about what they had done to me and eventually found out that I was off limits since I was the grandson of one of his father's clients in the neighborhood.

My mother came home and learned of the story and was determined to move us back to Glendale. We had to wait for our tenant's one-year lease agreement to expire. Meanwhile, I finished up my schooling at Sierra Park Elementary. From then on it was like I had a red light on my head. I was never harassed. In fact, most of the gang members left me alone and actually greeted me as they passed by me in the neighborhood. Despite this free pass, I was still scared and kept a watchful eye out for trouble.

One of our family Portraits (Author's collection)

As the lease of our Glendale home was about to expire, my mother reached out to the family to inform them that we were ready to move back into our home. The family who rented our home refused to leave or give us back our keys. This became another obstacle for my mother. This was another case of others trying to take advantage of a single mother. Nevertheless, we eventually took back our home and moved back to Glendale. This was the turning point of my life. My mother reminded me that one day when we were sitting in the kitchen and she was dealing with lawsuits and working multiple jobs, I told her, "This is just not fair to you. I feel so bad that I can't do anything to help you." I believe it was at this point that I decided that I wanted to be able to rescue people in need.

MIDDLE SCHOOL MADNESS

Leaving elementary school and transitioning to middle school meant leaving behind immaturity in some areas and becoming a more astute person. For me, it became a new way to manipulate others to my way of thinking and fighting the bullies. I learned to lie and hide the truth because I did not know what to do with the truth. I exaggerated about everything to make myself look better than I really was at the time.

I loved all sports. Many of my friends were participating in baseball, basketball, and football. I was not able to play because I was not invited to play, and I was not going to ask my mother for money she did not have for league fees and uniforms. I knew I had to make the best of a situation over which I had no control. Instead, I went to my friends' games and sat on the bleachers fantasizing it was me at the plate or catching the ball for the touchdown or making the last-minute shot into the hoop that won the game. I lied to girls when they asked what I was doing and told them that I had to be at a baseball or football game. They thought I was on the team, and I was not about to correct their misunderstandings and be thought less of a man.

To make matters worse, I was an asthmatic who needed a breathing machine and medicine. I was also allergic to many foods, pollens, dust, and animal hair that caused me to have asthma attacks, welts, and hives all over my body. Whenever I spent the night at a friend's home, I would have to bring along my nebulizer for treatments. Fortunately, our home had a pool, and I was able to improve my fight against asthma by swimming.

FIGHTING THE BULLIES

By middle school I really hated bullies, and many of them rode the bus from Wilson Junior High School to their homes in Glendale. I knew from traveling in the same buses, that they loved to sit in the back and toss things at the back of the other students' heads. They also would punch and kick them. Lord knows there were many days I came home with bruised legs and sore arms from being punched and kicked myself.

I knew a way to pay back these bullies and humiliate them in a way they would never forget. On hot days the bus driver would have all of the windows down for air flow. One nice hot day I left school early with a group of friends (the water balloon brigade). These friends of mine had been victims of the bullies' schemes a few times themselves. We prefilled several dozen balloons with water from the front lawn areas of homes near the junior high school and placed them into our backpacks. We then rode to the top of Glenoaks Boulevard just east of Verdugo Road. That was a difficult feat due to the steep hill. It was an exhausting ride on our bicycles. At the top of the street where the road peaked, there was a stop sign. We hid on a private driveway. We could see the yellow school bus slowly coming up the steep street. Black diesel smoke emitted from the rear of the bus. The noise of the engine was unmistakable. We pulled out our water balloons from our backpacks and placed them into our wrist rockets or sling shots while we waited for the bus to stop at the peak. I gave instructions that the balloons had to be shot as the bus stopped. We each had to aim for a different part of the bus near the back, so we would be sure we hit the bullies with water as the balloons impacted the window frames or by luck entered the bus. The roar of the diesel engine edged closer, and my heart pounded with excitement. I never gave a thought to the consequences of my actions or the chances of the bullies learning who did this to them. The bus reached the peak, and I gave the command, "fire!" We let the balloons fly. They hit their intended targets with a splash. We then ducked out of sight. I heard the bus move forward a little before we heard the sound of the air brakes.

I shouted, "Let's get out of here." With that, we placed the backpacks over our shoulders, mounted our two-wheelers, and raced away from the crime scene. Glenoaks Boulevard was such a steep hill that going down was easy and so was gaining speed. I never remember even stopping at

Verdugo Road. We must have been lucky enough to catch a green signal because I made it safely through the intersection.

We had so much fun that our brigade decided to do it again the next day but with one exception. There was no way we were going to ride our bikes up there again. The next day we hitched a ride home after school and took our motorized minibikes powered by gas powered lawn mower engines to our crime scene. This time, we had to keep an eye out for the Whirly Bird, the Glendale Police helicopter. We sped down Greenbriar Road and headed for Glenoaks Boulevard. On the motorized bikes, it was only a ten-minute ride.

Looking up every so often for Whirly, we kept moving until we arrived at the crest of the hill and parked our bikes. We didn't realize that the bus had already turned the corner right after we crossed Verdugo Road. It may have been a good idea to look behind us as well as up. We barely had time to dismount before the bus arrived, and we only had time to throw the balloons at the bus by hand. We still hit our targets, but this time we were upright a little longer. We could hear the kids yelling in our direction as the balloons exploded. We quickly

Me preparing for my anti bullying campaign. (Author's collection)

mounted our motorized steeds and sped away, looking out for Whirly the entire time. We all made it home with a sigh of relief, but we could see that Whirly had arrived on scene near Glenoaks Boulevard. We ducked inside our homes and headed right to our homework.

Keeping a secret was not a skill possessed by most middle schoolers. It was not long into the snack period the next day (first break) that some of the bullies that were on the bus sought me out and found me at the basketball courts. They knew this is where I hung out with my friends. I was picked out of the lineup, and of course no one from the water balloon brigade was there to back me up. I was not sure if they knew what was about to happen and hid or were busy inside the school. There were no teachers present to stop the altercation. Several of the onlookers pushed me into several of the bullies who punched and kicked me, and I blocked their attacks as they shouted, "You'll never do that to us again, you dick!" I was able to land a couple of good blows before the assistant principal and some teachers moved in our direction to break up the melee. Of course, before the staff arrived, we all broke apart. The staff pleaded with many onlookers as to who was involved. No one cooperated because they wanted to see more fighting after school, and there was no way anyone would mess with the possible rematch.

To my surprise, no one threatened me the rest of the day, and no one "invited" me to the bridge where most of our fights took place after school.

The water balloon brigade turned into a berry brigade. There were trees around the school and throughout the neighborhood that dropped seedlings that were hard and small enough to be more accurate with sling shots and wrist rockets, and they hurt when you were hit by them. This could assure us that we never miss our targets.

Our new brigade changed membership. Now those who refused to stand up and fight when caught or who snitched on us for mischievous deeds were out and those who were well-deserving of such punishment were in. Our next attack strategy involved targeting the bullies as they rode past on their bikes. We hid in the front yards and as they approached, the sound of carob tree pods being crushed by bicycle tires gave them away.

You could also smell the fresh carob emitting from the pods.

As the bullies passed, we hit them in their backs, legs, and heads. The buttocks were the bullseye reserved for the sharpshooters. This caused many of them to stop or nearly fall off their bicycles. They were in such pain and anguish they had a hard time contemplating what was happening to them. Because many of the trees in the area dropped the same seedlings all over the sidewalks, the bullies were confused and thought the seedlings may have fallen from on high. The sight was so hilarious we had a hard time not bursting into laughter. The seeds were much more effective than the water balloons.

It wasn't too long before the vice principal found out about our target practice, and we were called into his office. I still do not know how he found out. We all received five swats for our felonious ways. That wooden paddle hurt. I think I was more frightened about the principal's description of the paddle and seeing it than I was of the anticipated spanking. This ended my career of attacking bullies—for now.

The worst bully I knew was Greg W. He and his father were part of my Y.M.C.A. Indian Guides Tribe when my father was alive. My father was the chief of the group. His Indian name was Thunder Cloud and mine was Little White Cloud. My father and I spent months making an Indian chief head dress with feathers. This thing was beautiful and the envy of several dads and their sons. Greg and his father asked to borrow the headdress one day shortly before my father disappeared. After my father went missing and was presumed dead, my mother and I requested the headdress back, but he and his father refused to return it.

Greg was a tall boy in junior high and one of the bullies. One day he started punching one of my friends, Ron S. I jumped on Greg's back and let him have it. I punched him several times all over his back, head, and face. Distracted by my attack, he stopped attacking Ron and focused on me. He was able to elbow me in the stomach and knock the wind out of me. Greg looked at me and said, "Rich, what are you doing?" I answered, "I don't like my friends being picked on." To my surprise, he said, "Ok," and walked away. I don't think Greg ever picked on anybody else again, or at least I never heard any more about him. I also never saw him again or my headdress.

THE PEBBLESHIRE PIRATES—"SHOW SOME RESPECT"

I lived in a cul-de-sac on Pebbleshire Road in an upper middle-class neighborhood of Glendale, California. I had the best neighbors and most of the homes had swimming pools. There was a group of us in the neighborhood that loved to hang out with one another. We loved to create havoc as long as we never got caught. We overheated our friend's pools to spa temperatures and tossed rocks into other neighbor's pools. We were referred to as the Pebbleshire Pirates. The group was named by Edwin Bowes who came up with the slogan "Show some respect." We would make fists and would cross our arms in front of our chests like the cross bones on a pirate ship flag as we chanted our slogan.

Gun Battle, Kick the Can, Jump the Kids, Ding Dong Ditch, Freestyle Skateboarding, Fake Accidents and Teasing the Local Police were some of the games we enjoyed on our block. We loved when our parents had parties because we would volunteer to tend bar and, of course, taste test the beverages.

We all had cap guns and would have massive gun battles where those who were shot fell off the rooves and onto the grass. It's a wonder none of us ever broke any bones, or our necks, in these battles. The girls in their bell bottom pants played too. Sometimes they were better than the boys in our hang ten shirts and jeans. When the neighborhood girls first wanted to play, most of the boys were against it. I suggested we battle them for supremacy. If they won, they would be allowed to play. They won, and the supremacy war raged on for weeks. I must be honest here; I think the girls won more battles, so we decided to split the sexes in order to win more often.

We played Kick the Can. Basically, it was hide and seek, but any player who was found had to go to jail. If a hiding player could kick a can without getting caught, then all the jailbirds would be set free. We played that game more than most. I remember being really good at hiding and was rarely caught. We used one of those large Folgers and Chock full o'Nuts coffee cans, and we had to replace it every other week from all of the abuse it took.

Several of us built a jump ramp for bikes. We would ask the little kids to lie down on the other side of the ramp and see if we could jump the kids. We became so good that we lined the kids up in a row to see how many we could jump over. Thinking about this now, it was really a

Practice for *jump the kids* (Author's collection)

stupid idea. I am surprised no one was ever hurt by this activity.

Ding Dong Ditch was fun. We picked our victims carefully. We would ring their doorbell and run from the scene. We'd watch the unsuspecting inhabitants look out in frustration as no one was waiting at the front door when they arrived. Some of my friends would light fire to brown paper bags filled with dog excrement. When the occupants opened their front doors, they were met with a bag of fire. On instinct they'd stomp on the bag, and the dung would ooze out onto the front porch or end up on their shoes or both. Tiled porches were the best. The dung would really fly and scoot across the landings with speed. Some of the kids would fill porch fountains with laundry or dish soap before we rang the doorbells.

Greenbriar Road was the large thoroughfare that connected most of the residential streets in our neighborhood and had a steep hill. Those of us daring enough would bomb the hill (ride straight down without stopping or swerving back and forth to slow down). Of course, yours

truly was a dive bomber, and I did not even own a skateboard. I promised my neighborhood friends they could ride my minibike as long as
they allowed me to use their skateboard. I got plenty of road rash from
that stupid activity.

One of the worst pranks we played on our neighbors was our fake
accidents. We would pile our bikes in the middle of the roadway and
pretend to be hurt by laying in the roadway blocking traffic. For effect,
we would use fake blood that we placed on our heads and drooled out
of our mouths. People would stop their cars, get out to check on us,
and call for help on neighbor's telephones. We would lie motionless
until we heard the sirens coming. Then we would all stand up and ride
off in different directions before the police and fire arrived on scene.
We did this only a few times until the neighbors caught on and started
shooing us away or Whirly started patrolling the area.

Halloween was one of my favorite holidays in our neighborhood.
We would take king-size pillowcases from house to house. We'd fill them
up with so many treats they would be too heavy to carry. Although it
was fun to trick and treat, we always had to watch out for the bullies.
The middle school bullies did not disappear; they just became high
schoolers. Now they had cars and could drive into our neighborhood.
They brought the fight to us, and of course I welcomed them with open
arms. They would toss eggs on cars, homes, and even on us. They would
also spray us with water fire extinguishers.

Several of us devised a plan to protect the younger kids, their parents,
the parked cars, and the neighborhood. My friends and I would visit
the markets and be sure that we had plenty of eggs. Some of us even
hid the eggs in our homes so our parents would order more. And we'd
get shaving cream from our parents' medicine cabinets.

We stood at the stop signs of Greenbrier Road and Misty Isle where
the bullies arrived in their hot rods. We would have the little kids cross
in front of their cars, which forced the bullies to yield to pedestrian
traffic. We would use this opportunity to crouch down along the sides
of their cars and spray shaving cream on the passenger doors. On other

occasions we would hide in the bushes, and when they were stopped, we would pelt their cars with eggs. The bullies disappeared for a short time and then returned to the same intersection. One time the bullies must have had a meeting because when they stopped at Greenbriar and Misty Isle, they all took the same defensive position. The passengers immediately jumped out of the cars with fire extinguishers in hand. Fortunately for us there were no cell phones, so they couldn't warn one another when we started pelting them with eggs. The bullies were angry and started yelling. This plan worked because the bullies stopped attacking the small children, their parents, and the homes and parked cars in our neighborhood. They did not return the following year.

My mother took me horseback riding, and I learned to ride English dressage. I entered a few competitions and played a little pollo for fun. I liked pollo, but the dressage riding and jumping did not work well for me. I was thrown from several tall horses and lost interest. My mother eventually sold our Pebbleshire home, and we moved into an apartment in Glendale near the end of my ninth-grade year. This was a sad time for me because I loved our childhood home, and apartment living was so confining.

Trying to find a hobby for me, my mother bought me a dirt motorcycle for my fourteenth birthday and that sidetracked me from antisocial behavior. She took me out to Indian Dunes outside of Valencia and Castaic off State Route 126. We went there every other weekend, and my mom transported my motorcycle on the back of her station wagon. Ridding motocross was such a great distraction for me. I lost interest in fighting the bullies and took up racing. This became a passion for me. I finished middle school and we moved from Glendale.

HIGH SCHOOL

My mother decided that it might be a good idea to move to Newbury Park for a new life. She bought a new home across the street from the high school. There were plenty of places to ride motorcycles in the hills surrounding Conejo Valley, CA. I was excited about living in a new home and a place where you could ride your motorcycle from your house.

On my Honda XR 75 at Indian Dunes, 1977 (Author's collection)

I did not count on the loneliness of not knowing anyone at the school. Being the new kid, meant I had no friends and a greater chance for being bullied. I found solace in a student who was also new to the school. Her school burned down in Thousand Oaks, and she was transferred to Newbury Park High School. She was a pretty girl and nice to me. Her name was Heather. We hung out for a short time, and this took away my loneliness at school. She was one grade higher than me. By hanging out with me, an incoming freshman, she probably took a social hit, but she didn't seem to mind. I met another kind person named Leslie. She was also terrific. Leslie was a good person and became a fast friend. I am not sure if Heather introduced us or not. Leslie and I are friends on Facebook to this day. She is an accomplished University Professor in Arkansas with a lovely family. Heather became a model and actress. I am no longer in touch with Heather.

We moved back to Glendale after living one year in Newbury Park. The commute was too much for my mother who drove to Los Angeles each day. I was saddened because I was starting to make new friends and loved our new home. I understood and knew the transition would be easier for me since I grew up in the Glendale School District. We moved back to the same apartment building (Verdugo Woodlands Apartments) we had left the year prior.

My junior year of high school was boring. I hung out with my friends, Joe Reuter and Dana Drew, who were also bored with the dumbed down classes. Joe and I would ditch class and head to the ski slopes in the winter and the beach in the spring. Despite my lack of attendance, I never missed turning in an assignment. I would receive credit for my homework and only showed up for tests, on which I scored high marks. Some of my teachers said nothing to the administration, while my US history teacher turned in my poor attendance to the principal. I had missed over eighty-six days of school and was made to be a teacher's aide in US history my senior year. By the end of my junior year, Joe enlisted in the US Air Force and tried to have me join him. I chose to stay and graduate with my class.

My senior year I saw that only the football players ever had chances with the good-looking girls. I was small but really fast and believed I could make the team. I wanted to hang out with the players at recess and lunch. I tried out for the team and ran the 40 in 4.6 seconds. The coach offered me to play my senior year as a cornerback. I hit the weight room and practiced running to prepare for hell week. The coach gave me the papers for participation. I was required to get a physical and needed uniform money and shoes to play. I figured that my past asthma may disqualify me, and there was no way I was going to ask my mother for money for shoes, a uniform and an exam. I walked out of the coach's office and tossed the application into the nearest trash can. I never returned to football and endured ridicule from the football players who called me a quitter. I loved basketball but knew that the same fate was awaiting me there, so

I never applied or tried out for the team or any other team sport again.

Many of my classmates were applying to universities and had their futures planned out. I spent so much time away from school and did not know what an SAT test was or what it meant for me until it was too late. I was too busy working different part-time jobs and was more interested in buying my first car than anything else. My father's mother had left me one thousand dollars, so it was time to buy a car. I found a '70s Dodge Challenger for a little over a grand, but my mother helped me with the balance. I loved working on cars and had secured a job at Jack Ellis Chrysler in Glendale through the school district's Regional Occupation Program (ROP). I became so good at auto mechanics that I began servicing race cars and collector cars. I was in auto shop and the teacher had me teaching the students how to work on some of the cars. The movie studios donated the *Smokey and the Bandit* car, and I showed the students how to work on that car too.

One of the car collectors, Dave Taylor, owned Fosters Donuts on San Fernando Road near Burbank. He owned a Plymouth Superbird and a Hemi Roadrunner that I personally repaired and tuned at our high school auto shop as students looked on or assisted. I would take students to the junkyards in the San Fernando Valley to find parts for restoration. I became so good at it that my auto shop teacher spoke to Arizona Automotive Institute and Central Wyoming College about one of their scholarships for gifted students. He eventually told me, but I was not prepared for the rigors of college. Instead, I took a job as a manager and cook at one of Mr. Taylor's donut shops and continued working on his cars.

The donut shop was located across the street from the California Highway Patrol (CHP) station. The cops from CHP and Glendale Police would visit me in the morning for a cup of coffee, which I gave to them on the house. I figured this favor eventually would pay off for me. One day I was racing and doing skids in a parking lot in Montrose when Glendale Officer Joe Andrews gave me a ticket. Instead of citing me for exhibition of speed, he ticketed me for speed in trade, which wasn't as costly. In my stupidity, however, I neglected to tell my mother of the citation that required a parent to accompany me to court. I knew that my mother could not afford to miss work, and I did not know what to do. The citation turned into a warrant for my appearance in Pasadena Juvenile court. I eventually showed up after a letter came to the house. My mother took me to court, and I pled guilty. I lost my car for a week. Officer Joe Andrews has since passed on. We used to joke about this ticket when I was a rookie. He said about recalling the situation. "I gave you a break because you admitted to your wrongdoing and were very respectful."

ARRESTED BY GLENDALE POLICE

Eventually terrorizing my old neighborhood caught up with me one day. I was cruising with a friend Joe S. in my old neighborhood when we ran out of fuel for my car. We were near my friend Ron's home. You may recall that Ron was the guy in middle school that I stood up for when bully Greg tried to intimidate him. I went to his house to see if he had any gas or could give me a ride to the gas station. I grabbed the metal gas can I had in my trunk, and Joe and I headed for Ron's house. I knocked on his front door, and no one answered. I then remembered that Ron had left with his parents to San Diego for a few days. I came up with a brilliant plan. I had a rubber fuel hose in the trunk of my car along with other tools from tinkering around with my carburetor a few weeks prior. I thought we could just siphon out some gas from Ron's truck that was parked in his cul-de-sac across from his house. I thought we'd get enough to run to the gas station, fill my can, and return to refill his tank. I figured I'd leave him a note as to what I had done. I was able to begin the siphon process, and all was going well when the neighbors heard us. The curious neighbor walked out front and confronted us. "What are you guys doing?" I explained to the neighbor what had happened. The neighbor explained that he did not know me or my relationship with Ron. He could see that I was taking gas from Ron's truck. "I'm calling the police," he threatened. I told the neighbor that I would stop and leave. The neighbor turned around and walked at a rapid pace toward his front door. I disconnected the siphon hose from Ron's truck. I turned to Joe and said, "Let's get out of here." Joe and I ran back to my car. I poured the siphoned gasoline into my empty tank. As I was adding the fuel to my tank, I heard the distinctive sound of a police car driving up Greenbriar. The air entering the front grill area near the siren gave off a whistling sound that I immediately recognized. I then saw the police car headlights make the top of the hill. I suggested that we run and hide in the shrubbery down the street. We were able to make our way to some dense bushes as the police car arrived on scene. The neighbor met the police at my parked car. I realized that we were not going to get away with anything because the police now had information about my car registration. Joe and I walked out of the shrubbery and met the police at my car. We explained what had happened. Since the police were not able to verify that Ron and I were friends, they took Joe and me to jail.

Being placed into handcuffs was not a pleasant experience. I did think it was cool to ride in the police car until we arrived at the Glendale City Jail. After being fingerprinted and photographed, Joe and I were placed into a separate jail cell away from general population because we were minors. The cell was painted yellow and had padding on the vertical bars. This cell was later utilized as the drunk tank. Joe offered to call his mom and have her take custody of us, so the police could release us to her care. I remember freaking out because I knew that my mother would eventually find out. With severe embarrassment, I told my mother after she found out from Joe's mother.

INTEREST IN THE MILITARY

One day in early spring of 1980, the military recruiters arrived at our high school and talked with us about jobs in the military. I was interested and decided to sign up for the Armed Services Vocational Aptitude Battery exam (ASVAB). I eventually took the test just before graduation. This was a pivotal point in my life when I decided to enlist in the US military. I needed a direction, and this was an option for a needy young man without a father.

GRAD NIGHT AT DISNEYLAND

Well, I finally graduated high school. Many of my classmates were going to be leaving for college. Not me. I was not sure where I was going after graduation. All that mattered to me was I was riding a bus to Disneyland and trying to figure out how my friends and I were going to sneak in beer. Most of my friends had smoked marijuana before we boarded and were passed out before the bus arrived at the Magic Kingdom.

I was super excited to see the Matterhorn Mountain lit up in the darkened skies of Anaheim, California. Our bus followed a line of buses attempting to ingress into the parking lot. By now, my fellow classmates were up, awake, and chugging beers they had snuck onto the bus. The popular girls we called socialites or soshes were putting on their makeup as they stared into their compact mirrors. I moved toward the back of the bus and knelt down in the darkened bus. I took some sips from the beer fest. The constant stopping and starting of the bus made me dizzy and I went back to my seat after downing one beer. Our bus finally stopped, and the driver stood up and turned on the interior lights. He instructed us to disembark the bus after he told us our bus number that was posted in the front window.

The front door to the bus cracked open and we all poured out like liquid exiting a soda pop bottle. We all ran toward the front gates of the amusement park. I lead the charge. "Follow me!" I shouted as several of the park security ordered us to stop running. We made it to the turnstiles and showed our high school identification. We were allowed to enter Mickey's house. I again led the group in a hurried pace down Main Street to Fantasyland where the giant mountain awaited our arrival. It was time to tame the bobsleds. The two popular rides at the time were the Matterhorn and Space Mountain.

It wasn't long before we were headed to Space Mountain. Our group was able to ride almost all the popular attractions in record pace as we ran from attraction to attraction while security would yell at us to stop running, which we ignored. We eventually slowed down our pace and looked for our schoolmates. We saw a group of girls that entered the line behind us on the people mover. The people mover is a slow-moving tram system that moves six people at a time in and out of attractions throughout Tomorrowland. We wanted to sit with the girls, but we knew they would probably turn us down. The ride was nearly over, and we wanted to hang out with the girls. We came up with an even dumber idea. When the people mover entered one of the buildings, we would exit and jump into the girl's car. When the ride entered the last building, we jumped out. We waited for several cars to pass us. When the girl's car entered the building, we jumped inside. Of course, we were welcomed with screaming. "Get out of here," they shouted in disgust. We apologized profusely as the ride ended. The ride operators tried to stop us because we were caught on camera exiting the ride inside the building. Oops. We ran down the escalators and ran to Fantasyland where we hid for several hours ridding kiddie rides and looking for schoolmates. The last several hours seemed to creep by. We were worried we were going to be caught by security. Several guards passed by, but no one tried to detain us.

We finally saw our classmates when it was time to return to the bus. We all shared our adventures in Wonderland. We told about being chased by security, but there was little interest as the popular boys bragged about who they had made out with on the slow rides. I just watched the girls stare in our direction as they made goo-goo eyes at the popular boys. We eventually entered the bus after roll call and left. As we drove onto the interstate, all I could think of was my life was going nowhere, and I was desperate to change that situation. I just didn't know how.

IN REMEMBRANCE

I would like to take the time here to say something to the Pebbleshire Pirates we lost too early in their lives. Thank you for blessing us with your short presence. You will always be in our hearts and memories forever. Our way of showing respect to you will be the way we lived our lives.

The Pebbleshire Pirate children: Kelly, Debbie, Jon, Michael, Tara, Rich, Beverly, Mark, Joe, Tim, Frank, Kathleen, Paul, Cathy, Julie, Patricia, Russell and Anne.

Our lost Pirates: Lori and Stacy.

In 2008, I lost my friend Ron who died from medical complications—I could not rescue him.

LESSONS LEARNED

So many people like me have grown up with a single parent. That one parent is just trying their very best to provide food, shelter, and the necessities of living. There are many options for today's youth to participate in school sports at little to no cost.

When you see a young person in need of socialization, do not shut them out of your lives. Bring them into your homes. Share life's blessings with them. Do not look down upon them because they are not as fortunate as you to have an intact family unit. Protect them from the bullies.

The needs of a young man or woman to have a father figure cannot be overrated. My need was huge, and I know there are others who needed a good example. Choosing a good father figure in a dating relationship is crucial to your child's needs. Your children are watching you.

Some anti-social behavior is a way some children cry out for attention. Communicate with your child about their needs. Talk with their friends and learn their desires. Take them to counseling when you go for yourself so they can open up and be given important life skills if you do not possess them as a parent. If you have a parent who is suffering and struggling to make things work, try and seek out counseling for tools to help you from feeling helpless as a child.

2

SERVING MY COUNTRY

"If you choose courage, you will absolutely learn failure, disappointment, setback, even heartbreak. That's why we call it courage. That's why it's so rare."
—BRENE´ BROWN, DARE TO LEAD (2018).

FINDING A ROLE MODEL

My mother was working so hard it was difficult for her to provide opportunities to model leadership from a man's perspective. I was desperate for a male role model or anyone who could provide me mentorship on how to become a man and a leader. My mother dated several men after the loss of my father, but most of them had no interest in my road to success. There was one exception: Edouard. He was my mother's second husband. Edouard was from Belgium and had served in his country's military. He knew what I needed to do. He showed me how to shine my shoes and drove me to different places to run and timed my workouts. I really did appreciate his help; it prepared me for military service.

After graduating from high school, I attended Glendale Community College. Because I had no idea how the college system worked or where college could take me, I was a lost student. There were no role models at college, only uncontrolled testosterone and a lack of focus. My male classmates spent most of their time figuring out where the next parties were and how to score with the women. I questioned why my classmates were attending college, and none of them provided any concrete answers. I did not think for myself and search for meetings or study groups at the college to help me. My successful school friends—the ones who had intact families with money—were sent to universities and were well on their way to a successful life. I had no idea how to accomplish such a task. I just sank in despair and projected failure.

AIR FORCE CAME CALLING

One day I received a call from an Air Force recruiter who said that I had tested very well on the Armed Services Vocational Battery exam (ASVAB), and the military would like to speak with me about a job. I was intrigued by the fact that the military called me and paid people to fight the bullies. I had no money and worked only minimum wage jobs that were never going to lift me out of poverty. I did not know what to do about college. The military offered free college tuition during my active service and money for college when I finished my enlistment. I had no father figure and needed affirmation. Would the military provide this for me? Could the military provide mentorship and purpose? I hung up the phone and talked to my mother about it. She thought it would be a good idea as long as I attended college at some point. I contemplated the idea of serving my country and promised her I would attend college sometime in the future.

At the time, my mother, her current husband, and my sister were living in La Crescenta, California. I knew that if I was to enter the military, I had to get myself into good physical shape and that meant running. By now, I had outgrown my childhood asthma. I began running and training hard to pass the physical requirements for military service. I ran the track at Glendale High School and Glendale Community College, and around my neighborhood.

In May 1981 I met an Army recruiter in the Glendale office. We reviewed my test results. He offered me several choices for good jobs in different branches of the military. I was attracted to the special forces. I told the recruiter I was interested in serving in the Air Force. He introduced me to the Air Force recruiter, and we talked about being in pararescue or a combat controller. Para jumpers, also known as PJs, and combat controllers were the special forces of the Air Force. These elite group of special operators must attend specialized training that include parachuting, scuba diving, field medic, and survival courses. There is a high failure rate for these specialty schools that last two years. We also talked about loadmaster and air freight/air cargo training. After some discussion about the available jobs the military had to offer, I chose loadmaster as my career field.

WAS I 4F?

The term 4F is used to describe failure to pass a physical and dental exam for the military. It was established in 1948 as part of the Selective Service Act. The recruiter and I drove to the Armed Forces Evaluation Center for physical and mental testing. I passed all the exams. I had excluded childhood asthma from my medical history form because I felt that I had outgrown this condition, but I told the military doctors about my childhood issues with asthma. They wanted to disqualify me for service. I asked how I could prove I was ready and qualified for service. They told me that I needed a letter from my pediatrician stating that I had outgrown my childhood asthma and have the letter delivered to my recruiter. This was a crushing blow. I felt horrible that my honesty might disqualify me from serving my country; however, being truthful was more important to me. In those important moments doing what is right takes courage even if it means it may cost you your hopes and dreams for the future. For me, it meant putting on the line my becoming a man and standing on my own.

THE LETTER OF APPROVAL

My mother called my pediatrician, Doctor Garcia, and explained my situation to him. He drafted a letter and sent it to my recruiter, and the medical examination board allowed me to enlist. The job of loadmaster included loading aircraft with cargo and personnel, air rescue and recovery of downed aircraft and pilots, and moving the different branches of the military to special operations and missions wherever the Military Airlift Command sent me. The idea of special forces took a back seat because I did not want to risk another setback as the one I had just experienced. I signed my enlistment papers the following week and entered the delayed enlistment program with a ship-out date of July 28, 1981. I remember crying so hard when I made it. It was like being allowed to play sports in school, and I was going to be paid $501.00 a month and have a roof over my head and all the food I could eat. I would be out of the house and on my own. I was nineteen years old.

At the time of my enlistment, I was still attending Glendale Community College, taking business, social studies, and math classes. I passed two of the classes but failed the geometry class. I was really distracted by my upcoming military service. I did poorly in the math class because I ditched so many days my junior year of high school. I eased my angst by working on my Dodge Challenger. With the help of my friends, we upgraded the engine size and converted the automatic transmission to manual. This task filled the time before I had to leave for the service.

SHIPPING OUT

The day for me to leave home arrived. It was June 28, 1981. I had packed my bag the night before but did not sleep due to my excitement. As I left the house, I made my mother promise me she would not cry. It was too difficult as it was. My mother kept her promise as we said our goodbyes. Edouard drove me to my recruiter's office, and we headed back to the processing center. I hugged Edouard and thanked him for helping me. I had one large suitcase, a smile on my face, and loads of nervous energy. I was ushered into a large room along with other young men and women. Many of the men had long hair. I had forgotten that women were signing up to serve in the military, too. I wondered how many people there were trying to find their purpose in life, or their manhood like me. Was I the only one? One guy I met said he was joining the military to avoid serving time in jail. "That's an option?" I asked. He nodded in the affirmative and told me the courts had been doing that for a long time. After several minutes of meeting other potential recruits, a man dressed in a fancy Marine outfit entered the room. He yelled something that sounded like, "Atten hut!" We must have had dumb looks on our faces because he yelled for us to get to attention and explained that we were to stand erect with our hands to our sides until we were moved to form a few straight lines he called columns. There were some really stupid people in the room who did not listen. After refusing to obey, those people were whisked off to some other place with their luggage in tow. I never saw them again. I had no idea where they went, and I really did not want to know. I stood still until I was told where to stand and thought "this can't be too bad; just do what you are told." After we lined up in straight columns, we were told to raise our right hands to take the military oath of service. I remember hearing the words "protect the United States Constitution" and "so help me God." That was all I could remember, and I must confess that I had no idea what I was swearing to do or what it meant. I was just excited to see what awaited me.

After we finished our oath, we were told to enter a hallway with several openings with the branch of service posted over the top of each entrance. I headed for the one marked "Air Force." The Air Force line was small in comparison to the others. I remember something my recruiter told me when we were going over my test score and what jobs I was able to select. He told me I could have any job in the Marines, Army, Navy, or Coast Guard because their standards were lower than the Air Force. That's why there were only four of us in the Air Force line compared to the other branches. The other recruits pointed at us as if we were weird. Our group was escorted to a bus marked LAX. I gazed out of my window seat at the other recruits. Some of them looked very nervous and focused on our bus as they stood waiting to be escorted away. As our bus pulled away from the center, I was relieved.

We finally arrived at Los Angeles International Airport. I do not recall the airline, but the sign read San Antonio, Texas. By now, I was becoming hungry as I relaxed. I loved to fly, but one of my fellow recruits hated it. I thought to myself, *why did this guy sign up for the Air Force if he hates to fly?* We eventually boarded the plane and were separated from one another. As we parted ways, I said, "see you in Texas."

I was looking forward to seeing Texas again. In 1968 my family visited the World's Fair in San Antonio. It was called the HemisFair. That was a great memory for me. The river and floating restaurants on boats were interesting. My sister had a different experience. We got stuck on the Ferris wheel, and she was frightened. It was hot and humid, and our hotel room had large crickets that freaked out my mother. Despite the bug infestation and the Ferris wheel incident, my father remained calm and was the type of guy that made good out of most situations. He was a military man who served in the Army at Fort Ord, California. That was the same place where Elvis Presley served and about the same time. They may have known one another. I never had the chance to ask him.

WELCOME TO BASIC TRAINING

The food on the plane was okay, and I remember thinking this military adventure was fun. Little did I know. I was in for a surprise. We landed on July 29, 1981, around 10:00 p.m. (2200 military time). I remember walking out the back of the plane and was hit with intense humidity. I started sweating before I walked a hundred feet. I stood on the tarmac and waited for my new friends to join me. We entered the terminal and were met by an airman who held an Air Force sign. He introduced himself as he escorted us to a dark blue bus parked near the exit. We placed our luggage next to the bus as instructed and entered. We took the only few seats that were available. Several of the passengers asked where we were from. We said we were from California and were greeted with a hearty "welcome aboard." The airman entered the bus and walked to the center isle as he shouted, "This is not a social bus. If you talk, you will be escorted off the bus and have to walk to the base. Do you understand me?" Only a small group surrounding me answered, yes. The airman directed everyone on the bus to reply, "Sir. Yes, sir." More of the passengers shouted it at the top of their lungs several times until the whole bus was in unison.

Little did I realize this would be the extent of my verbal responses for the next few weeks. This airman was preparing us for what was about to take place. This bus was old and smelled like the buses I rode in elementary and middle school. The diesel smoke and noise were enough to make you sick, and we could feel every bump in the road. This short bus ride seemed to take hours. When we arrived at the building he referred to as our new home, the girls were escorted to another area. We placed our luggage in a square painted area and then were positioned into columns of four and sorted from tallest to shortest. I was about the middle in height, so I was placed in the middle of the column and grateful not to be the tallest or the shortest of the recruits.

OUR NEW HOME AND PARENTS

After we lined up, a military man rounded the corner wearing a green, well-pressed, short-sleeve fatigue shirt and a "Smokey the Bear" hat. He said his name was Sergeant Christ. He was intimidating to me, and I am sure he was to others as well. "Welcome to squadron 3-7-1-1, your new home for the next six weeks. (This was minus zero week, one week for processing). You have no parents here. I am your mother and father. I'm your drill instructor (DI). Welcome to my family." He pointed to our luggage and said, "Take a long look at your luggage. You won't be seeing your civvies for quite some time. Grab your toothbrush, toothpaste, deodorant, and any toiletries you have with you." Someone in our group made a comment or did something wrong or stupid and our DI was soon yelling. Guys were holding their toothbrushes, soap, and deodorants individually because they did not have a bag or some sort of container in which to carry them. When someone dropped a deodorant can, they were ordered to do push-ups. It was a crazy scene. Deodorant cans and other items rolling or scattered on the ground. Recruits doing push-ups, and the DI yelling instructions. I felt rather safe since I was near the rear of my column and chuckled to myself. What I didn't realize was that most of the recruits were doing push-ups except me, so I stood out. It didn't take long for the drill instructor to be on me like flies on shit. "What's so funny, worm? You think you can squiggle out of this predicament?"

"No, sir" I replied in a squeaky voice.

"It's Sir, no sir! Get down and give me twenty!" I needed no explanation as to what that meant. My fellow recruits and I did a lot of push-ups. I did so many I could tell you how many cracks were in the concrete of the drill pad by the time I left basic training.

After being introduced to who was in charge, and how screwed up we all were, we began marching in single file columns to our dormitory or barracks. We entered a large room with beds lined on each side of the room. There were gray lockers at the head of each bed. Each of the mattresses had neatly folded sheets and blankets on top. We were told where and how to stand at the foot of our beds. Then came the bed-making instructions. We were taught how to fold the sheets into "hospital corners." This was all new to me but interesting. Only then were we allowed to open our lockers and place our toiletries onto the top shelf. I paid attention and loved how we all looked when our beds were made. I felt a sense of accomplishment and pride, and I was only a few hours into the process. We were told to fall out, use the latrine (bathroom), brush our teeth, and hit the beds for sleep. It was 2:00 a.m. (0200 hrs.).

REVEILLE

At 0430 a bugle sounded from the carefully placed speakers that echoed across the barracks. I sat up in my bed as others were stirring from the dreadful awakening. Within seconds, our DI was walking the middle isle banging a trashcan lid with a stick, yelling, "Get up you lazy bastards!" This made me question why I joined the military. After we stood at attention in our underwear, our DI made the "rounds of humiliation" for those that still had cartoon-print skivvies or simply refused to scatter out of bed. The laughter in the dorm was followed by more push-ups for all. This went on for about an hour until we settled down and were tired of the continuous recital of "Sir. Yes, sir."

After allowing us to dress into our dirty clothes from the prior night, we were led to the drill pad under the covering where we lined back up in columns of four. This was our first march. I had no idea where we were going early in the morning. We were all marching nowhere, at least that's what it seemed like. "Left right left. Squadron halt!" The DI shouted from behind us. We rounded the building to the other side. There were the girls. They were lined up too. There was a man dressed in Air Force blues who stood at the front and shouted, "Report!" Each of the drill instructors shouted back, "All present and accounted for!" Soon each of the other squadrons were following orders: "Column files from the right, march!" Then they marched forward in step through a door that led somewhere. It was our column's turn to move to the front door. As soon as I neared the opening, I could smell the food. I was not even thinking of food with all that was happening to us. It was the chow or mess hall. I was starving. I realized I had not eaten a thing since the flight to Texas. We grabbed trays and were instructed to get two glasses of water in addition to any beverage that we wanted. We were ordered to drink those two glasses of water before we could eat, but not until we all arrived and were seated at our table. I arrived at the order area where I had a choice of eggs, potatoes, and toast. Made to order breakfast. Really? Is the nightmare over? There had to be some trick. "There was no way in hell this is the military." I thought we were being fattened up for slaughter. I chose one egg, and one piece of toast. I was not about to vomit my first meal on a forced run. We walked with our trays held tightly to our chests as we arrived at our table. Our DI was standing at our empty table, giving one of the recruits orders on what to do next. When we all encircled our table, we were instructed to place our trays down and stand at attention. Then we were given the command to be seated, "Ready? seats!" Looking through my peripheral vision, I could see other tables doing the exact same thing. I could also see that our DI moved to a table with other drill instructors. We all drank our water together and then started in on our food. Several of the recruits remarked about my small portion. I explained that I was not sure what they planned to do with us after breakfast. The others decided to eat only half their meals and discarded the rest in a nearby trash can as we exited the chow hall. Everyone met outside and lined up in formation.

WEEK ZERO

On day one of week zero we went right from the mess hall to the drill pad and began to march. This was fun because we were all collectively learning to march as a unit. From the cadence of "left, right, left, right, one, two, three, four" to the singing of jodies:

Where We Go

Everywhere we go, people wanna know

So we tell them we are the Air Force

Mighty, mighty Air Force, rough 'n' tough AF

Straight shooting Alpha better than Bravo,

Big baby Bravo, better than Charlie Chicken

Charlie chicken better than Delta

Dumb-dumb Delta better than Echo

Icky icky Echo We are the Air Force; mighty, mighty Air Force

Source: drillpad.net

We kept marching and trying to stay in step until we reached the building marked Medical Clinic. The other flights (squadrons) I had seen from the mess hall were standing in formation waiting to enter the clinic too. We eventually entered the wooden building ourselves and formed a single file line. As I came closer to the medical staff dressed in white coats, I could see that one of the technicians placed a large metal gun-shaped object against the left arm of the airman a few positions ahead of me. I heard a click sound from the gun and the airman winced as if it hurt. The rumors swirled in line that these were shots. It was now my turn, and it was not as bad as it was intimidating by the size of the gun used. I exited the building to join my fellow airmen who were all rubbing their non-dominate arm near the shot site. We were eventually told by our DI that we were receiving inoculations against different viruses such as yellow fever in case we were deployed in time of war. "Suck it up and get into formation!" he yelled. We did as we were told and formed our columns of four to prepare for our next destination.

We arrived at a white building with a sign marked Barbershop. There were six stools and about half of us were forced into the shop like sardines. We had nothing to do except watch as our fellow airmen had all their hair buzzed off. There was some sort of psychological explanation for this. I was sure of it. These are other moments when you question why you joined the military: first the shots and then humiliation by haircut. After the buzz cuts were completed, we met outside to form our squadron line-up. There was a wall of mirrors near the exit, so you could see your bald self in full view. Seeing that I had no hair, I reached up to feel if what I saw was true. Our DI exited the barber shop with a big grin and shouted, "Now you look more fit for military duty!" We then marched off to our next destination.

THE WEIGHT OF THE WORLD

We eventually arrived at a very large concrete building that resembled a warehouse. We entered the building and arrived at several stacks of large green duffle bags. It was shopping military style. They had underwear, T-shirts marked with 3711, shorts, socks, fatigue pants, and boots. We loaded these large bags to the top with these "free" clothes. We were then instructed to use the straps attached to the sides of the bag to place the bags onto our backs. These bags were heavy. People were struggling to hoist the heavy duffels onto their backs. Our DI, never short for words of wisdom, shouted, "Welcome to the weight of the world on your back! The safety of those we protect!" It made sense to me, and the heaviness of the bag melted away as I thought that I was going to learn how to protect my country, my family, and my friends. I felt that I had a purpose in my life.

The sense of pride distributed the heavy weight with the thought of this important message. I could see a lightness in the faces of my fellow recruits. We marched off to our dormitory with pride in our hearts. We marched flawlessly in step and with a purpose I had not seen before.

We arrived at our dorm and were allowed to retrieve our running shoes from our suitcases. After a mad scramble to find our bags and retrieve the shoes, we entered our barracks and placed the bags into our lockers. As if by instinct, we knew to head back to the drill pad in formation. We accomplished this with lightning speed and were ready in no time for more instructions. It was near lunchtime from what I could sense. We were not allowed to wear watches, but my stomach reminded me of my small breakfast. We marched in the direction of the mess hall. I smelled food and imagined what I was about to consume. By now I was starving. I ordered as much food as I thought I could eat. I was so excited to eat that I almost forgot about the mandatory water consumption. After chugging down the two glasses of water, I consumed my food at high speed. I was not alone. I cannot recall what it was that I ate, but I very distinctively remember earning an appetite that day.

After inhaling our lunch, we marched back to the barracks. Our DI instructed us how to mark our clothing, and how to fold our shirts and underwear. Then we were told how to organize our lockers for inspection. The entire process took us to dinner and eventually to bed. That night I had never heard such loud snoring. Everyone was exhausted, and this was the end of day one of week zero. I thought to myself, *basic training has not even begun.* As soon as that thought left my mind, I was awakened by the call to reveille and the banging of a trash can lid by our DI. It was day two.

OUR ROUTINE

We jumped from our beds at 4:30 in the morning and were allowed to dress in workout clothes with instructions to use the latrine (bathroom) and file onto the drill pad outside. We stepped outside into a severe lighting storm. There was so much lightening I could smell the electricity in the air. It was also a very hot and humid Texas summer morning at 0500 hours. We stretched in formation after roll call and began to jog around the drill pad. That was followed up by some calisthenics. We were all sweating within minutes. I was pleased to see that we were getting some exercise beyond marching. After about a forty-five-minute repertoire of mixed movement, it was time to make use of the showers. "Use soap, you dirtbags," our DI shouted from the entrance to the latrine.

We dressed into our fatigues for the first time and headed back to the drill pad. The last ones to arrive were on the ground doing push-ups and yelling, "Sir. Yes, sir." After the first round of push-ups were completed by the late comers, everyone joined the push-up brigade for laughing during their penal phase. In the end, no one was left out of some sort of punishment: latrine squad, guard duty, and other chores around the barracks. After serving our sentences for laughter, it was time to head to the mess hall for the meal rituals.

This day, we marched to the same building with empty sacks on our backs and received our new dress blues, dress socks, and dress shoes. We were told to prepare the dress uniform, but we were not allowed to wear them for another few weeks. I helped some fellow recruits shine their shoes and iron their shirts and pants. We then had to place our prepared uniforms into our lockers for inspection.

After nearly three hours of uniform preparation, our DI entered the barracks and shouted, "Inspection!" Our squadron leaders were out front being humiliated by our lack of preparedness. The DI handed out team assignments for areas of the dormitory. It was not long before we were all face down completing our rounds of push-ups for our lack or readiness. The rest of the week involved trips to the medical center for vision tests followed by our confirmation of duties, tech schools and final base assignments (referred to as dream sheets). By the end of the week, I continued with my choice of loadmaster as a career. Our first weekend was here at last.

NO DAYS OFF

With most jobs, your weekends are yours to do as you please. That is what we all thought. Wrong! We spent most of the weekend cleaning the inside and outside of the dormitory and doing more preparation for inspections that would follow on days to come. When we finally had a moment to ourselves, there was no television, Xboxes, computers, radios, boom boxes, cell phones, or social media to keep us entertained.

We had books we could read, several decks of cards, chess or checker boards, or just each other to keep us occupied. Those who could not deal with this were outside smoking cigarettes.

CARE PACKAGES

The highlight of the weekend was the mail that arrived at our dorm. Many of the recruits had letters and care packages from family and friends that they shared with all of us. If someone received a love note from a girlfriend and someone found out about it, they read it out loud to embarrass the lovebird. Once someone's note was discovered, they usually never let it happen again. I was blessed to be one of those who received care packages filled with baked goods and letters from family and old neighbors wishing me the best. Sadly, there were some who did not receive one letter or package our entire time of training. We were the only family they had, and our DI was correct. He was their only mother and father. This was sad and really hurt me to see others suffer this way. I recalled how I felt when I lost my father and how isolated I felt. I made sure that these outcasts and forgotten fellow airmen were able to open my packages and read my letters. Before long, these lonely friends of mine were the recipients of letters from my grandmother (Gram) and family. This is what "team" meant to me. This is why care packages in any form are so meaningful to our military troops! Week zero was about to end and it was time to sleep because the next day was the first day of basic training.

THE FIRST DAY OF BASIC TRAINING

Somehow someone awakened and suggested that we wake up early and be standing at attention ready for the day before our DI arrived. As usual, our day began with reveille and the banging of a trash can lid. After two beats of the trash can lid, our DI realized we were waiting for him. He stopped banging the lid and smiled. He retreated to his office and our squadron leader shouted, "File out to the drill pad!" Each morning we began with workouts and running because of the high heat index of the Texas weather that occurred before noon each day. Our workouts were followed by showers and breakfast. We marched to classrooms where we were given custom and courtesies training for military behavior and ate K-rations and meals ready to eat (MREs) when we were away from the dorm during lunch breaks. We always had water to consume throughout the day and before meals. During one of our workout sessions, we braved the obstacle course. This was fun because it was challenging physically and mentally, and the obstacles were difficult for those who were overweight or not in good physical condition. Some were even injured and had to leave basic training while others were discharged for failing to obey orders or not being able to mentally handle the demands. I loved our weapons familiarization and shooting training. I received an award for my ability to shoot an M16 rifle. Thanks to my uncle Paul, who was a Marine sniper, he passed on some of his training to me that I carried forward throughout my life.

I remember about halfway through basic training we were allowed to visit the Armed Forces Exchange Service (AFES) center on the base. We could wear our blue uniforms and make phone calls to our families. We could also eat pizza and sandwiches! It was the first time we were unsupervised since arriving on base. We all thought we had died and gone to heaven. I called home and told my mom our graduation date.

She told me that she and Edouard would definitely be there. I was really happy.

REMEMBER THE ALAMO

As we neared the end of basic military training, we practiced what is known as pass and review. This is part of the military graduation where our flight (squadron 3711) would be introduced to our family and higher staff from the base. After our last practice, we were allowed to visit downtown San Antonio. I talked my airmen friends into allowing us to visit the site of the 1968 HemisFair. Some of the old buildings were present even though they had been abandoned over the years. There was still a cable strung between tall poles where the skyway chairs scurried across the fair at the time of its operation. After a short time trying to re-live my past, we all headed for some real history at the Alamo.

I had always wanted to see that adobe fort. I wanted to learn about the Alamo and the history of those two hundred brave men who fought against Mexican General Antonio Lopez de Santa Ana's large army of somewhere between two thousand and six thousand troops during a thirteen-day standoff. The defenders finally lost their lives on March 6, 1836, which some scholars claim took only twenty minutes to accomplish. Leaders such as Davy Crocket, James Bowie, and William Travis were among those who stood their ground and led the standoff against the Mexican Army. These types of stories interested me at the time. I felt that these brave souls knew courage in the face of overwhelming odds and fear. There was much to learn from their example. Were they on a journey of courage?

BAIT AND SWITCH

About a week from graduation, I was told to report to the Central Personnel Base Office (CBPO) regarding my job and tech school. I was informed that I had to consider changing jobs from loadmaster to air cargo specialist because they had detected some minor hearing issues when I went through my original testing months ago at the processing center in

Los Angeles. I was told that if I did not accept the job change, I would be discharged and sent home. Thinking about it now, I should have raised questions like, "If this is true why was this not brought up when I first tested? Did the Air Force hire too many loadmasters?" Since I was really enjoying my military enlistment, I accepted the air cargo job and left.

GRADUATION DAY

It was October 1981 and graduation day had finally arrived. We spent several hours after breakfast preparing our uniforms for graduation. I must have helped at least five or six guys shine their shoes. We completed our readiness, and it was time to march over to where the ceremony was being held. I was super excited that I had passed basic training. As we neared the ceremony drill pad, I could hear the band playing military music for the audience. I could see from a distance that there were many spectators, but I could not see my mother or Edouard anywhere. I told them to look for the 3711 flag in front of our squadron. All the squadrons lined up on a grassy area covered with retired planes for pass and review. I tried to remember the command "Eyes right" as we neared the field. I tried to remain in step so I would have the timing right. Focusing on the drum beat from the marching band made it a little easier to stay in step. We were all nervous. It was our turn. "Forward march!" our drill instructor shouted. We entered the large field and could see that the squadrons in front of us had made two left turns and then entered a concrete area where we would march by the spectators who clapped when they recognized their loved ones in formation. We remained in step as we approached the base commander. Then the command came, "Eyes right!" All the columns to the right of the first left column turned their heads to the right and looked at the base commander. The audience then began to cheer. After all the squadrons had completed their pass and review, they stopped at a waiting area in front of the base commander. The commander delivered his speech and introduced the best squadron of the training group. We all then took our military oath of office. After congratulations were announced, we tossed our bus-driver caps into the air, and the crowd erupted in unison.

We were free to meet with our families. I finally met my mother and Edouard in the crowd. Apparently, they found our 3711 flag and found me as a result. My mother's tears said it all. I knew she was proud of me. I told her that I had a few hours for lunch before I had to head out to my dorm to pick up my suitcase and travel to my next base for training.

With my mother at graduation from basic (Author's collection)

TECH SCHOOL

It was October, and I was headed for technical school at Sheppard Air Force Base on a small puddle jumper turbo-prop plane. This base was famous for its 80th Flying Training Wing. The trainers from this program are responsible for training NATO pilots how to fly combat missions, similar to the Top Gun Naval Aviator School in Miramar, California. In addition, the base is also known for all air operations: mechanics school, recovery, flight planning, load planning, and medical schools. While I was at the base, our country was training the Israeli Air Force. They were using F-16 fighter jets they had purchased from us.

Wichita Falls, Texas, is located near the Oklahoma Panhandle. It is very flat there, no mountains for miles. Our dorms were two-story wooden structures with basements in case of tornados. I was used to earthquakes, but tornados scared me. We were supervised by squadron leaders that marched us to and from the chow hall and class each day.

WORK HARD, PLAY HARD

The weekends were our time to get into trouble—unless, of course, you fell behind in class and had to retake a test the following Monday. Friday and Saturday nights included endless pitchers of beer and loose women at the airman's club. Some of the airmen would make beer bongs out of oil funnels connected to rubber tubing taken from medical supply. They would pour a pitcher of beer down your throat until you choked and spit up the overage. I tried it and got drunk quick. After about three episodes of that activity, I lost interest.

I had heard the officers club was worse, and we tried to sneak in there a few times to see if the women were better looking and livelier. The decorum was much nicer and the women were prettier, but the music was boring. Most of the officers were not interested in partying as much as the enlisted workers. "Work hard, play hard" was at play when it came time to party. The best part of officer base housing was the free booze in their temporary housing refrigerators. Enlisted personnel were in bungalows, while officers were in single-story housing. They also had no snoring roommates to deprive them of sleep.

BACK TO SCHOOL

The long break from school was over. I had two semesters of community college following high school but wasn't focused. Then I had basic military training for six weeks. Now I was going back to school. Even though it was technical military school, it still required basic math, writing, and reading. It did not take long to remember that my academic neglect had a consequence. I had to learn calculations for balance and weight in order to know how to load aircraft properly. Physics and engineering were the basis of that training. Oops! *When do we fight the bullies?* You may recall that the weekends were free except for those who had to study to retake tests on Monday. I became one of those airmen. As the schooling progressed, I spent less time at the clubs and partying and more time with classmates trying to pass exams.

MUD FELLOWS

It rained a great deal during my time at Sheppard AFB. One Saturday, it rained so hard it became a muddy mess in the common area that joined several of the dormitories. The rain stopped and a couple of guys started tossing a football around on the concrete pathways. The ball landed in the mud near another airman and splattered him. The mud-covered airman tossed the ball back in such a manner that it landed in a muddy area and sprayed the guy who first threw it. He immediately ran and tackled the guy who threw the ball back. Someone yelled, "Fight!" Soon the dorms emptied, and airman poured out onto the muddied area and some joined the wrestling match until a few of the lead airmen arrived to calm down the mêlée. Someone suggested we have a mud football game. The two fighters that started the skirmish became the team captains, and they chose teams. Not wanting to miss out, I made sure to get on a team. We played from just past lunch until it was too dark to see. The girls did not play but stood around laughing at us. We were all filthy. My eyes hurt from abrasions created from splashing debris and dried mud. We were all hurting, but no one cared. It was so much fun. I even scored several touchdowns. It was a great bonding experience. We were no longer just dormmates. We were *mud fellows.*

FINAL BASE ASSIGNMENT

During technical school, there was another chance to complete our choices for final base assignments. Your choice had to match the career field and the needs of the military where there were shortages in your career field. (In reality, you were going where the military wanted you unless you knew someone in high places.) Because my specialty was air cargo, I thought it wise to choose a base that moved the most freight and personnel. I selected Travis Air Force Base in Northern California.

It is known as the Gateway to the Pacific. I read numerous pamphlets on Travis from the Central Personnel Base Office (CBPO) at Sheppard. I was intrigued by Travis' honor guard and drill team that traveled the country and handled many large military ceremonies and marched in parades. My friend Joe who enlisted in the military before me, was stationed at Travis. This would be a great assignment for me.

Graduation from tech school arrived and there was no pomp and circumstance surrounding it. It was a small ceremony, and we all were given our final base assignment. I was assigned to Travis. I was surprised that my wish came true. It was time for leave. It was time to go home for a few weeks before reporting to base.

LEAVE TIME

After spending six months in Texas, I was ready to come home for leave. I really missed Southern California and my family. I took a flight to Los Angeles on what was Continental Airlines. The flight attendants moved me to first class and treated me with free food—all I could eat—and adult beverages as they thanked me for my service. The best part of the flight was listening to the Dodgers on the plane's radio. They were in the World Series and people were clapping as the Dodgers made great plays. We finally landed, and my family was waiting for me with cheers and hugs as I entered the terminal from the plane. (Back then, family could meet you when you disembarked the plane.) I was in my military uniform. This was the first time my sister had seen me since I left for the service. I was excited to see my family.

We drove home immediately. I wanted to come to the house and sleep in my own bed. Alone. My mom and Edouard said they had a surprise for me. They had sold my Challenger and bought me a Volkswagen Bug. This was not a fair trade. I lost a high-performance car I built from the ground up and got a VW. I was furious, but I think they thought it was in my best interest to have something smaller and more economical. I cannot recall what we did for the few days I was home. I drove up to my new base, Travis in Fairfield, California, in my VW.

TRAVIS AIR FORCE BASE, GATEWAY TO THE PACIFIC

If you were in the military and were sent somewhere in the Pacific region, there was a good chance you, your freight, and your battalion left through Travis. The base was known for transporting military personnel returning from different war theaters. Shortly after World War II, Travis hosted the B-29, B-36, and B-52 bombers. These bombers eventually moved to Beale AFB, and Castle AFB, California, when the 14th Air Division left the base.

Eventually Travis became the Military Airlift Command (MAC) with its large capacity cargo planes (C-5 Galaxy and C-141 Starlifter) used to transport military personnel to combat sights and Medical Evacuation operations. Today, MAC and Strategic Air Command (SAC) combined the operations to become the Air Mobility Command. According to Travis Air Force Base Heritage Center, "Travis maintains a workforce of approximately 6,976 active-duty military and 3,577 civilians to support its global mission. In addition, the more than 3,100 reservists assigned to the associate 349th Air Mobility Wing combine with their active duty and civilian counterparts to form a fully integrated Total Force team. The massive Travis work force makes an economic impact in the local community of more than $1.5 billion annually."

SETTLING IN

I had read all the data on Travis in the pamphlets before I requested Travis as one of the bases of choice. I had no idea as to the size of the base. The front gate was enormous, and the traffic was like going to Disneyland by the long lines of cars waiting to gain entrance. There were large C-5 aircraft landing and taking off frequently. I took a map from the law enforcement officers manning the gate after telling them that I was newly assigned and showed them my transfer papers. They sent me to the CBPO to learn of my assignment. After a short time there, I was sent to the 60th Aerial Port Squadron to meet my squadron commander, Major C.

Major C. was a nice man who wore black framed prescription glasses and spoke softly. He gave the background of the squadron's history that was way too boring to a young man lost in a giant forest. I do recall him talking about moving a lot of freight and passengers or something about the Gateway to the Pacific. We walked around the squadron, accompanied by his assistant. At some point, he sent his assistant to gather my residential assignment paperwork and asked me a suspicious question, "I read your background, and the Office of Special Investigation (OSI) wanted me to ask you about your father."

"What do they want to know?" I asked.

"They wanted me to ask what you knew about your father's disappearance."

I was caught off guard and not knowing what and why the Department of Defense was curious about my father, I played the death card. "I was told he drowned in a fishing boat accident in San Diego. That's all I know, and that's all I was told." The commander seemed content with my answers, and we finished the tour that ended back at his office.

Major C's assistant handed me some paperwork to give to the manager of the dormitory where I would be staying. I drove to the dorm that was on the other side of the base and parked. I met the manager and obtained a key to my room. I hauled my luggage up the wrong flight of steps/fire escape and eventually found my room after learning the numbering system. My roommate was home and not surprised at my arrival because he was told I would be coming. I put away some of my clothes and was ready to eat. My roommate pointed out our window to the chow hall that was located across the street. After some small talk, I left for dinner. I had the weekend off and thought it best to try and find my longtime friend, Joe.

FRIENDS REUNITED

I had not seen Joe since he left for the military. It was early November 1981. I knew he was stationed at Travis and was assigned to the 60th Avionics Maintenance Squadron. His unit was housed a few blocks from mine. I was able to locate Joe's room. It was a Saturday morning when I finally located Joe. His name was the only one on the door. "Break on Through" from The Doors was coming from behind the closed door.

Joe was playing music from a makeshift stereo system from a car radio he had put together with some friends who spent time in Japan to acquire the latest in HiFi components. These friends sold Joe the parts for near pennies on the dollar. He told me he did not have a roommate because he was in the honor guard and that was one of the benefits. I inquired about room inspections because my dorm manager told me that they occurred monthly in our dorm, and Joe's place was a mess. There were beer bottles, coffee cans, pizza boxes, terrariums, and trash strewn about the entire room. His bed frame was attached to the ceiling. Joe told me his room didn't get inspected. The management figured his room was kept tidy because of his guard participation.

I expressed to Joe that I was interested in a better stereo. He told me that I should check with some loadmasters in my squadron because they go overseas and can pick one up real cheap. After catching up, we decided to go to the Snake Pit (a small bar with food) and grabbed a sandwich and a cold beer. We shared our basic training and tech school adventures.

HONOR GUARD INTEREST

I told Joe that I had read about the base honor guard in a pamphlet during tech school and it seemed interesting to me. Joe explained the duties of the honor guard and the drill team. He told me about the benefits: no roommate, free movies, free dry cleaning, travel opportunities, officer quarters at other bases and favor amongst the base leadership. Each squadron had to provide volunteer personnel to the base honor guard. Joe's unit needed a volunteer, so he signed up. Joe was assigned to the military funeral details. He also explained that you also had to be on the base for at least one year before you could apply unless your squadron waived the waiting period. An honor guard assignment meant that you worked for two squadrons, and if you made the drill team, you were on the road marching in parades and air shows across the country. I told Joe that I was going to try out for the drill team. He thought I was crazy but, as usual, he said, "Go for it."

BACK TO WORK

My first day on the job I was sent to the Load Planning Department. The assignment was to plan and design the placement of cargo and passengers into the cargo planes without compromising the ability of the plane to fly safely. It involved advanced math calculations and spreadsheets done by hand—no Excel. Once the planning was calculated, the loads were put together by warehouse personnel who built pallets that were covered with plastic and netting, unless the items were rolling stock: vehicles, planes, or anything else that could not be placed onto a pallet. Once the pallets were built, they were placed in a giant storage and stacking conveyer system. The pallets would be picked up by large scissor-like vehicles called K Loaders that transported the pallets to the back of the cargo planes and loaded them with the assistance of the Loadmaster and Ramp Services.

The placement of the cargo had to match the planning sheet. Once I mastered the planning duties, I was transferred to the warehouse special handling group. People on this job handled specialized freight such as radioactive materials, chemicals, weapons, munitions, explosives, reconnaissance film, and anything that would require a special security clearance or specialized training to process. Because of this, I was sent for more schooling to receive certifications and clearances to handle such items.

BACK TO COLLEGE

I had promised my mother that if I went into the military, I would go to college. I kept my promise. Sort of. I was called into the squadron commander's office and told to go to the CBPO to talk with them about some testing. When I arrived there, I was told that during my tech school apprehension training, it was discovered that I had some reading deficiencies. The base management recommended that I take some reading classes at the base in their long-distant college learning program. They explained that the military would cover the costs. Believing that I had no choice, I signed up. The program was run by Chapman College (now Chapman University). I signed up for reading and intermediate algebra. I attended classes in late afternoon after my work schedule. I listened to audio cassette tapes and watched videos of professors lecturing. I loved the reading class, and it helped me. I struggled with the algebra course. I dropped the math class but finished the reading course. I did not realize that I was one of the first students to attend Chapman University's long distant learning programs at Travis AFB. Thirty-six years later, I graduated from Chapman with my BA in Criminal Justice (see Educational Road). I kept my promise!

VOLUNTEERING FOR HONOR GUARD DUTIES

Since my squadron was one of the largest on the base, I thought it would have the most volunteers serving in the honor guard. This was not true. When I met with Major C., I learned that we were lacking volunteer participation. I told our commander that I was interested in trying out for the honor guard, and I needed permission to visit the guard to see what the requirements were and determine if it might be something I could do. I was granted permission.

I had only been on base a couple of months. It was January 1982 when I arrived early the next Wednesday and met some of the honor guard members at their squadron. We sat in a classroom instruction area for a briefing. The sergeant in charge introduced me to the members as an interested participant who came to watch.

After a short briefing of upcoming events and travel plans for certain groups, we departed for practice. The guard practiced folding the American flag over an empty casket and other members practiced the color guard duties that included two flag holders and two riflemen. I had always been interested in learning how to fold an American flag. During our practice, a large group of men left the building with rifles in their hands. They were the members of the men's drill team. I tried to pay attention to the color guard practice, but it was hard to ignore the drill team. I was drawn to the noise outside. I heard loud stomping, metal scraping, slamming metal, and commands. The members of the guard knew I was seriously distracted and asked me if I wanted to go outside and watch. I nodded and we left the building. The drill team members were dressed in green fatigues with blue scarves in the openings of their shirts, honor cords across their shoulders and chest with special shinny boots with white ladder laced strings with taps on the heels and toes. These guys were in amazing shape to march in step while spinning rifles with bayonets attached. I was mesmerized by every movement. They even tossed the rifles back and forth to one another without dropping them. I had seen pictures of these guys in the Travis AFB brochures and pamphlets when I was at Sheppard AFB. I even recognized some of them from the photos.

Several guardsmen could see my curiosity and asked me if I was interested in trying out for the team. I nodded. They told me there was a lot of training and practice just to qualify to try out for the team, but I had to learn basic honor guard first. There was a rite of passage: You must serve on the basic guard.

When the drill team took a break, the guard members called the drill team leader over and introduced me to him. "This is airman Ulrich. He is interested in trying out for the team." Of course, the leader was very cordial and put out his hand to shake mine. He then shouted to one of the drill team members to retrieve a practice drill sheet and a practice rifle. The drill team member returned with the requested items. The leader handed me the paper in my left hand and the practice M1 rifle in my right. The rifle was heavy. It made a loud thud as the metal plate attached to the M1 rifle butt struck the ground. Several of the other drill team members snickered as I stood like a totem pole in silence. The drill team leader took the paper from me, folded it up, and placed it into my left front pocket. He then placed the rifle on my right shoulder and placed my right hand where it cupped the butt of the rifle. The rifle slid down my shoulder and the leader kept showing me the correct position. This went on for several minutes until I finally learned the correct placement on my shoulder. The leader shouted, "Fall in!" The members of the team lined up within seconds and stood with their legs spread shoulder distant apart. Their rifles were in their right hands held down by their right leg; their left hand was behind their back, and their heads were bowed down. "Drill team!" the leader called out. The men snapped up their heads, pointed their rifles forward as they extended their right arms. They remained in that position until they heard the command, "Attention!" Then the team slammed the butts of their rifles to the ground, which made a loud sound as the metal from the butts hit the asphalt. I was transfixed as the team stood at attention. The leader then motioned me over to him and said, "March behind us and see if you can keep up. Forward, march!" he commanded. I managed to stay in step until the command "right shoulder" was given, and the rifles again slammed the ground in unison and the team managed to place their rifles onto their shoulders while marching together.

Then they started swinging their left arm down by their side and then up across their chest. They looked like soldiers from another country. I lost focus by trying to emulate this movement and found myself immediately out of step. I was glad that the team was marching in between several buildings and out of public view. I got back in step with the team until they started doing drill maneuvers while marching. When the team stopped to practice spin and toss routines, I stopped and marched in step and out of the way. Apparently, I was doing the right thing because the leader gave me the thumbs up.

After about thirty minutes of practice, we stopped in front of the honor guard building. The leader told me to take my rifle, paper, and go inside to practice some basic manual of arms (right shoulder, left shoulder, present arms, order arms) and other basic maneuvers that most guard members knew how to do. The drill team leader said he would teach me the other maneuvers later. By the end of the practice, I was very sore. I realized that I needed to be in much better condition in order to perform basic maneuvers. I wondered if joining the drill team was beyond my abilities. I believe the drill team leader was testing me or at least trying to show me what type of work was expected of a drill team member.

I met back with Major C. and told him of my interest to meet with the honor guard every Wednesday and I attended honor guard practices each week for about a month. I reported back to squadron leadership that I enjoyed the honor guard and the practices. I explained that I was still in training and not a member. Work was easy for me compared to the honor guard and rifle practices. I took my practice and training rifle home and practiced every day for hours. I decided to begin a regiment of push-ups and sit ups and began weight training, squatting, and anything to build stamina and strength. I must have spent several hours every day until I learned all the basic moves for the guard. Joe was impressed with my improvements and helped with practice. Within a month, I was able to join the guard and participated in my first funeral.

It was early on a spring Saturday in 1982 when we met at the honor guard unit. To my excitement, the drill team got on the bus with us. I found out later that they attend special funerals and are responsible for the twenty-one-gun salute part of the funeral. We were going to a funeral for a retired Army general. We drove to the base-police weapons vault and the drill team exited the bus and asked me to join them. Inside the vault were several wooden crates on the floor. "We are taking these with us," one of them said to me. They then removed several boxes of blank ammunition and clips and placed them into the metal ammo boxes. We grabbed the crates and took them to the bus and drove off to the Presidio in San Francisco. During the drive, the drill team began loading the M1 magazine clips with the blanks. They also removed their chrome helmets from their flight bags to polish them. I volunteered to help several of the drill team members.

I watched as the drill team opened the wooden crates. Inside were black- and chrome-plated restored M1 Garand rifles with white straps. Each of the rifles had bayonets attached to the top. I learned that these were the performance rifles that are capable of firing live rounds. I was allowed to hold one. They were much lighter than the practice ones.

It was a foggy morning in the bay as we arrived early for preparation. We practiced folding the flag, and I was assigned to be a pallbearer. Our job was to meet the deceased at the hearse and march, while carrying the coffin, to the burial site. This was my first time carrying a casket and folding a flag in front of a family. I was nervous. During the ceremony, while we folded the flag, the drill team would fire off the rifles and the bugler would play taps. Sergeant Grays would then present the family with the folded American flag and three of the expended shell casings from the twenty-one-gun salute.

The hearse arrived and everything went according to plan. Our sergeant told us the funeral was a success. The family took the time to thank each of us and voiced how grateful they were for our presence. From that day forward, I understood the importance of being a member of the honor guard. It was about the respect of military service members and their families.

MAKING THE DRILL TEAM

It had now been four months since I joined the honor guard. I had performed in several military funerals, worked out regularly, and practiced all the drills on the learning sheet with members of the men's drill team. It was time to try out for the team. In the fall of 1982 I arrived early for Wednesday practice in nervous anticipation of being grilled by the drill team leader. During Sergeant Grays' briefing he added that I would be trying out for the drill team and welcomed all members to stay around the classroom for my tryout. He obviously saw the worried look on my face and said, "He will have to get used to performing with people watching if he wants to make the team." The classroom was cleared of chairs, and all the guard members stood against the wall with drill team members. "Front and center Ulrich!" Sergeant Grays shouted. I swallowed the saliva in my mouth and stood at parade rest (left hand behind my back, rifle in my right hand, the butt of the rifle down, with the rifle extended away from my body, looking straight ahead). I felt like a pioneer wagon surrounded by a band of Indians waiting for the attack.

The drill team leader stood in front of me at attention and yelled, "Attention!" I pulled the rifle along the side of my body. "Right shoulder!" I slammed the butt of the rifle down made snap movements as I placed the rifle onto my right shoulder. The guard members liked my movements and clapped. That was all it took. I was like a well-oiled machine performing for a now-friendly audience. "Spin to parade rest. Twelve count manual, thirteen count manual, kill time manual, carousel manual ..." At the end, everyone was cheering. "Honor Guard members attention!" Grays shouted to end the applause and ordered "Drill team and Ulrich file outside and into formation!" At first, I just stood there until the team leader told me to move outside too. Once outside, the drill team formed up. I was placed in the middle column second man back. I was then told that I had to march with the team for the final part of the tryout. I kept thinking to myself, "*I'm halfway there. Feed off the team. Stay in rhythm.*" We were off and marching. Now I had to perform the same commands with the team. I had been practicing with them, so I knew I could do it fairly well. Before I knew it, we were back at the honor guard

Congrats on making the team Rich (*center*). First detail, Travis Airshow. (Author's collection)

building. "Halt!" Sergeant Grays shouted. And then "Fall out!" he commanded.

Sergeant Grays called everyone into the honor guard building except me. It was the longest wait in my life. After what seemed like eternity, Sergeant Grays emerged from behind the front doors and called me inside. Before everyone, he congratulated me on making the honor guard and drill team. Everyone came over and shook my hand. Practice ended, and I couldn't wait to tell Joe I had made the team. I went to the nearest pay phone and called my mother to tell her that I had made the team. I then went back to my dorm, sat in my chair, and cried. I then lay down and fell asleep.

PARADES & PERFORMANCES

Our drill team became well known among the entire military, dignitaries in DC, and large parade organizations. We marched in parades in California and Washington State. The biggest parade was the Torchlight Parade in Seattle. The Columbus Day Parade in San Francisco was a large one too. We performed in air shows throughout California. We performed at halftime shows or before sporting events at the Oakland Coliseum and the old Candlestick Park. We even flew on the President's support planes to events. My favorite performance

Photo by TSgt. David C. Skeen

Travis Drill Team Best in California

The men's drill team from Travis AFB, Calif., poses for a victory portrait after winning the state drill team competition. In the first row, left to right, are A1C Joseph Chavez, A1C Michael Villa-Blais, A1C Richard Ulrich, A1C David Palmer, A1C Romulo Maulino, and Amn. Matthew Rehlander. Standing, left, are SrA. David Stringer and A1C Thereyarn Pressley. Kneeling in the second row, left to right, are SrA. Orin Thomas, A1C Hudson George, A1C Orin McCammon, and A1C Robert McConnell. Standing, right, are SrA. John Lima (rear) and A1C Daniel Gamboa. Holding the championship banner, left to right, are SSgt. Christopher Chong, assistant NCOIC; SrA. Ronald Snell, team commander, and TSgt. Jarvis Grays, NCOIC. To prepare for the competition, the team participates in approximately 35 parades each year.

California State Champions Drill Team photo (Courtesy of the *Tailwind* newspaper. Photo by TSgt David C. Skeen.)

was the Miss California Beauty Pageant. We performed on television and then escorted the contestants to the Boardwalk for the day. Each year our drill team would perform against other branches of the military, competing for Best in California. We won every year I was on the team (1982, '83, '84). Our success was well known from the West Coast to the East Coast. The Washington Honor Guard from Bolling AFB used our unit to handle White House details west of the Mississippi. This relieved much travel for the Washington, DC, Guard. We handled President Reagan's visits to California.

OPERATION URGENT FURY

I rotated to different assignments within my squadron until I learned that I could sign up for mobility duty. This would allow me to handle different air cargo assignments within the Military Airlift Command by way of Temporary Duty Assignment (TDY). I traveled with the Army. I really became acquainted with the 82nd and 101st Airborne units of the Army. I also worked with the world-wide medivac units. I would allow the other branch members to borrow my dining hall card so they could eat great meals, and the guys gave me meals ready to eat (MREs) for camping. They were so grateful.

In 1983, Maurice Bishop was assassinated by Cuban rebels who had taken over the country of Grenada. There was a large group of American medical students attending St. George's Medical University at the time of this communist takeover. Then President Reagan thought it best to evacuate the nearly eight hundred students from the island before they became hostages.

In a joint military operation that included, the Air Force, Marines, and Navy we successfully secured Pearl Airport and the surrounding areas near St. George's, the capitol of Grenada, to begin the process of extracting the medical students from the university. Travis AFB's 60th Military Airlift Wing provided security for the airport along with troop and cargo support to the mission. The mission was a success. We got all the students off the island safely.

OUTCASTS OF THE SQUADRON

In early 1985, my honor guard and drill team duties were coming to an end. I would be promoted to sergeant within a few months and discharged from the military halfway through the year. I met with my squadron commander to see where I could finish out my time. I was currently assigned to ramp services and worked the night shift when I was back on base because I spent most of my time on travel duty with the honor guard and assorted missions. Ramp services was responsible for meeting arriving and departing aircraft on the flight line. The personnel would offload or onload freight from the planes to the storage docks and back. I told my commander that I wanted to remain in this assignment. He told me that most of the ramp services personnel were like outcasts. I asked him why, and he explained that many of them had discipline issues for being drunk on base, drunk driving on base, fights, and even domestic abuse and other anti-social behaviors. Some of the airmen were awaiting possible dishonorable discharges. This group of airmen was supervised by civilian supervisors who had little vested in the military or helping these outcasts. The commander tried to change my mind. I insisted that I be given a chance at ramp services. He allowed me to stay.

HIDDEN POTENTIAL

My uniform was clean and newly pressed. My boots were shined and I looked like a model soldier as I arrived back. Ramp services was located in a mobile trailer outside the warehouse. "Well, look here. A guy that has never worked before," exclaimed one of the civilian workers as I opened the door to the trailer. The military airmen just stared at me and sneered from their seats at the table. The group then turned back to their card game. It was a scene out of a western movie. I took a seat on the couch next to another civilian worker who was not playing cards but reading a magazine. He introduced himself and told me he lived in Suisun City outside the back gate of the base. He loved fishing and wanted to know what kind of trouble I had gotten into to cause me to be transferred to ramp services. When I said that I volunteered for the assignment, the airmen at the table stopped playing cards to pay attention to what I was saying. "You must have done something wrong to end up here," he opined. I insisted that I wanted to come to ramp services. "When is your discharge from the service?" He inquired.

"July 1985."

"What do you know of what we do here?" he asked. After telling him I knew very little, he stood up and said, "Let's begin your training." He walked me to the front of the trailer where there was an operation board with flight numbers of planes that were going to land. He showed me the load plans and how to load up the K-loaders with freight in preparation for the upload team and the empty K-loaders the download team used to empty the landing aircraft. There was a lot of down time between operations.

The first aircraft of the shift arrived, and I rode out with the download team. The guys' uniforms were filthy and unkept, and their hair cuts were out of regulation. However, they worked hard and were good at their jobs. I was surprised at the accuracy of their work. As time went on, I really loved working in this section. It was my favorite work assignment in the squadron. I kept asking myself, "*What happened to these guys? Why are they outcast amongst our other squadron members? Can we change the perception here?*"

PROMOTION TIME

It was May of 1985 and I had been in the Air Force for four years before being promoted to a non-commissioned officer (NCO) and taking my place among the supervisors. I was working in the most disrespected section of the squadron with some of the greatest and funniest group of guys I had ever worked with in the military. It really bothered me that everyone looked down on them.

Shortly after my promotion to supervisor, I had all the guys meet me outside the trailer for roll call. I asked them if they wanted to change how people viewed ramp services. I asked them if they would like to make this the most sought-after assignment in the entire squadron.

"Sure," some of them replied. Others asked, how. "I don't know how," I told them. "I'm working on it."

"Okay, Sarg," they said, placating me.

NO MORE OUTCASTS

I went to the squadron commander's office with an idea. "Major, I have an idea. I would like to change the perception of ramp services and make it the best example of the entire squadron. Airmen will beg you to transfer them to our section."

"If you pull that off," he challenged me, "I will recommend you for a commendation medal for meritorious service to add to your other accolades from the honor guard and special operations."

I asked for a box of customs and courtesy manuals from personnel. When they asked why, I told him that the men in my unit need to know how to behave before they can have a standard by which to live and work. I also need money for uniform upgrades. The men need to change their appearance. Their uniforms are way below standards. "You know that I know about uniforms from the honor guard," I said. "Give me a month and I will show you the most amazing change!" I left the office challenged and not sure if this would work.

The next morning, I met with the guys in front of the trailer with a box of manuals. By now, they were asking if our briefings were going to be out front each day. I explained the meetings each morning were to change our lives and the perceptions that others have of us. "Gentlemen, these manuals are known as custom and courtesies of the Air Force. Some of you have not seen these since basic training. By the looks of it, most of you have forgotten these rules and regulations. We are known as the outcasts of our squadron. Not anymore. I plan to change what people think of us, and I hope you would like to change that perception as well. When we are done, you will look different. You will act different. You will be different. Some of you will become airmen of the month, quarter, and year. You will be the envy of the squadron. Airmen will beg command to transfer them to our unit. What do you say?" I sure knew what it was like to grow up without leadership. "It's my turn to give back what the military did for me," I told them. The silence was deafening, but the looks of surprise were priceless. "What do you have to lose?" I asked. After some more silence, they all nodded and said they would give it a try.

THE IMPORTANCE OF RECOGNITION

Each and every day we lined up for a meeting with our manuals in hand. Each man took turns reading sections of the manual and then I verbally tested them on previous sections. I met with all the shifts to make a change. I bought flight scarfs and taught the guys how to wear them with their uniforms. I showed them how to blouse their pants and made sure their boots were shined. At first, some of the guys complained that they were not in the honor guard, but after other squadron members started complementing them, they accepted the uniform upgrade with pride. Even the civilian workers and supervisors began to compliment the changes. We were changing perceptions.

Over the next couple of weeks, the guys began to really improve their uniform appearance. They started to understand the manuals they had been studying. I had the senior airmen from the other shifts lead the meetings when I could not make the night shifts and report back to me. All the shifts were improving greatly. I moved to a special shift that started at 5 a.m. and ended at 1 p.m. This allowed me to keep an eye on multiple shifts. The improvement was so impactful that I needed to find a way to recognize our unit for their hard work.

After a month, I returned to the squadron commander's office to see if there were any plaques, trophies, or awards I could use to recognize the changes made by our unit members. The major pointed me to a storage locker in the main office. The locker had a few wooden squadron plaques that had blank metal plates and they were covered with dust. He gave them to me. I found an engraving machine at another squadron on the base and engraved the recipient's names. I made up an Airman of the Month and Airman of the Quarter award and gave them to our commander to hand out at the next all-squadron meeting, so our guys could be recognized in front of their peers.

SQUADRON MEETING OF RECOGNITION

It was now July 1985 and the day came for our unit to be recognized in front of the entire squadron. Our squadron commander called our entire unit up front and announced, "This is ramp services. The most improved unit in the history of our organization." He explained why. He then called out several of our members who really changed themselves and won Airman of the Month and Airman of the Quarter. Several of these men had reversed their pending disciplines and re-enlisted for another term! Many of the guys returned to their wives. One of the men went on to be promoted and took over my job. Just prior to my discharge one of my guys had won Airman of the Year in the entire Air Force! We all sat down in our seats after a standing ovation. I felt so proud of them all.

Our meeting was about to close when our commander called me to the front. He awarded me with the commendation medal for the overall meritorious work in our squadron, work in the honor guard, and other military operations. I had forgotten his promise to me about turning around ramp services. By the time I discharged from the military, ramp services was the most sought after assignment in our squadron. If you wanted to make

Recognition from Major C (Author's collection)

improvements in your life, you requested ramp services. Working there changed my life too.

LESSONS LEARNED

I was so honored to serve our country with the amazing men and women in all branches of our military. Most of them realize that their service may cost them their lives. Many of these brave men and women were like me—looking to find themselves, to become mature, independent men and women. Others were there because it had been a way of life for their family for generations. Some chose the military rather than spend time in jail or prison. Some felt it was their patriotic duty to serve. Some liked to rescue others. Some have no one at home, and the military is the only family they have. Whatever motivates these amazing servants, they are worthy of our gratitude. The importance of affirmation cannot be overstated. The men in my unit thrived on being recognized for their talent and abilities, and it changed their lives forever. I was so proud to serve alongside of them and to be a catalyst for them to find amazingness. They had really fixed themselves for a better us.

3

THE RESCUER

"Real heroes don't wear capes. Real superheroes wear uniforms and badges and stethoscopes!"

—DEAN CAIN

ABOUT US

You just heard an intruder enter your home. You call 9-1-1. The rescuers, not knowing what they may encounter or what dangers they might face, are on their way in a matter of minutes to protect your life and property. Your car was just involved in an accident, you are injured and trapped inside. You're terrified and you're hurting. The Rescuers arrive to smash windows and pry open a door and extricate you and get you immediate emergency treatment. You hear the siren as the ambulance arrives and the next group of Rescuers are on site to provide emergency assistance and transport you to the nearest hospital.

A bank is in the process of being robbed. The masked bandits have guns and have threatened everyone in the bank. The Rescuers arrive, armed and ready, to do whatever it takes to take down these criminals while they do their best to protect the patrons and employees inside.

Someone planted an explosive device in an airport. Everybody out!

Soon the Rescuers are on scene to diffuse the device before anyone is injured.

Our country is at war. Several Rescuers just bailed out of an airplane at thirty thousand feet into enemy territory to locate and rescue a captured US soldier—your son or daughter.

A house up the street caught fire. The fire truck just arrived, and while some Rescuers are armed with fire hoses to douse the flames, another Rescuer charges inside the burning building to save the family dog!

On September 11, hijacked commercial aircraft flew into the Twin Towers in New York. As terrified people were rushing down the stairwell to safety, the Rescuers were entering the building to save as many as they could. Unfortunately, that story had a very sad ending and we lost almost 412 emergency personnel that day. (This does not account for the deaths related to health issues systemic to the incident).

A homeless man just had his few belongings stolen from him. He's sitting on the sidewalk weeping. The Rescuer sees this and, although it may be too late to capture the thief, the Rescuer will take the homeless individual to a local store and purchase food and other necessities out of his own pocket.

In any of the above instances, the Rescuer's first tasks are to protect, help, and save the victim. This characteristic seems to be inherent in certain individuals. It is common to find Rescuers in the following occupations: firefighter, police officer, nurses, EMTs, and US military. A Rescuer, however, can also be a lawyer, businessman, store clerk, counselor, or even a politician. Rescuing takes on many forms aside from just rescuing someone in life-and-death situations.

Sometimes "run-to-danger" trait of the Rescuer can cause them to be pulled into situations that might be detrimental to the Rescuer, but in the Rescuers' mind, it is their duty to provide help and assistance, albeit they may not even wish to do so. This is where my story begins.

POLICE ACADEMY PREPARATIONS

I really missed the camaraderie and *esprit de corps* of the military. I had been out of the military since July of 1985. I had worked odd jobs at UPS, Ralph's grocery, and some security details. It was now the summer of 1987. I never contemplated that a job as a first responder may be able to fill that loss. I heard that the Los Angeles Police Department (LAPD) held academy prep classes on Tuesdays and Thursdays at 6:00 p.m. at the police academy in Elysian Park adjacent to Dodger's Stadium. I showed up at the police academy on a Tuesday night to see for myself. The academy staff explained that in order to participate in the academy prep class, I needed be an applicant for the Los Angeles Police Department. I also had to pass a physical agility test that included a mile and half timed run, fifty push-ups, ten pull ups, and an obstacle course with a solid-wall climb. I saw cadets lined up in the center of the track and watched them march and then run. It reminded me of basic military training. I realized that I really missed the military. I decided to take the physical agility test and told the staff that I would return on Thursday night.

Thursday came and I arrived early to take the test. I passed the tryout and was told that I needed to obtain a white T-shirt with my last name printed on the back in black block letters and a pair of navy-blue shorts that could be purchased at the academy store. I was not sure how to apply, but I was about to find out.

Although, I didn't know exactly what being a policeman involved, I knew the work was risky but exciting. I had a little experience with the police during my youth. I did not see much negativity in this career choice. I did some research and found out that I would have to attend a police academy and field training and endure a probation period of one year. The Los Angeles Police Department had a great reputation. It appeared that most police departments had similar guidelines for hiring and retention rates. I learned that the city of Los Angeles offered hiring preparatory classes at the LAPD headquarters at Parker Center (named after Chief Parker, 1905-1966). I called the city personnel department, registered for the classes, and applied for the job of police recruit. I obtained my workout clothes and a letter of proof that I was enrolled in a prep class and had applied for the job.

I arrived about thirty minutes early the day of my first academy prep workout class and showed my letter to the staff. They told me I could participate. I was excited. The applicants formed four rows on the center grass area of the academy track. I had no idea where to stand. It seemed that everyone already had their positions assigned to them. I decided to stand in the back of one of the rows. One of the instructors saw me and shouted, "We have a trespasser!" This brought me right back to basic military training. The instructor introduced me to the class without calling me a name or making me do push-ups. He then placed me into the formation by height. Before I could adjust to my new surroundings, we were doing push-ups and sit-ups. I learned that day that I had to do my stretches before workout classes began.

AFFIRMATIVE ACTION

Two weeks had passed, and I was settled in with the workout program. It was time to head to Parker Center to take the written exam. There were about forty applicants in the same classroom that was used for the hiring preparation classes. We were all given a booklet, a couple No. 2 pencils, a blank sheet of paper, and a Scantron test form. I think we had about ninety minutes to complete the exam. I was surprised at the simplicity of the written test. I finished first, turned in my test, left the exam room, and went home.

There was another component in the hiring process: the interview. I continued the hiring prep classes at LAPD headquarters to prepare for the oral interview. They taught us communication techniques that I still use to this day. At the end of the class, I was well prepared for my oral interview. I had to wait on the results of my written exam before moving on to the next phase in the hiring process. A letter finally arrived from LA city personnel with my written test results. I scored high and was invited to take the oral interview within two weeks.

The day of my interview I was a little nervous. I arrived at Parker Center early and I was dressed in a conservative, navy blue suit and did my best to remember all that the interview preparation class had taught me. I felt I was ready. There were several people sitting next to me, and they all appeared nervous as well. I had been drinking a lot of water and headed to the bathroom.

While in the bathroom, a guy standing at the sink looked right at me after washing his hands and said, "Good luck. They aren't hiring white guys today."

"What do you mean?" I asked.

"You'll see." He left the bathroom. I did not see him in the interview waiting room. He may have been an interviewer because he looked like he was in his forties. I sat back down in the waiting area for a few minutes while I contemplated what that guy in the bathroom had just said to me. I had no idea what he was talking about.

"Richard Oorick. You're up!" shouted a female who appeared in the waiting room carrying a clipboard. I stood and followed her to a small room with five people sitting at a long table across from a single empty chair. I knew the empty seat was reserved for me. "Let the interrogation begin," I thought!

I was a little nervous but loosened up as they started with simple questions to verify my identity. They asked all the questions I had been forewarned about in the hiring prep classes. There were no surprises. I was well prepared. The interview seemed to take only a few minutes. The interviewers smiled at me and shook my hand as one of them opened the door for me to leave. At the end of the interview, I was confident I had done well.

Several weeks had passed before I received a letter from city personnel. I was anxious to move on to the next step, but to my disappointment, I had failed the oral interview. I was out of the process but could re-apply within a certain number of months. I was devastated. I felt like an outcast, like when I was not invited to play sports with my friends when I was younger. Was the guy in the bathroom, right? What happened? Was I discriminated against? I had no idea, but I was determined to find out.

I showed up for workout practice early and questioned other

applicants about their answers to the oral interview questions. Everyone had given the same or similar responses, yet some had passed their orals. But not the white male applicants. They all had failed their orals, too. What happened here? I was concerned the instructors would remove us from practice as soon as they found out we weren't in the hiring process anymore. Several of us who failed our orals were pulled out of formation and asked if we wanted to remain in the workout group. They were all white males. Since we were allowed to re-apply, we were allowed to remain in the class. I was relieved and informed the instructors of my intentions to remain.

I learned later that Los Angeles lacked a true minority representation in its police force and the city council had mandated that the city hire more minorities. I was caught in the middle of this change known as affirmative action. I felt discriminated against because of my race and gender. I decided to try and attend a police academy on my own. I thought I would have a better chance of being hired if I had already attended a police academy.

RESERVE OFFICER ACADEMY AT RIO HONDO

Many cities hire officers who graduate from the Rio Hondo Community College Police Reserve Academy. I could either re-apply for an officer position or attend the academy unsponsored. I was impatient and decided to apply for the academy on my own.

Rio Hondo has two academies. They have a full-time academy and a reserve academy (now called an extended academy). The full-time academy met Monday through Friday (now Tuesdays through Saturday) and the reserve academy meets Tuesday and Thursday nights (5:00-10:00 p.m.) and all day Saturday.

It was now late 1987 and I signed up for the reserve academy. I was working at the University of Southern California Public Safety Department at the time. Many of the full-time cadets and reserve cadets were sponsored by municipalities. Only a few of us were not sponsored. USC did not sponsor academy recruits. The academy does their best to help each unsponsored cadet have a job before they graduate, so they can wear the agency's uniform at graduation. To attend the police academy, you must pass a physical agility test:

a. 99-yard obstacle course

b. 165 Drag 32ft

c. Chain Link Fence Climb 6ft

d. Solid Wall Climb 6ft

e. 500 Yard Sprint

(https://www.riohondo.edu/public-safety/police-academy/newcadetinfo/ policeacademytesting/)

In addition, you must pass the requirements of the California Government Code section 1031, which includes the requirements to:

(a) Be a citizen of the United States or a permanent resident alien who is eligible for and has applied for citizenship, except as provided in Section 2267 of the Vehicle Code.

(b) Be at least 18 years of age.

(c) Be fingerprinted for purposes of search of local, state, and national fingerprint files to disclose a criminal record.

(d) Be of good moral character, as determined by a thorough background investigation.

(e) Be a high school graduate

(https://leginfo.legislature.ca.gov/faces/codes_displaySection.xhtml?section Num=1031.&lawCode=GOV)

And you must not be any of the exceptions found in section 1029, which includes the exclusions for

(1) Any person who has been convicted of a felony.

(2) Any person who has been convicted of any offense in any other jurisdiction which would have been a felony if committed in this state.

(3) Any person who, after January 1, 2004, has been convicted of a crime based upon a verdict or finding of guilt of a felony.

(4) Any person who has been charged with a felony.

(5) Any person who has been found not guilty by reason of insanity of any felony.

(6) Any person who has been determined to be a mentally disordered sex offender.

(7) Any person adjudged addicted or in danger of becoming addicted to narcotics.

(https://leginfo.legislature.ca.gov/faces/codes_displaySection.xhtml?lawCode=GOV&sectionNum=1029)

The academy is located in Whittier, California, on a hill away from the main campus near Rose Hills Cemetery. There are multiple classrooms, an outdoor shooting range, an obstacle course, and a running track. There is a fire road that leads to some water towers that is also used for running.

I showed up early the first day of the reserve academy. It did not take long for the academy staff to arrive and begin yelling at us to line up on the drill pad. Remembering basic training in the military, I moved quickly into action and helped others line up into four columns. I loved the discipline and really missed this training. After learning that I had a military background, the staff singled me out. Each time the class failed to follow instructions or made mistakes, I was down doing push-ups for them. After each mistake, I stood up and worked on straightening out my classmates while the staff sat back and enjoyed the side show. I immediately moved into drill team mode and began marching the class around the parking lot and drill pad areas. We eventually ended up in one of the classrooms where we were given our expectations for police academy life, what it would take to graduate, physical training (PT) gear, and our schedules. After hearing all of this, I was really looking forward to the training in the classroom, the firing range, and the workouts. I gave notice to the LAPD workout group I would be attending the reserve training academy.

The routine was rather simple. We would arrive early in either PT gear or uniforms on the drill pad and wait for inspection or any other surprise the staff wanted to use to catch us off guard. After our workout, we would change and head to the classrooms with some small break between courses. Saturdays were a full day that usually included an hour lunch break. We were required to take exams on each of the subjects or what is now referred to as knowledge domains. We were required to pass each domain with a minimum score of 70 percent.

We had firearms training each week, which was fun and fairly easy for me with my military background. Mixed between the time on the firing range was the weaponless defense training and hand-to-hand

At graduation with Gram, Rose Hills Cemetery, 1989 (Author's collection)

combat. Lastly, there were the defensive and tactical driving courses.

Time flew by and it wasn't long before the academy training came to an end. In January 1989 I graduated from the academy, and USC allowed me to dress in their officer uniform for the ceremony at Rose Hills Cemetery Auditorium.

MY FIRST ARREST

It was January 1989. I had parked my car on the street and went to the front door of the apartment where my fiancé and I lived. As soon as I reached the top of the stairs, I heard a loud crash behind me in the street. I looked and saw that a large Cadillac had collided into the rear of my parked car. The crash was so violent that it pushed my car 180 degrees around and across the street. I yelled for my fiancé to call 9-1-1 while I ran downstairs to see if the driver in the Cadillac needed medical attention. His window was down, and I asked him if he was okay. The car smelled of alcohol, and there were several beer cans on the floorboard. Suddenly, the driver put the car in reverse and attempted to leave the scene. I yelled at him, "Stop! You hit my car. You're not going anywhere." He still continued backing up. Knowing this guy may kill someone if I didn't do something, I dove into the driver's window, put the gear shifter into park, and removed the keys from the ignition switch. The driver started punching me in the back of my head and shoulders to try and stop me. I yelled to my girlfriend, who was standing on the upper landing of the complex, that the driver is drunk and trying to leave. Within minutes, I heard the amazing sound of a siren approaching.

Officer Ron Williams from the Glendale Police Department arrived with his trainee, and they removed the male driver from the car. It wasn't long before two other police cars showed up. I explained to Officer Williams what I had seen and done. He told me he appreciated my intervention. What he said next changed the trajectory of my law enforcement career forever.

Williams explained that the previous summer, mid-July 1988, he was dispatched to the north forks, where the roads of Cañada Blvd and

Verdugo Road split in north Glendale, to investigate an injury traffic collision. Williams arrived to find four people had been killed instantly by a suspected drunk driver who was estimated to be travelling 80 mph south on Cañada Boulevard when he drove over the median and struck the victims. The driver had a blood alcohol level of 0.15 percent. Williams was quite shaken by the sight of two mothers with their children lying in the roadway. Williams shed tears when he recalled the scene.[1] He asked me what I did for a living. I told him that I just graduated from

Post academy group officers, April 1989 (*left to right*): Officers Lemay, Walker, Tsuruta, Ulrich, Linder, and Solis with "Whirly." (Glendale police yearbook first issue, 1990.)

Rio Hondo's reserve police academy and was looking to become a police officer. He asked me what agency I was going to work for. I told him that I was not sponsored but put myself through the academy. He said that Glendale was a great department to work for and that they have a great reserve unit. He told me to reach out to Agent Al Frazier who was

---

1   Stephanie O'Neill, "Shattered Lives : Families Grieve for 2 Mothers, 2 Daughters Killed by Careening Auto," *LA Times*, July 15, 1988, https://www.latimes.com/archives/la-xpm-1988-07-15-me-7032-story.html.

the hiring agent for the program, and he would put in a good word for me. I was on the phone with Frazier the next day.

I applied for the Glendale Police Department's reserve officer program. It took me about four months to complete the application process, and I was hired for a dollar a year! In April 1989, I began my field training.

THE DUSTERS

I was riding with my training officer (TO), Jim Lowrey, on the afternoon swing shift when a blue Cadillac was driving below the posted 25 mph speed limit. The vehicle was impeding traffic to the point that other drivers had to move around the car to continue. We pulled alongside the vehicle on Chevy Chase Drive before the railroad tracks that led into Los Angeles. As we pulled alongside the vehicle, I saw the driver drinking a beer. I told my TO what I saw, and he attempted to stop the driver. He turned the lights and siren on, but the driver still did not respond immediately. The driver eventually slowed and pulled to the side of the roadway, and the vehicle struck the curb as it came to a stop. I was so excited that I launched out of our car as soon as we came to a stop. The driver was looking in his rearview mirror as my partner approached the driver's side. I approached on the right passenger side. My keys were jingling, and my police radio volume was on high. My approach was not very stealth. Upon hearing me approach, the driver slowly turned his head in my direction and stared at me like the movie *The Exorcist*. I was really mesmerized by this blank stare. Within a few seconds, I felt a tug on the back of my shirt collar. My TO said, "Back up. He's a duster." A few seconds later, I heard several sirens approaching our location. Several police units arrived behind our unit, and before I could contemplate what happened, the driver was in hand cuffs and detained.

My TO explained to me that the male being detained had taken phencyclidine (PCP) or angel dust or animal tranq (as it's known on the street). PCP is a dissociative anesthetic that can cause hallucinations or other distorted behaviors where your brain appears to dissociate from your body. Users have done atrocious things to themselves and others while under the influence of this drug. It was originally developed as an animal tranquilizer but was discontinued in the late 60s. Users ingest it by smoking a cigarette dipped in the chemical. Backyard chemists usually batch up PCP and flood an area with the chemical, which would explain why its usage comes in waves.

Our academy instructors had told us about the strange behavior exhibited by persons taking this drug. My TO went on to explain that the southwest side of the city had been experiencing multiple calls regarding PCP users. Within the week, I saw other males exhibiting bizarre behaviors. One man removed a manhole cover and tossed it like a frisbee. Another guy was crawling around like a snake slithering on his stomach. Several other males were seen running around naked and rolling around on people's wet front yards. These incidents lasted two weeks and then stopped until the next wave started.

THE PILLOW PYRO

Officer John and I were dispatched to a burglar alarm set off by a glass breakage sensor. Glass break sensors are usually very reliable. We arrived on scene and the business was engulfed in flames. I requested fire department response. John and I kept the spectators at bay while the fire was extinguished. John told me that although the fire was out, we had to wait on the fire captain to determine if there needed to be a police report. I stood next to John as the fire captain decided that the fire seemed to be suspicious in nature and warranted a police report. I was enthusiastic to learn how to conduct my first real arson investigation. I remembered from the academy training that a fire occurs when oxygen, heat, and a fuel source are combined. I was curious how the fire captain determined the fire was suspicious. He told John that he had requested for the arson investigator to come to the scene and verify his suspicions. Within a few minutes, the investigator arrived. The captain and John greeted the investigator and talked about the fire as I stood out of the way. Eventually, John and the fire captain moved away, and the investigator entered the burnt structure. John and the fire captain were conversing and not interested in me, so I stood at the opening of the business and discretely watched the investigator. He kept looking back at the fire captain and John as if he was being careful not to be seen. He then went immediately to the rear area of the structure and picked up something. He then headed in my direction at a rapid pace. I moved quickly away from the entrance and turned my back, so he wouldn't think I had been watching him. He approached the captain and John, held something up, and bragged, "I found it. It's definitely arson. We will need a report." I was really looking forward to writing an arson report and approached the group and proudly said, "Okay. We will write an arson report for you."

The investigator spun around and snarled, "nobody writes arson reports here but me! You will write 'Fire Other.' I determine if the report is changed to arson!"

"Yes, sir," I meekly replied.

He went to the trunk of his Chevy Caprice and removed a metal can and placed the object inside, put a lid on it, and handed it to John to be placed into evidence. I never saw the item. We went to the evidence and property room. John labeled the metal can "incendiary device" and placed it into evidence. I wanted to tell John what I had seen the investigator do that was suspicious, but I was so embarrassed and humiliated that I never brought it up. I thought being a rookie, I would be scolded again.

Years later, I learned that the arson investigator was John Orr. He was under surveillance by the ATF (Alcohol Tobacco and Firearms) *pillow Pyro* task force for causing multiple fires and charged with four counts of murder from a hardware store fire he started in South Pasadena. I shared what I had seen that day with the task force.

BECOMING A FULL TIME POLICE OFFICER

During my next reserve officer meeting (November of 1990), officers from the Professional Standards Bureau interrupted our meeting to announce they needed to hire twenty-one full-time officers. After asking for volunteers, I raised my hand. I walked out of the reserve meeting and followed the Professional Standards Bureau officers to their office. I applied for full-time duty, went through the hiring process, and within a matter of weeks, I had an academy date and a letter of hire.

The academy began in late December (1990), and I was glad to avoid the heat. Although I had already attended a police academy for reserve officers, at the time, the state of California still required a full-time academy attendance. They later changed that requirement when they realized the state was wasting money and resources.

The academy was held at the Los Angeles County Sheriff's department in Whittier, California, about an hour's drive from Glendale. The commute was the worst of it, but carpooling made the trips tolerable. One of my academy drill instructors was Dennis Smith from the Glendale Police Department. He was a great runner, leader, and teacher.

The sheriff's academy was no different than Rio Hondo with one exception: more hours. The academy was a converted high school. It had a dining facility, which meant that we did not have to pack a lunch each day. Our driver's training course was at the Pomona Fairgrounds, and the shooting range was at Pitchess Honor Ranch in Castaic, California.

Near the end of the academy, Officer Smith told the staff I had once been in the Air Force Honor Guard and Drill Team. He brought the staff outside and handed me a M1 Garand honor guard rifle. "Do something," Smith said. "Show us what you can do." I performed a few maneuvers, and at the end, acting Sergeant Ornalis suggested I perform in front of the academy classes inside the gym or forfeit graduating. I thought he was joking, so I said, "sure." I just wanted to graduate from the academy. Then Sergeant Ornalis snatched the rifle out of my hand and ordered me back to the classroom.

The day of training in the gym arrived. The staff was discussing graduation and other upcoming events with several of the classes. I saw the entire staff but no sign of a rifle anywhere. I was rather relieved that I may have just been tested and there were no plans of me to perform. Wrong! Before I knew it, I was called out in front and handed a rifle. I tried to remember what I had done as one of the drill team solo performers. I was like a machine but a little out of practice. I started out slow but ended with a high aerial toss spin that I was able to catch into a salute and bow. The cadets enjoyed the performance. We broke into our academy groups and headed for lunch. I was relieved that the pressure was off. The sergeant and many of the staff shook my hand and patted me on the back. I was really out of sorts on how to react, but my staff seemed proud to have me represent them.

With my Uncle Carl on graduation day from the Los Angeles County Sheriff's (Author's collection)

GRADUATION DAY

One of our class members (Deputy Talent) was a former Marine Corps drill instructor from Camp Pendleton. Between the two of us, we drilled our class into perfection. With my drill team background, and Talent's experience in marching, we developed several amazing marching routines for graduation.

Graduation day finally arrived (May 1991), and our class was lined up for pass and review. We were one of the last classes to arrive and salute the sheriff and our families as we passed by.

After our class salute, we broke into our unannounced razzle dazzle drill. This caught many spectators by surprise, but we nailed it. The audience cheered with excitement. Our staff and families were very proud of us.

9-1-1 HANG UP

In fall 1991 I was completing my field training when my training officer, Chuck Lazzaretto, and I were dispatched to a single-family residence in north Glendale regarding a 9-1-1 hang-up call. Police dispatcher Christine Goebel received only one partial ring on the 9-1-1 system. Per policy, she attempted a call back to the residence, but no one answered. According to Christine, she had "a hunch, a feeling something wasn't right at the address and entered the hang-up call into the dispatch system." There was a history at the address. After dispatcher Annamaria Taylor did a premise history check of that residence, she learned that a few weeks ago our department had to check on the well-being of a female, Janet, who had been harassed by her ex-husband, Dave. The previous call had been cleared with no problems detected.

We arrived at the home and parked down the street. We approached the home from the side for safety reasons. We took positions on both sides of the front door. I was on the right side and Chuck was on the left. I knocked on the front door and waited a few seconds. There was no response. I knocked again, and this time I heard footsteps. The noise increased as someone or something neared the front door. I mouthed to Chuck, "I think someone is at the door." Chuck acknowledged me. I heard the footsteps stop and then start again as if they were now walking away from the front door. I knocked on the door again. The same sound of footsteps moved toward the front door. The voice of a male asked, "Who is it?" "Glendale Police. We received a 9-1-1 call from this residence and are here to make sure you are okay." The footsteps walked away from the front door again. I checked the door to see if it was locked and the lock was engaged. I knocked again and the footsteps moved toward the front door again. "Who is it?" the person on the other side of the door asked. I repeated that we were the police responding to the address because of a 9-1-1 call. This time I requested, "Please open the door so we can make sure you are okay." The male on the other side of the door said okay and slowly opened the door leaving only a sliver of an opening. "Sir, I need to make sure you are ok. Please open the door." He opened the door some more. He was a tall man, well over six feet, with an athletic build. I asked him, "Are you alright?" As he opened the door, I saw a great deal of blood splattered on the walls down the hallway. "I have blood on the walls," I shouted to Chuck. I kicked the door fully open and saw a man at the end of the hallway jumping up and down. He was yelling "help me!" I unholstered my service pistol, pointed my weapon at the man at the front door, and ordered him out of the house and onto the front yard. He mumbled to himself as he followed my commands and lay prostrate in front of my partner and I on the front lawn. I yelled to Chuck, "There's a guy inside asking for help!" Chuck radioed for emergency assistance. The assisting units arrived, and the male was placed into handcuffs while I searched the house with Chuck. There was a woman (Janet) in the living room bleeding from a gash on the right side of her head. I requested medical assistance for her. The male down the hallway had his hands tied in front of him and his legs were bound with an electrical cord from a vacuum cleaner he had dragged into the hallway.

After separating him from the vacuum, the male victim told me his name was Jim, and he had come to Glendale from Atlanta, Georgia, to meet Janet, the owner of the home. He met Janet on a dating group. Jim had been staying at Janet's home for the last few days. He planned to fly back to Atlanta at the end of the week. She had recently been divorced from the male suspect Dave, who lived in Burbank. Dave was recently visiting his family in Chicago and had expressed to Janet that he wanted to reconcile their marriage. Janet had told Dave numerous times that she was not interested in reconciling because of his anger issues. When Dave flew back to Los Angeles, he decided to drive from the airport to Janet's Glendale home. Dave came over to the house since she stopped taking his calls.

That day, Janet had decided to do some shopping and have her hair done while Jim remained at the house. About an hour after she left, there was a knock on the front door. Jim opened the door and Dave asked to see Janet. Jim said she was not home, and Dave pushed the door open nearly knocking Jim to the floor. He walked around the house searching desperately for her. "Where is she?" he demanded to know. Jim told him that she was out shopping and having her hair done. "Who are you?" Dave questioned. "I'm just a friend," Jim answered. "When is she coming back?" Dave asked. "She told me she would be gone about four hours and that was an hour ago," Jim answered.

Dave walked rapidly through the house as if he was searching for someone. He tore out all the phone cords from the walls and then grabbed Jim by the arm and forced him onto a kitchen chair. Dave removed a meat fork from a kitchen drawer and started poking Jim in the chest. "What are you doing with my wife?" he questioned. Jim tried to explain that he and Janet were just friends. This enraged Dave even more who prodded Jim even more with the fork and threatened, "I will get the truth out of you." Dave then grabbed Jim by his arm and led him to the living room and sat him down on the couch. Dave then started throwing furniture around the room demanding that Jim tell him how he met Janet. Jim broke down and admitted that he met Janet through a dating group. Dave became enraged and smashed the glass coffee table into pieces. He yanked Jim off the couch and pulled him to a bedroom. He threw Jim onto the floor and then bound his hands and legs together with the cord of the vacuum cleaner. He stuffed a small hand towel into Jim's mouth and then picked up a piece of the broken glass from the coffee table and said, "I'm going to cut off your @#$%. You will never have sex with my wife again!"

Just then Janet opened the front door and called, "James. I'm back." Dave removed the gag from his mouth and ordered Jim to answer, "I'm here in the bedroom." Jim complied. Dave then shoved the towel back into Jim's mouth. Dave grabbed an iron from a nearby dresser and stood by the door awaiting Janet's arrival. Just as Janet arrived at the bedroom door, Dave hit her across the right side of her head, splitting open her head. Janet screamed as Dave pushed her down the hallway while shouting obscenities and calling her a whore and slut.

In the living room Dave seemed to calm down a little. Since Dave was distracted by Janet's presence, Jim wanted to try and escape or at least call for help. He tried to wiggle his hands free from the cord but was unsuccessful. He shimmied across the floor and was able to reach the phone that Dave had torn the wires from the bedroom jack. Jim was able to move his fingers, so he moved toward the phone jack and was able to connect the telephone wires to the wiring harness. Once the wires were connected, he dialed 9-1-1 with his chin. Just as there was a ringing sound, the wires came off the terminal. Jim then removed the towel in his mouth with the phone receiver. When he heard the knocking on the front door, he moved to a bedroom wall and used it to stand up. He could hear the police knocking and shouting on the other side of the front door demanding to check on things.

Dave kept going back and forth from the front door to Janet telling her that she needed to tell the police that she had fallen and cut her head. Dave had forgotten about Jim and was distracted by the police. As soon as the front door was open, Jim entered the hallway and shouted, "help me." He jumped up and down so the police could see over Dave's large body blocking the police officer's view of inside.

The real hero in this tragic story is Christine Goebel. If the 9-1-1 system rings one full time, the dispatcher will attempt a callback to the location. If there is no answer on the callback a "check the well-being" call is entered into the system and the police are dispatched to the location. On this occasion, there was not a full ring. A "blip on the radar screen" that disappeared is the best way to describe the scenario. Christine had a "feeling" that a response was warranted. Speaking recently with Christine she humbly stated, "That call always made me think of the what ifs? What if I had thought, 'half a ring, just a glitch?' What if you and Chuck had not been as thorough? All clear, all quiet. Back in service. Rich, I was just doing my job."

THE NORTH HOLLYWOOD BANK ROBBERS

In the fall of 1993, Sergeant Grimes of the Special Enforcement detail saw and heard a red Ford T-Bird squeal its tires as the vehicle tore out of a Shell service station. He checked the license plate as he followed the car northbound on Pacific Ave. The vehicle was registered to a rental car company. Grimes decided to stop the vehicle for the unsafe start. He flipped on his lights, and the driver took his time pulling over. Grimes stopped the vehicle just before the State Route 134 freeway.

He walked to the right rear of his unmarked patrol vehicle and approached the suspect vehicle to contact the driver. When he asked for his driver's license, the driver, named Phillips, told Grimes he had left his license at home. Grimes then ordered Phillips out of the car. Phillips met Grimes at the back of the vehicle, where Grimes searched him and found a Glock pistol in his waistband. Grimes secured the handgun, withdrew his own service weapon, pointed the weapon at Phillips, and ordered the right front passenger, Mătăsăreanu, to place his hands onto to the dashboard and not to move. Grimes then called for emergency backup. I was dispatched to assist him.

By the time I arrived on scene, several officers were there detaining the other occupant. I assisted with clearing the vehicle of any other occupants, removing evidence and took the original report portion of the investigation.

Inside the car the following evidence was found: another loaded Glock 17 pistol, Norinco MAK-90 semi-automatic rifle, Poly-tech semi-automatic rifle, Colt .45 pistol, Springfield .45 pistol, over 1,500 rounds of 7.62 x 39 mm FMJ rifle ammunition loaded into 30 round triple (banana clip) staggered magazines taped together with gray Duct tape, 3 round magazine drums loaded with the same 7.62 rounds, a mix of 9 mm and .45 JHP rounds, a stop watch, 3 smoke bombs, 3 different California license plates, 2 programmable scanners with earpieces, 2 gas masks, 2 ski masks, 2 sets of gloves, 2 wigs, 2 cans of gray hair spray paint, 2 level III bulletproof vests, and nearly $2,000 in US currency (1s, 5s, 10s). It took hours to process all the items into evidence.

Phillips and Mătăsăreanu were booked for suspicion of robbery, grand theft, transportation of weapons, and possession of modified weapons. Phillips spent 99 days in jail and Mătăsăreanu did 71 days. After Phillips finished his time in jail, he and Mătăsăreanu returned to the police station where all their registered weapons were returned to them. I was working the front desk of the police station when they showed me the paperwork from the court, signed by a judge, ordering the return of their unmodified weapons.

Over the years following their Glendale arrest, several Bank of America locations and armored trucks in California were robbed. An FBI agent who learned of Grimes, arrest believed the suspects in these robberies may have been Phillips and Mătăsăreanu. The FBI agent shared this belief with the FBI's Bank Robbery Squad.

On February 28, 1997, Phillips and Mătăsăreanu entered the Bank of America at 6600 Laurel Canyon Blvd in North Hollywood, California in full body armor and ski masks as two LAPD officers saw them and broadcasted that a robbery was in progress. Phillips and Mătăsăreanu forced a customer to go inside the bank and fired off rounds to announce they were robbing the bank. Phillips and Mătăsăreanu eventually exited the bank and engaged LAPD in a 44-minute gun battle. Phillips eventually committed suicide on an adjoining street and Mătăsăreanu was shot in the legs by a SWAT team member and died at the scene behind a car he was using for cover.

A few days later, I was asked to come to the watch commander's office. There were two FBI agents there. They placed a Glendale Police report in front of me and asked if I was the officer that authored the report. I recognized the report as the one I had written from the arrest of Phillips and Mătăsăreanu by Sergeant Grimes. The agents told me that the guys who robbed the Bank of America in North Hollywood and were in the gun battle with L.A.P.D. were Phillips and Mătăsăreanu.

Organizing evidence from Sergeant Grimes' stop and arrest of suspects Phillips and Mătăsăreanu, October 1993. Pictured with me are Special Enforcement Detail (from *left* to *right*) officers Bickle, Lytinski, myself, Grimes, Cisneros and Breckenridge. (Author's collection)

THIS IS A STICK UP!

One night on graveyard shift I decided to grab a cup of coffee at a local donut shop. I parked in the rear to avoid people thinking I was there for donuts. I saw a small white sedan parked in the alley facing the main road as though ready for a quick getaway. This seemed suspicious to me because there were available parking spaces in the front of the strip mall. I could see someone was in the driver's seat. Thinking he could be waiting for an accomplice who might be robbing one of the stores in the strip mall, I asked for a backup unit. With backup I cautiously approached the driver's side with my duty weapon unholstered and in my right hand. I illuminated the interior of the car and saw a male asleep. On the right front passenger's seat was a chrome-plated revolver and a piece of paper that read "give me all your money." It didn't take much to realize what this guy planned to do. I called for more units to assist me while I kept a close eye on this armed male.

When more backup units arrived, I told my fellow officers to box the suspect vehicle in until we can order him out of his vehicle safely.

Some of the other officers checked on the businesses in the strip mall to see if there were any suspicious activities. After clearing the shopping center, the surrounding police vehicles illuminated the suspect's car with overhead take down lights. I then ordered the man to get out of the car with his hands up and not to reach for his gun. The man opened the car door and was under the influence of a narcotic like heroin or other opiate drug(s).

During the interview, he admitted that he had come to rob the donut shop because he needed the money to support his drug habit. He wanted to wait until the other businesses in the center closed after 11:00 p.m. He had injected some heroin and fell asleep waiting for the time to pass. He was booked for suspicion of robbery, possession of a loaded firearm in a vehicle, under the influence of a controlled substance, and suspicion of driving under the influence of a controlled substance. I had to ask him what he was thinking doing this at a donut shop where cops go to eat donuts. He admitted that he was stupid and did not think about that and started laughing. We both laughed.

THE SLEEPY GUN

One night I was working the graveyard shift when I saw a man seated alone on a bus bench. His head was tilted back and off to the side, and he appeared to be asleep. I stopped to check on his well-being. The man was asleep with a revolver on the bench next to him. I unholstered my weapon, backed away from the guy, and summoned assistance quietly on the radio. After units arrived, I devised a plan to secure the male and the weapon so no one would get shot. One officer would grab each hand, I would reach under the male's armpits and pull him backwards and over the back of the bus bench and another officer would grab the gun. The officer who had the duty of grabbing the gun counted to three using his fingers, and we all moved together like a well-tuned machine. After he was taken into custody, we determined he was under the influence of heroin and was suicidal. He had planned to kill himself but passed out from the drug he had taken. It is interesting to note that incident happened a few days after the donut shop incident, one block away and another case of heroin use.

THE CAR DEALERSHIP TAKEDOWN

Responding to a threatening customer at a Ford dealership's service center, I got the rundown from a service assistant who witnessed the threats and observed that the customer had a gun tucked into his waist band. The service assistant told me that his supervisor, the service manager (SM), returned from a test drive with the customer. The SM told the customer that he was not sure what was causing the transmission problem because he couldn't replicate it during the test drive. The SM told the customer he would try to diagnose the problem. The assistant and the customer then drove the van to the parking structure that houses cars awaiting repairs. The customer was furious and said in Spanish to the assistant that if his car doesn't get fixed, he would "come back and shoot up the place!" He patted his waistband, revealing the handle of a gun covered partially by the man's jacket before storming off through the garage.

The SM told me that the suspect complained of a check engine light that kept coming on and causing the van to sputter and jerk. The service manager took the suspect from the service line and the two of them drove around the block attempting to replicate the problem. The suspect complained that he is tired of having this problem with the car and the dealer doesn't appear to believe him. Unfortunately, the problem did not repeat itself during their test ride. The SM told the suspect that he might not be able to fix the problem if he doesn't see it happen. This was before the suspect became mad at the assistant. The SM told me he had discovered there was a recall on the computer that communicates with the transmission, but he hadn't had a chance to tell the customer of his findings. Instead, he reported the threat to the general manager (GM) of the dealership who called the police.

I briefed the GM about what his workers had reported to me and said I would devise a plan to get the suspect and his weapon into custody. The GM provided me with the suspect's contact information and history of the car service from the dealership.

Back at the police station I called the suspect and introduced myself as the director of service for the dealership. I apologized for the frustration he was feeling from the issues he was having with his van. I let him know about the recall with the computer and that we had already started to replace the computer. I asked if he could return to the dealership within a short amount of time so we could return his van to him. He said he could have a friend bring him after work at 5:00 p.m. I told him that the dealer closes at 5:00 p.m. and I needed to know what type and color of car he was coming in so the service center would let him inside. He said he would be coming in a yellow convertible Cadillac. I completed my call and wrote my report.

With permission of the police supervisors and management, we devised a plan: At 4:00 p.m., several officers and I would respond to the dealership. We would send workers and customers home and lock all the doors. Officers would keep an eye for passersby who may want to enter the dealership for shopping. All the roll doors would be down and locked. The special enforcement detail (SED) team would be in undercover vehicles with high powered weapons parked a block away from both sides of the dealership. We would be ready for a takedown of the yellow convertible and the suspect.

It was five o' clock, and the suspect had still not arrived. I was about to call him on his cell phone when I heard the SED on the radio stating they had a yellow convertible stopped at a signal a block away. The GM was standing next to me as I told him that we may have spotted the suspect. I stood with the GM as we awaited the updates. The suspect and the car were stopped at gunpoint and safely detained. There were three other persons in the car with the suspect. The suspect and one other male had loaded handguns and two of them had outstanding warrants.

The suspect was arrested for terrorist threats and possession of a loaded, concealed firearm without a permit. Another suspect was arrested for possessing a loaded firearm in a vehicle and an outstanding warrant. The third was arrested for an outstanding warrant from LAPD.

I entered the jail wearing my uniform and introduced myself to the suspect. "Hi, I'm Rich Ulrich, the director of service for the dealership."

The suspect recognizing my voice put his hand on his forehead and said, "Wow! You got me!"

I told him, "You should never threaten people who are trying to help you."

I'M GONNA JUMP

We got a call one night of a male creating a disturbance and threatening suicide in his townhome. My trainee and I responded. The family said their adult son was under the influence of methamphetamine. He had been throwing things around in his room and threatening to kill himself. According to the family, they had not seen him with any weapons. We entered the house and went upstairs to his room. His bedroom door was ajar, and we could see him standing next to the window. In the most calming voice, I called his name, "Jimmy." He took one look at us and dove through the glass window, shattering it to pieces, and clung to a tree. He then shimmied up the tree and onto the roof. I looked to see where he had positioned himself. "Jimmy are you okay? Come on down so we can talk," I pleaded.

"Back off or I'm gonna jump!" he demanded.

I radioed in and requested a fire department response. The family told me that he suffered from depression and needed to take his medication, but he refused. I also learned that he was on probation for a drug offence. I tried to plead with Jimmy by telling him that he is not in trouble and that all I wanted to do was talk with him, but I could not go up on the roof. Jimmy said that he would come down only for his probation officer.

I called the station sergeant and explained what was happening at the house and that Jimmy was threatening to jump, would come down only for his probation officer. Our field supervisor, Ernie Garcia, came up with a brilliant plan. He changed into his civilian clothes and wore a baseball cap to cover his face. He then drove to our location and parked down the street. It was nighttime so Sergeant Garcia would not be distinguishable in the darkness.

My partner and I placed Jimmy's mattress below the window so we could tackle him onto the mattress when he came back through the window. "Jimmy!" Garcia shouted as he walked in the street.

"Who are you?" Jimmy questioned.

"It's Mr. Mack."

"You don't sound like him," Jimmy challenged.

"I drove all the way here from the valley to talk with you so you would come down. You want me to go back home? You know what. I am going home." Garcia challenged back.

"No. Don't. I'm coming down," Jimmy shouted. Jimmy shimmied down the tree and into the window. As soon as Jimmy came through the window, my partner and I tackled him onto the bed. Jimmy was covered in blood from the broken glass that cut his forehead and arms. We handcuffed him and took him to a mental health facility for a seventy-two-hour observation.

MY HUSBAND IS TRYING TO POISON ME

One time I was called to the emergency room at one of our hospitals because a patient was claiming that her husband was trying to poison her. I met with the patient to investigate this claim and document a report.

The emergency room doctor told me that the patient was feeling sick to her stomach and suffering from migraines. She had been experiencing these symptoms over the last twenty-four hours after drinking bottled water delivered to their family home. The patient was in good health and saw her primary care physician each year. The patient had been experiencing tachycardia (high heart rate) and hypertension (high blood pressure). She was given beta blockers to slow down her heart rate. Blood work did not show any signs of drug induced metabolites. Since the women told the doctor she thought her husband was trying to poison her, the doctor was required to call the police to investigate.

I located the patient in one of the treatment areas. Immediately,

I saw that her pupils were dilated, and she had eyelid tremors. Her pulse ranged between 120 and 140 beats per minute (60-90 is average). I took out my pupilometer to compare her pupil size with normal sized pupils. Hers were approximately 9.0 mm. (The normal range is 3.0-6.5 mm.) Using the examination light from the wall mount, I directed the light source into her eyes to see her pupillary reaction to light. Her reaction to light was two seconds slower than average. The room was rather temperate, yet she had goosebumps on her arms.

The patient tried to explain that her husband had been slowly poisoning their drinking water. She was unable to provide me with a motivation for the poisoning. She claimed to have a good marriage and stated that she was confused as to why her husband would do such a thing to her.

I asked the patient if she had any previous medical problems. She answered that she did suffer from migraines from time to time. When I asked her if she had recently had any sleeping issues, she said that she had not slept in three days. When I questioned why, she told me that she had been suffering from the migraines. She seemed a little delusional, which probably was due to her lack of sleep. "How long have you been dealing with migraines?" I inquired.

"For years, but they come and go," she answered.

"Do you take any medications for these migraines?"

"Yes," she said as she reached into her purse and removed a prescription bottle. The bottle was a prescription for Cafergot and was filled four days ago. The bottle of a hundred pills was nearly empty. I excused myself and took the bottle of pills to the physician's desk area of the emergency room. I looked for Cafergot (ergotamine tartrate and caffeine tablets) in the Physician Desk Reference (PDR). The PDR stated that it was a migraine medication or vasoconstrictor used to shrink the uterus post-delivery if breast feeding is not implemented. It was to be administered orally upon the first signs of a migraine. I looked it up online. WebMD stated that an overdose could be due primarily to the ergotamine component. Symptoms can include vomiting, numbness, tingling, pain, hypertension or hypotension, among other things. It went on to say that the "compound also has the properties of serotonin antagonism." The one word that stuck out to me was *serotonin*. If serotonin is restricted by antagonism methodology, the downside could be a flooding of serotonin. When the brain is flooded with serotonin, a patient can hallucinate. I went back to the patient and asked her to tell me what color she saw when she looked at the wall. She told me that the wall was loud. I asked her again to make sure.

"Loud," she replied the second time.

She clearly had symptoms of synesthesia (the crossing of the senses), which is seen with hallucinogenic drug influence. She had overdosed on her migraine medication and was hallucinating.

I returned to the doctor, handed him the bottle of pills, and rendered my opinion of his patient. I explained that Dr. Linnda Caporael had hypothesized that the Salem Witch Trials that occurred in 1692 may have been a result of ergotism poisoning. Ergot fungus can develop in grains of rye. This fungus alkaloid has similar actions as lysergic acid diethylamide (LSD) in humans. Later, LSD was derived from the same fungus.

This rye used to make bread was consumed by Salem township occupants. Ergot causes vasoconstriction, but also causes nausea, cramps, hysteria, hallucinations, tachycardia, and other "fight or flight" sympathomimetic responses. Dr. Caporael pontificated in her hypothesis that the behaviors and gangrenous green visual cues would be the result of the influence of the poisoning but seen as demonic possession worthy of death by the clergy of that time.

The ER doctor looked at me and inquired as to how I figured out this diagnosis. I told him about the Drug Abuse Recognition programs officers can attend in their advanced education and that it had really helped me in the field to rule out medical symptoms and diagnosis drug influence instead.

It was at that moment I realized I should use this training to help people to see the harm they are doing to themselves by taking drugs. I told the doctor that I was glad he called me and glad I could help. I had many encounters in that emergency room with the same doctor over different drug overdoses, and he was very supportive of me and always asked for my opinion. He would call police dispatch and ask for me personally. We became good co-partners in diagnosis, and he hardly ever questioned my opinion when it came to poly-drug use. I learned a great deal from our relationship.

"STOP LYING TO MY DAD"

It was my son Rolfe's fourteenth birthday, and he wanted to take a ride in a police car. It was a quiet morning, but we were eventually dispatched to Glendale Memorial Hospital emergency room to interview a victim who had been shot by an unknown gang in the parking garage of the hospital. My district partners searched all of the surrounding parking structures for evidence and possible witnesses. None were found. With all the traffic of a late morning, it was apparent that the shooting did not take place where the victim claimed.

Rolfe and I met with the victim for a statement. He told us that he was driving northbound on Interstate 5 when he accidentally cut off another driver. The other driver kept tailgating him, flashing his headlights, and honking the horn at the victim. The victim displayed his middle finger at the suspect. The suspect driver then started swerving to ram the victim's vehicle. The victim exited onto Los Feliz Road and drove east until he reached the hospital. He pulled into the parking garage to try and hide. The victim exited his vehicle, thinking he had escaped. That's when he heard two gun shots followed by pain to his back and buttocks area. He realized he had been shot and ran into the emergency room for help. The entire time the victim was speaking to us, Rolfe kept tugging on my sleeve asking if he could say something to the victim. I finally introduced Rolfe to the victim, "This is my son Rolfe. He would like to say something to you."

Rolfe said, "*Stop lying to my dad.* Tell him the truth."

The look on the victim's face was priceless. We were both caught off guard and then, pointing to Rolfe, he said, "I can't lie to you."

The victim admitted that he had gone to the Avenues, a local gang, to sell some weed to a friend. The Avenues saw him there and chased after him. He tried to get to his car but was shot twice in the backside. He drove to San Fernando Road because he knew there was a hospital in Glendale just a few blocks away. LAPD responded to the hospital and took over the investigation.

"HANDS UP OR I WILL SHOOT"

A trainee and I were driving on the west side of Glendale one night. I told my trainee that the area was a tributary of crime that spilled over from Los Angeles. No sooner did I say that, when a man waived at us to stop. "I was just kidnapped, robbed, and dumped right here," he said. "And that's the car that did it to me!" The victim screamed as he pointed to a light-colored sedan slowly driving away from our location. The victim told us one of the suspects was armed with a large knife, and they had taken his sports bag with personal items such as a wallet and clothing. The sedan must have seen the victim contacting us because they suddenly took off. I notified police dispatch to send an officer to meet the victim and took off after the sedan. They turned off their lights to avoid detection. While driving across the bridge over the LA River, they tossed the victim's sport bag out of the car and into the river. I entered Interstate 5 and could see the shadowy outline of the suspect vehicle that had already entered the freeway and remained in the far right lane. I notified dispatch that I was in pursuit. The suspect was still driving without lights, creating a dangerous situation. Drivers were moving to the right to yield to our emergency lights and siren and nearly hitting the suspect vehicle in the process. The suspect must have realized that driving without lights was more dangerous than advantageous because he eventually turned them on.

The pursuit continued for a short time until the suspect vehicle exited onto Forest Lawn Drive where they entered the underpass tunnel and stopped. Making matters worse, our closest back-up units were still en route. The suspects were armed with at least a knife, outnumbered us, and were smart to use the tunnel. I told my trainee that there was probably a good chance that we can expect to be involved in some alter-cation. I used the public address (PA) speaker and ordered the suspects to put their hands up. They did not comply. I ordered the suspects a second time and again they did not comply. I then said, "Hands up or I will shoot!" The suspects still did not comply. I asked my trainee to hold the button down on the PA while I racked (loaded) a round in the shotgun. The noise of the shotgun racking a round echoed loudly off the concrete walls. The suspects immediately put their hands in the air. I then heard the welcoming sound of sirens approaching.

With backup, we easily were able to remove each of the occupants and place them into custody. I went back to the scene to meet the victim and learn more about the crime. The victim had been on foot soliciting sex just inside LA city limits when the crime occurred. The sedan had pulled up, and one of the occupants exited the car, held a knife at the victim's throat, and ordered him into the car. The victim complied. The suspect held the knife at the victim's side while they drove to a large, unlit parking lot in Glendale. The victim was forced to give all the suspects oral sex. They pushed the victim out of the car and kept his sports bag. Although the original kidnapping took place in Los Angeles, Officer Mazadiego offered to take the report for me and LAPD so his trainee could gain some experience. The three males were arrested for kidnapping with the intent to commit forced oral copulation and robbery.

THE FUEL THIEVES

A Chevron service station reported a large theft of gasoline utilizing stolen credit cards. I met with the owner who told me that several small pick-up trucks have been coming to his service station at various times and days during the week. The little trucks would somehow fill up with hundreds of gallons of gasoline. The credit cards used for the purchases of the fuel would not clear for payment because they were stolen. To be sure that his pumps were operating correctly, he called the Los Angeles County Weights and Measures unit to come out and make sure his equipment calibrated correctly. A Weights and Measures investigator responded to and verified that the service station equipment was indeed calibrated correctly. The investigator was there to provide me more detailed information and obtain a police report number. Several banks sent the owner letters stating that the credit cards used in these large transactions were reported stolen. This had been going on for months with different cards used at various service stations.

The investigator told me that there has been a rash of thefts county-wide involving these trucks who have been stealing gasoline and charging the purchases to stolen credit cards. I reviewed the video from the station cameras and was able to see a clear picture of one of the males and a partial California license plate of a blue Toyota Tacoma with a camper shell. The license plate started with 5P. I was given a copy of the video and pictures of the suspect and wrote my police report.

Two weeks later, I was driving northbound on Interstate 5 when I saw a small blue Toyota SR5 pickup with a license plate that started with 5P. The vehicle exited Lankershim Boulevard in Sun Valley. I followed the truck off of the interstate while I memorized the license plate.

The truck pulled into a small private service station that appeared to be closed. I drove home immediately and called the police dispatch who gave me detective Mario's cell phone. I then called him to tell him what I had seen. He asked me if I had seen an address for the station. I told him that I could go back there and obtain the address since I lived only a few miles away. I returned to the location and took note of the address, the parked Toyota next to the building, and the name of the station—Zimm Fuel. I called Mario back and provided him with the address, full license plate number, and name of the business.

Over the next several weeks, the detective bureau, our special enforcement detail, LAPD and other government agencies conducted several surveillances. It turned out the three suspects had three Toyota pickups that were modified with high-capacity fuel tanks in the rear beds of the trucks that were covered by small camper shells. The suspects would fill their regular tanks with fuel and then fill the large capacity tanks at different service stations. Somehow they obtained blank credit cards from a plastic company and then coded the cards with identity they had stolen from valid credit cards that had been scanned from readers used from customers at other retail establishments, ATMs, or any place credit cards could be read and scanned. Once the trucks were loaded with fuel, the suspects would go to Zimm Fuel where they would dump the fuel into the reservoirs where it would then be pumped into a fuel tanker. They would then sell the fuel at wholesale price to other service stations.

The operation covered many victims throughout Southern California, and there were at least twelve locations that were about to be raided by law enforce-

Ten arrested in gasoline fraud ring

By Ed Kamlan
Glendale News-Press

Investigator Mario Yagoda at a press briefing July 23, 1993. (*Glendale Newspress* weekend edition, July 24-25, 1993.)

ment teams. I was invited to participate in the service of warrants since I helped solve the case. It was a massive undertaking that required a great deal of coordination. I was surprised by the number of involved officers from LAPD. Detective Mario showed me five large black binders of warrants, places needed to search and gather evidence. This was a great example of law enforcement agencies working together. There were subsequently ten suspects arrested for fraud, forgery, grand larceny, and utilizing a computer to commit fraud and grand theft.

"YOU LEFT YOUR LICENSE PLATE BEHIND"

Sometimes suspects can be smarter than the police. And sometimes they are not. My district partner and I responded to a silent alarm at a

Ready Teller (now ATM) machine at the corner of Wilson and Glendale Avenues. When we arrived to investigate, there was a large metal chain affixed to the ATM machine and on the other end was a rear bumper of a truck with the license plate attached. It didn't take long to figure out that the truck was being used to try and pull open the ATM. Instead, the bumper tore away from the truck, and the suspect drove away without the bumper. I took the bumper to the station as evidence and asked dispatch to check the plate for registration and warrants. The plates were not stolen and there were no warrants.

A couple of officers went to the registered owner's home to see if the truck was there or to see if the truck had been stolen to commit the crime. About thirty minutes later, a red Ford truck occupied by two males arrived at the address, and the officers detained them. After admitting they had tried to break open the ATM utilizing the truck, they were arrested. The truck was impounded and sent to the police tow yard. I met the suspects at the jail. The driver asked me, "How did you find me?"

"You left your license plate behind," I answered. His partner then cussed him out while we tried not to laugh.

THE LOSS OF A FRIEND AND EX-PARTNER
Charles "Chuck" Lazzaretto began his career at the Glendale Police Department about one year before me. I was one of his partners after I completed my field training as a reserve police officer. After I became a full-time police officer, Chuck became my field training officer who completed my training. He eventually left patrol and landed the job of arson investigator. Ironically, we both had applied for the arson position but Chuck was granted the spot. The arson detail was transferred to the Robbery Homicide Bureau. Chuck and detective Frank went to a video warehouse in Chatsworth to follow-up on a domestic violence incident where the suspect worked.

It was the morning of May 27, 1997, and I was eating breakfast with my family when the phone rang. It was police dispatcher Michele Byrne. She told me to turn on the local news. There was breaking news out of Chatsworth, where a gun battle had just ended with LAPD SWAT and a lone gunman. My entire family had gathered around the television when she informed me that my ex-partner and friend Chuck was killed in the incident! Just as she told me this, I saw the body of a police officer lying on the hood of a LAPD police car.

He was surrounded by SWAT members. The chyron read "Glendale Police Officer's Body Removed from Chatsworth Warehouse." There was no name of the officer. I remember hearing the dispatcher say, "Are you alright?" I stood there in silence and dismay. Chuck was a ten-year veteran of our agency. He was married with two young boys. I hung up and sat down on the couch. I was in shock. My children surrounded me in an effort to provide some comfort. I explained to them that I had just lost a friend of mine, but I did not tell them how he died. I do not remember any more after that. Within the next few days, I was preparing for his funeral.

There is a sense of denial for all of us first responders. We all know that someday we may lose our lives in the line of duty. After donning my class A police uniform (long sleeve shirt, tie and hat), I checked out a police car and took three other officers with me. We lined up with other Glendale police cars that were formed in and around the streets that surrounded the police station. Somewhere in front of our vehicles was the body of Charles and the family limo.

We eventually started moving forward. Parked along streets and standing outside their police cars were officers from Burbank, Pasadena, Los Angeles, San Gabriel, South Pasadena, Azusa, Monrovia, and Arcadia.

The other officers were there to work patrol, so we Glendale officers could attend the funeral. They all were standing at attention and saluting us as we passed. I shouted out, "Thank you," to each of them on my loudspeaker as I passed.

We then drove through downtown Glendale to Incarnation Catholic Church for the service. There were a lot of attendees, and we had to park blocks away from the church. Cardinal Roger Mahony presided over the service.

After the service, we headed toward the freeway. In the high-rise buildings, I saw people standing against their windows holding posters that said, "Thank You, Charles." People were lined in the streets holding signs like "Thank you for your service," "You will be missed but never forgotten," and other tributes. Once we entered the freeway, a motorcade of police officers riding motorcycles led the funeral procession. There were so many police cars and civilian cars following behind our police cars. People were standing on the overpasses holding signs of thanks and many were saluting. Firefighters saluted us while standing in front of the stopped fire engines. My eyes teared up as I gazed at the amazing sight before me. The press estimated that there were about 2,000 attendees at Chuck's funeral.

We finally arrived for the funeral service at Forest Lawn of Hollywood Hills. We all tried to find solace in one another by sharing our grief. There was a 21-gun salute and taps played afterward. A helicopter fly-over with the missing man formation was above our heads and one of the fire dispatchers announced Chuck's last call broadcast. Here's the family approved paraphrase:

> Attention all Glendale Police and Fire Department Personnel this is the Last Call for Investigator Charles A. Lazzaretto…
>
> Charles Lazzaretto began his career with the city of Glendale Police Department in 1987 as a reserve police Officer and in 1988 he became a full-time police officer. On May 27, 1997, he paid the ultimate price by losing his life in a Chatsworth warehouse searching for a domestic violence suspect.
>
> Officer Lazzaretto leaves behind his wife Annamaria and their two sons Andrew, three, and Matthew, two. Chuck was loved by all who knew him. It was believed by many that someday he would become the chief of police. Goodbye Chuck. You will be missed by all of us. This is your last call.

That was a moment when almost everyone broke down. After interning Chuck to the Hall of Heroes Plot, we returned to our black-and-whites and headed back to the city of Glendale.

As we were arriving back at the city, we heard a visiting police unit in pursuit of a stolen car just a few blocks from our location. I turned up the street to face the suspect head on. I turned the car sideways and the four of us jumped out. The suspect stopped his vehicle and got out and started running in our direction. He was so distracted by the pursuing police vehicle that he did not see us standing in front of him. When he finally looked in our direction, he stopped running and put

Officer Charles Lazzaretto (Glendale PD yearbook 1990)

his hands in the air. The pursuing officer, who had been chasing him on foot, took him into custody and thanked us for the backup.

We finally made it back to the police station to either change into our civilian clothes or relieve the assisting officers. The officers who came to help us while we attended the funeral said they were having the time of their lives. According to them, it was the most action many had ever seen. Some of them said they had a great time and did not want to leave. I was very impressed and told them I would love to repay them for their willingness to volunteer, just not under the same circumstances.

MOONSHINE MAKER

Occasionally the officers had to work dispatch to relieve the full-time dispatchers. One time while I was filling in, I answered a phone call on the non-emergency line. The caller told me that he had had problems with his neighbor being too loud in the past, but things between the two of them had improved over the months. He told me that today he saw smoke in his neighbor's backyard. When he looked over the wall to investigate, he saw a fire in a stone fire pit in his backyard. On top of the fire was a metal rack and a large round metal can sitting on top of the fire. I asked him if the fire department should be called," he told me. "I'm not concerned, but backyard fires are against city ordinance." I told the caller I was an officer filling in and would respond myself since the address was in my work area.

When I arrived with officer Hunter, I could see smoke billowing up from the backyard, so I asked for the fire department to respond. We knocked on the front door and the owner answered. I explained to the owner that we were there regarding the illegal fire in his backyard. The owner walked us to the side of his house next to his open garage. There were grapevines along the entire side gate. He opened the gate to his backyard. I saw everything the caller had reported to me. In addition, the metal can on top of the fire was a beer keg with copper tubes running from the keg to a collector. It was obvious that the owner was making moonshine. The owner walked me through the whole process. I wish now I had videotaped it. In his garage he had ten 33-gallon plastic trash cans filled with a liquid substance. Five barrels were for wine he had made from his grapes. The other five were potato mash he had been fermenting to develop into vodka. There was a weed whacker next to one of the cans. He used it to stir the contents. There were stockpiles of potatoes he had grown in his garden, harvested, and placed into storage containers. I did my best not to laugh at this moonshiner. I called the station sergeant, and he sent out many officers who wanted to see this operation. Soon after, Alcohol, Tobacco and Firearms (ATF) arrived to collect the evidence and charged him for operating a distillery without a license.

THE OLDEST ROOKIE

One day management told me I was going to be training a very experienced older rookie who had worked for a law firm as a managing partner. He was very athletic and, at fifty-five, did really well in the police academy as one of the oldest police cadets to attend the Rio Hondo academy.

Bill Bottger arrived early for training one morning and stood out in the front row. His uniform was immaculate. I introduced myself to him before joining the experienced officers in the back of the briefing room. Bill was eventually called to introduce himself to the group. It was clear he was a professional speaker who had a quiet and humble demeanor about him. Bill was a sponge with the adage of wisdom and life experience that made teaching him police duties very easy. With his Army Ranger background, officer safety was never an issue. Writing police reports was a simple task for him. His prose was the best I had read, and it was obvious he was an experienced writer.

Each week, management would ask me what I thought of Bill, and I would report back that it was such a pleasure to have someone in our midst with maturity and experience in life. "He will be a great addition to our ranks," I opined.

Bill and I showed up for court several times. Bill always arrived early and was reading a book or training manual. He frequently wore seersucker suits with bowties. Bill's court presence was something to watch. I had to attend his testimonies in order to put it in his evaluations. To say Bill was amazing on the witness stand and that would be an understatement. He sat in the witness chair and looked directly into the eyes of the person questioning him as he answered in amazing detail. The defense lawyers appeared frustrated that they had even asked him questions. I wish I could have videotaped that moment!

After three years of working with our department, Bill left us to work with the US State Department and was part of the team of litigators that tried Saddam Hussein in Iraq.

Unfortunately, William C. Bottger Jr. passed away January 16, 2018, in Pasadena, California. He was seventy-eight years young! He was the oldest rookie of the Glendale Police Department but had the youngest heart. It was an honor to train Bill. Heaven now has our oldest rookie.[2]

THE DECORATED MARINE

Leandro Baptista was a Marine Corps veteran who had returned from the war in Iraq in 2004. Leandro had always wanted to be a US Marine. He was born in Rio de Janeiro, Brazil and moved to Florida to stay with friends of his family until he was able to enlist. After his discharge he earned a criminal justice degree and decided to become a police officer. He moved to Orange County after his discharge and heard that Glendale was hiring, so he applied. After graduating from the academy, he was assigned to me for training. His safety tactics were impeccable.

One day we were sent to the hills of La Crescenta to cover lunch relief for the district cars. We had just exited the freeway when Leandro's cell phone rang. It was a call from his first sergeant who was working at the Pentagon in DC. I told him he could answer the call. I stopped at the 7-Eleven, so he could get out and speak in private. After about ten minutes he returned to police car with a concerned look on his face. "Everything alright?" I questioned.

"I have a dilemma," he answered. "Over the last couple of weeks, the Department of Defense has been considering the formation of the first Marine Corps Special Forces Unit. When I discharged, there were only rumors that this might happen, so I discharged and decided to pursue a career in law enforcement. My sergeant told me that the funds have been appropriated, and they are now forming the unit. I have been asked to supervise the unit as their staff sergeant. I just started this job. What should I do?"

"What does your wife think about this re-enlistment?" I questioned.

"We talked about it. She said I could do whatever I wanted to do and that she would support me. I am asking you because I respect your opinion, Rich. You are a vet, too. You understand."

---

2   See Bill's obituary: https://www.legacy.com/obituaries/sgvtribune/obituary.aspx?n=william-c-bottger&pid=187939325

"Leandro, you obviously love our country and saving lives. What would be the better choice: protecting the lives of Glendale residents or the people of the United States and the world, which needs rescuing. You can always come back and be a police officer anytime. This is an opportunity of a lifetime, and obviously the military values your work enough to ask you to re-enlist. Go! Re-enlist and make us proud!"

That evening, Leandro went home and talked with his wife. He then put in his two-week notice. On his last day with me, he handed me a signed copy of Major Chuck Larson's 2008 book called *Heroes Among Us: Firsthand Accounts of Combat from America's Most Decorated Warriors in Iraq and Afghanistan*. The chapter called "Balancing Act" is about him. The author details several war heroes that received medals of valor and silver stars for their bravery. Leandro was one such recipient.

In the Hall of Valor a citation about Leandro reads as follows:

The President of the United States of America takes pleasure in presenting the Silver Star to Sergeant Leandro F. Baptista, United States Marine Corps, for conspicuous gallantry and intrepidity in action against the enemy as a Team Leader in Second Platoon, Company B, First Reconnaissance Battalion, First Marine Division I, Marine Expeditionary Force, U.S. Marine Corps Forces, Central Command in support of Operation Iraqi Freedom on 7 April 2004. In the Al Anbar Province, Iraq, 60 enemy combatants in fortified positions ambushed Sergeant Baptista's 25-man reconnaissance platoon, wounding six Marines and disabling two vehicles. When the attack commenced, Sergeant Baptista immediately dismounted his vehicle and led his team to flank the enemy positions. Avoiding enemy fire, Sergeant Baptista sprinted across a shallow canal, climbed a 10-foot berm, and charged towards the enemy. Drawing fire from enemy machine guns, he silenced one emplacement and then continued to press the enemy by hastily forming a three-man assault team. With disregard for his own safety, he advanced over another berm under heavy enemy fire. He disarmed an improvised explosive device, and without hesitation, charged forward, uncovering 11 enemy combatants. He ferociously attacked the surprised enemy, single-handedly eliminating four insurgents at close range while directing the fire of three Marines against the remaining seven enemy insurgents. While under fire from different enemy positions, Sergeant Baptista provided cover for his team to withdraw safely. By his bold leadership, wise judgment, and complete dedication to duty,

Sergeant Baptista reflected great credit upon himself and upheld the highest traditions of the Marine Corps and the United States Naval Service.[3]

There are other such articles and a podcast about him. It was obvious where he needed to be. I was honored and fortunate to work with a humble man and true war hero who chose service to our country over his own desires. Hoorah!

Leandro F. Baptista

BOTH SIDES OF THE PLATE

It had been a long day in court and I'd had very little sleep prior to reporting for the graveyard shift. I was in need of a strong cup of coffee, so I requested a meeting with my district partner, LeRoy Hite. No sooner had we swallowed that cup of java did we receive a call.

We were dispatched to a local motel regarding a suspicious male the manager had seen wandering the property. We met the motel manager who said he received multiple calls from his guests who were awakened by a man knocking on their doors. The guy appeared to be

---

3   (https://valor.militarytimes.com/hero/3793)

lost. He was described as a tall, thin-built black male wearing a white shirt and black pants.

We located the man on the stairs near the motel lobby. I asked him to come downstairs. He followed my instructions but appeared to have some difficulty navigating the stairs. Officer Hite searched him and found a California driver license in his right front pants pocket but no wallet. I had him sit on the stairs. He was not able to tell me his name but thought he was from Highland, California. He recalled that he may have taken a bus. He was not aware he was in Glendale. His ID said he was Ellis Narrington Burton born in 1936. He was fifty-nine years old. I checked his name through the law enforcement database and learned that he was a missing male from San Bernardino, and he might have Alzheimer's. He had been missing for at least a day, and we were to contact his daughter, Nadine.

I took Mr. Burton back to the police station and called Nadine. I told her that I had found her father in Glendale at one of our motels, and he had no idea where he was. I explained that I found her information in the missing person system and needed someone to come to Glendale to pick him up. It was 11:30 p.m., and she did not have a car at the time.

Sergeant Halvorsen allowed me to meet San Bernardino Police halfway to exchange Ellis' protective custody to them since they were the reporting agency. I notified Nadine and she was beyond grateful. Officer Moloney and I met halfway, and he took custody of Mr. Burton. I said goodbye to Ellis and reminded him to stay in touch with Nadine who reported him missing. He thanked me and we departed.

Years later, I was writing a police report when I received a call from our Press Information Officer (PIO), Tom Lorenz. He told me that he needed me to come to the police station the following day at noon to meet the media for an interview. Tom explained that a grateful man wanted to thank me for saving his life six years ago. I asked him who in the world would be thanking me six years later. Tom told me he would have records make me a copy of the police report. I stopped writing and went immediately to the station.

The police report was titled "Assist the Police." I saw the address of 6700 San Fernando Rd. I then saw the name of Ellis Narrington Burton. How could I forget the name Narrington. I immediately recalled the details of the missing man at the motel. I do not remember saving Mr. Burtons' life. I just drove him halfway home.

The next day I parked my patrol car in front of the police station and walked into the lobby. There was one photographer from the *Glendale News Press* and Mr. Burton, who had his back to me talking with the officer at the front desk. Mr. Burton turned around and smiled as we looked at one another. We shook hands as the photographer snapped photos of the two of us. Mr. Burton thanked me for saving his life. I asked him how, and Mr. Burton explained that he had suffered a stroke that affected his memory. He somehow wandered away from a medical facility and hopped onto a bus that led him to Glendale. He believed that if I had not found him that night and returned him to his daughter's home, he would have been killed, run over by a car, or worse. He always told his daughter if he regained his memory again, he would like to meet and thank the officer who saved his life.

Mr. Burton continued to explain that it was not long ago that he was a star athlete who played major league baseball. He then handed me a couple of his major league baseball cards. I was beginning to see how difficult it must have been, losing his memory and then regaining it. The two of us took pictures on the front steps of the police station that landed on the front page of the newspaper the next morning. We exchanged phone numbers and agreed to meet again.

One of Ellis' favorite eateries was Pinks in Hollywood. He loved the chili dog, Lay's potato chips, and a bubble up soda in a glass bottle. I met Ellis there about two times a year. We met with some of his high school classmates, baseball players who played ball with him in the Deputy Auxiliary Police (LAPD) program in the 1950s sponsored by Hollywood legend Mickey Rooney. Ellis loved baseball and NASCAR racing. He even came to my boys' pony baseball opening day and spoke as our guest of honor and signed baseball cards.

When Ellis was young, he attended Seventh Day Adventist private school in Glendale and then Jordan High School in Los Angeles. Ellis played minor league ball until he was drafted by the Colt 45s. He eventually was traded to the Cubs and the Cardinals. He was one of a few players who hit a home run from *both sides of the plate* in one game (meaning as a right hander and a left hander). Ty Cobb was the another.

Thanks, officer — six years later

■ Man who suffered stroke returns to express gratitude to Glendale cop who helped him.

Amber Willard
News-Press

NORTHEAST GLENDALE — Ellis Burton doesn't really remember meeting Glendale Police Officer Rich Ulrich, but said Friday that he credits him with saving his life.

In 1995, Burton suffered a stroke and was taking several medications that caused him to be very disoriented. He wandered away from his daughter's home in San Bernardino County and ended up roaming a Glendale

SEE THANKS PAGE A8

JLT. KARNIC9 / NEWS-PRESS

In the summer of 1995, Ellis Burton, left, suffered a stroke and became disoriented as he wandered away from his daughter's home in San Bernardino County. Officer Rich Ulrich not only helped Burton, but he tracked down Burton's daughter and made arrangements for him to be picked up in San Dimas — Ulrich drove him.

Glendale News Press article of reunion with Eillis Burton (*top*) signed Topps baseball cards

On October 5, 2013, I received a phone call from Nadine, Ellis' daughter. She called me to say Ellis had passed away October 1. It was the family's wish to have me speak at Ellis' funeral. I graciously accepted. It was a true honor to speak about Ellis' life and our friendship. I was rather humbled at the number of professional ball players from his era, along with his family's lifelong friends, who were in attendance. With all the people who could have been chosen to speak, I had to ask, "Why me?" Nadine told me Ellis had the highest opinion of me as a person and one who saved his life. "He confided in you some of the most intimate moments of his life; he trusted you," said Nadine.

When the day came, I was concerned that I would not be able to keep myself composed, but I did manage to hold it together as I spoke about Ellis. I sat down for the rest of the ceremony. The ceremony was about to conclude when the reverend called up Nadine to speak. She spoke of her father's presence in her life and then called me back up to join her. She then spoke of Elli's love for me and how I saved his life. It was a very humbling moment. I could not fight back the tears as people stood to their feet and applauded. At the reception, I was greeted by every attendee. I saw Ellis' friends with whom I had many lunches at Pinks and friends and family I had never met before. What a privilege it was to be his friend.

THE STATION BOMB
One day while working the front desk at the police station, a woman walked inside the lobby and placed a bag on the front desk. She told me that her husband had just passed away and she was cleaning out his side of the closet when she found a metal object and thought to bring it to the police or fire department to ask what it was. I looked inside the paper bag and there was a one-inch galvanized metal pipe with two end caps and a fuse at one of the ends. It was a pipe bomb. I was a little shocked, but the woman appeared to have no clue what she had in the bag. I called dispatch and had them enter a bomb threat call and requested assistance at the front desk to clear the block of pedestrian traffic. I called the station sergeant and asked him if he could notify the

Los Angeles County bomb squad. He joined me at the front desk. After we cleared the front of the station and the surrounding streets, we placed the bag onto the sidewalk in front of the station while we awaited the arrival of the bomb unit. After an hour, they arrived, took custody of the bag and the device. It was placed into a metal chamber and detonated.

DIVORCE BY DEATH

I came to the records bureau to pick up a report for court and decided to walk to the lobby to visit an officer working the front desk. As we were talking, an older gentleman, probably in his eighties, entered the police department lobby. He looked very upset and spoke only Armenian. We called dispatch and were put in touch with an Armenian translator. The man spoke while crying on the phone to the translator. He then handed the phone to the front desk officer. "What did he say?" she questioned the translator. I watched her as she listened with an expression of unbelief. I asked her what he said. She covered the phone with her hand and said, "He told the translator that his wife asked him for a divorce, so he hit her with a knife."

"Where do they live?" I asked. The man got back on the phone and said where they lived in Glendale. I ran out of the station and drove to the residence on Salem Street to check on the man's wife. I arrived at the small, single-story house and found the front door unlocked. Officers Hunter, Murray, and I entered the residence and found an elderly woman lying on the floor in a white nightgown in a pool of blood. She was deceased. The elderly man was arrested for her murder. The knife used to commit the murder was found in his right front pants pocket. The investigation revealed the man dressed his wife in the nightgown after he killed her so she would "look pretty."

LESSONS LEARNED

As you can see in this chapter, the process of becoming a police officer varies, and the types of calls to which we are exposed differs greatly. All rescuers are intertwined with one another.

Many of us become rescuers for numerous reasons. Most everyone who chooses this line of work is willing to possibly lose his or her life and may also sustain severe injuries in the process. Most of us knew the risks when we signed up for the job. The majority of us love teamwork and the camaraderie that rescuers share. Most of us are assertive and run towards danger while others run away from it. Rescuers must rely upon each other with strong interdependency.

Rescuing others is a life of self-sacrifice. Because of the trauma and pressure on many calls, some of us suffer from post-traumatic stress disorder (PTSD). Along with the mental pain there can also be physical pain from carrying or wearing heavy tools for the job or injuries sustained in the line of duty. We sometimes avoid doctors and funerals because they remind us of our vulnerability. Many of us try to cope by turning to alcohol or drugs or adultery. The stress can lead to spousal abuse and isolation. It's important for rescuers to have a strong support group around them to help them cope with the stress of the job, especially with the aforementioned issues we all face in varying degrees. Most of us loved the job and would not trade it for any other form of employment.

Becoming a rescuer for me was easy. I was committed to rescuing when I was a child. I struggled as a rescuer in my private life because I could not stop rescuing others. This became an obsession with me until I learned to confront the little boy who was hurt and damaged seeing what happened to my father and the suffering my mother had to endure, while I remained in a helpless crisis.

4

KIDDIE COP

"There is no keener revelation of a society's soul than the way in which it treats its children."

—NELSON MANDELA, FORMER PRESIDENT OF SOUTH AFRICA

MANAGEMENT'S PREFERENCE

Early one morning, I was driving to a movie detail with two other officers, and we were discussing our desires to transfer to other assignments within the police department. I was the senior officer in the car and was explaining how the process works. I had attempted to leave patrol duties over ten times and was unsuccessful. You could say I was an expert at what not to do. I explained that even though you may want to transfer to a detail and have the ability to handle the assignment, you will not transfer unless you are recruited by management because it is their job to determine the best use of resources for the agency. It took me ten years to figure that out. I told my partners that I had just turned in a transfer request to work vice narcotics, but I felt it best to be transferred where management believed I could make a difference for the benefit of the agency. The other two officers argued with me. They didn't believe it was true. After about ten minutes of debate, dispatch requested that I call a manager from the juvenile bureau. It was 6:30 in the morning. I made the call and activated the speaker on my cell phone, so my fellow partners could hear the conversation. After some small talk the lieutenant said, "I realize that you would like to work in vice narcotics, but we have a need in the juvenile bureau. We believe you are just the person to fulfill that role. Roosevelt Middle School had seen some turmoil over the last two officers that were assigned there, and we need a good resource officer." The lieutenant continued, "If you are successful, as I know you will be with your teaching background, that vice detail will probably be waiting for you around the corner." I thanked the lieutenant for his invitation and asked if he would mind if I talked it over with my family and called him back later that day. He agreed cheerfully, and we terminated the call.

My partners looked at me and said, "No way. I can't believe that. No way that just happened."

"Well, now you know the way it works," I gloated. The two of them talked about this for hours.

You would think that I would have been excited, but the reality was far from the truth. I did not want to be a *kiddie cop* working at the school. I wanted to be where the excitement was. I craved the danger and risk associated with working undercover. Little did I know being a resource officer would turn out to be one of the best assignments in my career. After discussing this with my family, I called back the lieutenant and accepted his offer. He was thrilled.

BACK TO SCHOOL- A NEW ASSIGNMENT

It was now late summer of 2001 and I had formally transferred from patrol to the school. The new school year was beginning. I had my school resource officer (SRO) uniform on and radioed to tell dispatch I was in-service.

There I was, standing in front of Roosevelt Middle School as the students arrived. My job was to keep a watchful eye for gang members trying to recruit the younger students into their fold, child molesters and other predators preying on the kids, and drug offenders. Traffic was another problem. Parents would stop their cars in the middle of the street to drop off or pick up their kids. There were many accidents. As a result, our traffic motor officers worked many of our schools to assist with these dangerous risks created by parents. I moved toward one of the gates students and teachers were walking through. One of the dangers of working in a school is the fact that you have a firearm strapped to your waist and middle schoolers are very interested in weapons. You have to keep your head on a swivel and have eyes in the back of your head. Weapon retention and safety is paramount with this detail.

SCHOOL LEADERSHIP

After the bell rang a man dressed in a long sleeve shirt and tie walked briskly toward me. "I'm George," he said. "Are you our new SRO?" I nodded. He spoke rapidly about some of the non-compliant parents. I could see that he was a bit frustrated. He had keys strapped to his belt and a lanyard that read Assistant Principal.

"Well, George, it's nice to meet you, sir," I said. I asked him if he wanted to grab a cup of coffee and talk. He showed me the teacher's lounge and the coffee maker. I grabbed a cup and followed him to his office.

George had piles of papers all over his desk, and I could tell he was very busy due to the constant interruptions during my short visit. Before I could even ask a question, George was complaining about the last school resource officer. I eventually inquired as to what he felt were the issues facing the school and what he felt I could do to help him.

He appeared shocked and after a long pause said, "You're the first officer to ever ask me that question."

"If I'm going to help make a difference here, I will need to know what is happening," I declared.

He smiled and began to list his concerns. "We have vandalism almost every day. Fights at snack and lunchtime. Kids bring knives to school; ransack the bathrooms by stuffing the toilets with paper towels; engrave graffiti on the mirrors, lockers, desks; and ditch class to smoke tobacco and marijuana. They drink alcohol with their high school friends off campus. The high school students come to the fence and pass marijuana and other items through the chain-link fence next to the grass field. It was so bad that we had to place black sheets of plastic cloth along the entire south side of the fence." After about ten minutes of listing problems, he looked at me and asked, "Aren't you going to write all of this down?"

Pointing to the side of my head I said, "I have it all down, George." I stood up and asked if I had an office. He walked me out of his office and introduced me to Karen, the assistant to principal. She handed me a key. At that moment, a man dressed in a security guard uniform approached us. Karen introduced me to Robert. He had a great smile and spoke in rapid, broken English. He was a very muscular man with tattoos on his neck and arms. He looked like a gang member, but didn't act like one.

Karen asked Robert to show me my office. On the way, Robert pointed out the classrooms and other areas within the school. We walked by the auditorium and up a flight of stairs. We were now above the auditorium and standing in front of a door without a number. I opened the door with the key Karen had given me.

"Officer Rich, this is your office," Robert said as he extended out his right arm and reached inside and around the corner of the entrance where he turned on the light. There was a desk and a few chairs inside. Robert told me that it was the old projector room for the auditorium. Robert slid open one of the metal doors opposite the entrance and showed me that I could see inside the auditorium. The desk was small, and the room was stuffy and dusty. After sitting down for a few minutes, Robert's radio crackled, and someone named Jimmy asked Robert to come quickly because two boys were fighting in the hallway. I suggested that I go with him, and he thought it was a good idea. We arrived in one of the hallways and by then the two fighters were tired and out of breath. Robert grabbed one of them by the arm and asked me to escort the other boy. After arriving at the administration office, we seated the boys in some chairs while we waited for George to call them inside. We all ended up in George's office, and the boys were told to write statements. George let me know, "this is what I'm talking about." Robert asked Karen if I could have a school radio. Karen handed me one and showed me where the charger stations were. I went back to George's office and read the statements from both boys. I told both of them that they could be arrested for fighting on school grounds. George smirked and made it clear that both would be suspended. The suspension seemed to be suitable rather than an arrest since the only injuries were bruised egos.

THE LAY OF THE LAND
Robert and I walked around the school (inside and out). He showed me all the entrances to the school. The bell rang for snack time and within minutes we were surrounded by hundreds of children leaving their classrooms to play on the field or grab a quick bite to eat. I was amazed at how much the children loved Robert. They were constantly coming up to him and greeting him in Spanish and English. Robert must have talked with several hundred students before the bell rang again. Within minutes the campus was empty of students, with the exception of a few stragglers who got tardy slips.

AN EX-GANG MEMBER
During the next couple of periods, I spent some time getting to know Robert. We were constantly being interrupted as he kept getting requests for student escorts or to assist with disturbances in and out of the classroom. His radio traffic was busier than my police radio. I learned that Robert was an ex-gang member from Pacoima. His old crew was Paca Trecé (thirteen). Robert left the gang lifestyle (was jumped out) when he became a father. He loved children and needed a job with health insurance. He acquired a job from a security company that had a contract with the school district. His mother was a stay-at-home mom looking after his other siblings, and his father was a landscaper and gardener. Their family came to America from Mexico in hopes that Robert and his siblings could have a better life. Over the years I wound up going to many of Robert's

family gatherings in Pacoima, which is a west suburb of the San Fernando Valley of Southern California. This neighborhood is infused with high gang membership and some low-income residency. His neighbors were wonderful, hardworking, and lovely people. Some of Robert's old gang members came by a few times to visit him as they drove through the neighborhood. Robert never hesitated to introduce me as his friend. They did not know I was a policeman. It seemed that most of his old friends were proud of what Robert was doing at the school.

At lunchtime the bell rang again, and the campus filled with students having meals and playing games or other activities after eating. I was amazed that the students segregated themselves at lunch. This reminded me of prison and really bothered me. Almost every lunch there was some sort of disturbance or fight. These disturbances were usually carried over to an off-campus area where they would resume after school. Sometimes these disputes made their way to the gangs in the neighborhood and ended in serious violence.

During my first year as an SRO, I spent time learning about the criminal issues associated with our school, the children who attended, and the dynamics of the student body. I made many arrests with nearly half of them constituting felonies, including possession of edged weapons on school grounds, assaults causing great bodily injury, possession of controlled substances for the purpose of sales to minors, terrorist threats, arson, stalking others, threatening phone calls, underage drinking, possession of drug paraphernalia, tobacco possession, and vandalism. To add to this problem, most of the arrests were repeat offenders who were on juvenile probation. I arrested parents for child abuse and spousal abuse. This place was in some serious need of change. The suspension and expulsion rates were out of control. I spent my time responding to issues with very little ability to proactively help. The teachers and administrators at the school were amazing. The counselors were the best I had ever seen. Robert was the best security officer I had ever known. What was causing these problems to occur? What could we do to help turn these problems around?

A DAY OF TERROR

We were only several weeks into the school year when it happened. It was September 11, 2001 and I was driving into work when there was an emergency broadcast on the radio from New York. Several planes had just crashed into the twin towers in Ney York City. I listened intently all the way to work. When I arrived at the police station, officers were crowded around the televisions watching the aftermath of this terrorist act. After watching the news and conversing with others about what was happening, officers began coming in for briefings. I met with my supervisor to see what assignment would be given to me based on what had just transpired. I was told to report to the school and provide support for the staff, students, and parents.

When I arrived at the campus, it was the quietest I had ever seen the school. There were no fights or disturbances. It was as if an invisible fog had overcome the usual activities. There was a severe disruption in the status quo. The administrators were walking around in a daze; they appeared to be in shock. I visited the teacher's lounge at snack time, and the teachers had the same look. I realized then that most of the people had never seen such shocking things as I had been accustomed to in my job. I spent most of the day calming down the staff and the children. Many parents came to the school to pick up their children because they were frightened. We all eventually made it through the day.

CHILD ANNOYANCE

I returned for the second year and hit the ground running. I responded to an incident at one of the elementary schools that feeds into the middle school to take a *child annoyance* report. After I created the report, a girl at the middle school reported the same type of annoyance by a suspect matching the description and behaviors as the first suspect. The behaviors included making sexual comments to the young girls as they walked to school. The following day I decided to wear civilian clothes to appear as one of the parents and walk the route where the suspect was seen. On the second day of walking the area, I spotted a male matching the description from the police reports walking behind a group of young females from the elementary school. The girls kept looking back at the male and hurrying their pace to widen the gap, but the male picked up his pace and continued to follow them. I was across the street walking parallel to the group trying not to be seen. I requested back up on my police radio (hidden underneath my jacket) and crossed the street behind them. I knew as soon as this male figured out I was following him, he may take off running. The male looked behind and saw me crossing the street. Sure enough, he took off running. I gave chase and notified police dispatch that I was in pursuit of the male matching the report. He was taller than me and his legs were thin and long which gave him an advantage. I had to work hard to close the gap between us. I could hear the wonderful sounds of sirens approaching. The male entered an apartment building as the police units arrived at my location. We gave chase into the building and followed the male up a flight of stairs. The male entered an apartment, and we were able to detain him. We contacted the girls and were able to verify that he was in fact the one harassing them with sexual statements. We arrested him and then conducted a protective sweep (looking for other persons needing help) of his apartment but found no one in need. It turned out that this male was a registered sex offender. He was on parole, so the arrest sent him back to prison.

Years later (2009), I responded to a horrific traffic collision in Glendale. I was needed to conduct a drug influence exam on a male driver that had fallen asleep behind the wheel and hit a young girl on her bicycle, nearly killing her. The man was under the influence of multiple drugs and after reviewing his records, I learned that he was the same guy I had arrested previously for annoying children. I testified in his preliminary hearing in Los Angeles Superior Court. He eventually pled guilty and was again returned to prison. History repeats itself and so do criminal's behavior. This is what we call *the revolving door* in law enforcement. Some people just never learn.

AN AMAZING PARTNER

Robert, our security guard, was an amazing wealth of information. He knew all the gang members and their siblings. He knew who the taggers (graffiti artists) were, and he knew the word on the street, which helped us offset the gang violence. I kept Robert up to date on suspects our agency was looking for at the time, and he told me how to find them. One day Robert and I had to travel across town to assist at Hoover High School.

After completing our detail, we headed back to our school. Then I got a robbery call at a 99-cent thrift store on my police radio. Robert and I were one block away. We responded to see if we could help. Apparently, the male suspect had robbed several victims in the store of their purses and other personal items, and witnesses had followed him to the restroom where he attempted to hide. This information was not provided on the call. Several employees approached us and motioned us over to the suspect's location. Robert and I went to the back of the store where the man was locked in the restroom. The closest police units were miles away, and I told Robert that we would have to act quickly and probably before the other units arrived. No sooner had I updated dispatch, than the male exited the bathroom. Robert and I tackled him, and Robert handcuffed him. Patrol officers arrived and took custody of the suspect, and we drove back to the school.

Robert's keen eye for criminal behavior was the best I had ever seen. We solved almost every vandalism case at school and were a team to be reckoned with. The school officials were very pleased with our progress of solving crimes and bringing forth the perpetrators. Even with all this success there was no end to the criminal and anti-social behavior among the boys at our school. The girls even had fights on occasion, but I only made one arrest of a female student the entire time of my assignment. She was drunk in public and in possession of alcohol.

MAN WITH A GUN

The most dangerous call Robert and I had together was to investigate some gang members who were loitering across the street from one of the gates near the administration building. Robert received the call and radioed me for help. He said one of the males may be armed with a handgun and they were to get revenge for an off-campus altercation that apparently had happened over the weekend. I met Robert near my office and notified police dispatch to send a couple of units near the front of the school. Then Robert and I headed toward the front of the school to gather any information we could. Using parked cars for cover, Robert and I could see three Hispanic males loitering in front of an apartment across from one of the main gates. I provided dispatch a description and location of the males. I was able to surprise and hold the males at gunpoint. The responding officers arrived within seconds and all three were detained and a loaded weapon was recovered.

ROBERT ATTENDS COLLEGE

Robert attended the security courses at Mission College and graduated top of his class. I wrote the college about what Robert had done for our school and our police department. College administration wrote me back and asked me to have Robert consider speaking at the security graduation. Robert was reluctant but said he would if I helped him write the speech he would consider it. Here is his speech:

A SERVANT'S HEART

Dear Faculty, Staff, fellow students, and families:

It is truly an honor to represent the students at Los Angeles Mission Community College and those enrolled in the Security Guard Training Program. I would especially like to thank Kathleen Bishop our director, Instructor Philip Smith and Officer Rich Ulrich of the Glendale Police Department for their support and leadership.

When I was a teenager, I thought that being a gang member was the only way of life. I thought that I could help guys in the neighborhood to become men. I have since learned that there is a better way to serve my community and my friends.

In 1999, I acquired a job as a security officer. I was assigned to the Glendale Unified School District. It was at these schools that I understood the true meaning of being a man—by being a servant. Here I was an ex-gang member surrounded by teenagers who wanted to become involved in gangs. They, like me, thought it was the best way to find their manhood. I watched the violence from the prevention side and found the experience very distasteful and disheartening. I did my best to turn these youths around from a life of crime and violence to a life of peace and prosperity. This continues to be a real challenge to this day!

It was this experience, that motivated me to go back to college and re-educate myself. I wanted to be in a position of leadership that would make a difference in the lives of others. I returned to my own community a changed person. The difference in my life has caused those around me to take a look at themselves. It was this journey that gave me a servant's heart. I have learned that it is much better to serve others and be an example than to be served myself. It was this lesson that gave me my true manhood and joy in my life.

Thank you for this opportunity,

Roberto E. Jr.

Robert's speech was chosen. I was so thrilled for him. Robert told me that he was honored to be selected but his English is poor and difficult to understand. He did not want to embarrass himself or delay the graduation. I called administration and relayed the message to them. They told him he could give it in Spanish, and I offered to deliver the speech too in English. Robert was ashamed of his abilities and not excited about public speaking. Despite the many generous offers of assistance, he declined to speak. I heard later that Robert was honored at graduation and his speech was read to the class by the director!

THE TIPPING POINT OF CHANGE

Back in the spring of 2001, I was still working patrol when I received a call of a combative mentally ill man causing a disturbance at the family home. My partner and I arrived on scene and the family was pointing to a male in the front yard who was yelling obscenities to the other family members who were inside their home. During this call I injured my neck. The numbness never completely stopped in my left hand. I eventually had surgery to release the carpal tunnel and relieve nerves in that area. The surgery was unsuccessful, and the numbness continued. I made several trips to the emergency room for shoulder and back pain radiating from my neck. MRIs showed some injury in my back. No MRI was taken of my neck.

I continued working through the school year until summer break. In the summer, most SROs not assigned to the high schools were assigned to the detective bureau or patrol. I was assigned to the juvenile bureau to close out open cases. I cleared many cases that summer and became familiar with the juvenile district attorney's office. This relationship proved to be very advantageous for me in the near future.

In December 2002 I was on patrol while school was on break. I eventually ended up in the hospital and emergency surgery was performed on my neck (more on this in chapter 6). I returned to the school a month after surgery and some physical therapy to visit the staff and Robert. They all tried to be positive, but they looked worried that I wouldn't be able to return to their school. I remember going down the hallways and praying, "Lord if you allow me to come back here, I will finish this job the right way and change my attitude. I will find a way of fixing the problems at this school." I left the school with the promise, "I'll be back." It worked for Arnold Schwarzenegger. Right?

Meanwhile, Robert had cleared over seventy-one vandalism cases while I had been away. Our police chief was so impressed, he recommended Robert receive a special accommodation for his work and an offer to join our police agency volunteer program! Robert accepted the chief's invitation and served our agency for five years. Robert earned accommodations from Los Angeles County District Attorney's office, the county supervisor's office, and the Glendale Unified School District. The school district offered him a job a few years after I left.

A PRAYER REMEMBERED

I returned to work four months after my surgery. The look of shock on the police staff's face was something to behold. They were stunned and speechless. The school staff was no different. Robert greeted me with a huge hug and big smile. Robert and I were back in business. This time things were different. I shared with Robert my prayer and promise. He said he wanted to help me fix things too.

One morning after grabbing my morning coffee, I took a stroll in front of the trophy cases that lined the walls near the auditorium entrance. There was a strong prompting for me to take a closer look into the trophy cases. I pulled out each trophy and looked closely at them. Most of them were drill team and marching band trophies. There were four cases. It took me about 30 minutes to view all of them. Robert found me as I reached the last case and asked me what I was doing. Wanting to sound like a great detective, I said, "I have no idea." In the very last case was a blue and silver one that read, "1968 Boys Football Champions." I learned later that my captain, Ray Edey, had been on that team! I showed it to Robert. We just looked at each other. As if hit by lightning, I said to him, "This is the problem."

"What?" he inquired.

"Robert. There are no sports trophies here but this one from 1968. This is also the only one that is for boys. Don't you get it? Our school is missing some identity, and our boys need something to be proud of. Our school pride is gone. Who are the Rough Riders?" Robert stood there with a real look of intrigue. I needed to do some digging, and I knew who I needed to talk to.

RON GRACE, MY MENTOR

Ron was our head counselor, who had a heart for helping children. He was very intelligent and insightful, and I needed his help. I made an appointment with Ron through the main office. When it was my turn, I entered his office. After some kind words welcoming me back, Ron inquired as to the reason for my visit. I explained my attitude change and that I wanted to know if there were ever any sports programs at our school that involved our boys and girls competing with other schools in and out of our district. He told me that years ago he and some of the teachers drove the children in their private cars to other schools to play sports, but they stopped long ago due to liability issues. Ron gave me the names of three teachers (who chose to remain anonymous) who participated in this practice with him. I reached out to these teachers. They were very supportive of my idea to reinstate sports but questioned how I was going to transport the children. They decided to help me during recess and lunch times where we competed within our school only. Ron offered to referee the games. This was the beginning.

POLICE ACTIVITY LEAGUE (PAL)

The PAL program began in New York City when a young gang member threw a rock through a store window. "New York City Police Lieutenant Ed Flynn liked kids and was convinced that there had to be a better way to reach at-risk youth before they became involved in destructive and often harmful behavior. Lt. Flynn located the gang's leader and met with him to discuss the problems in the neighborhood. The gang leader spoke openly about his frustration of living in the inner city and constantly being watched by the law saying, "Man, we ain't got no place to play, nothin' to do. The cops are always hasslin' us. We can't even play baseball." Realizing this was the key, Lt. Flynn was able to rally many of the neighborhood storekeepers and his fellow police officers in support of his vision to start up a baseball league for the kids. He was able to raise enough funds to buy baseball uniforms and equipment and located a playground for games."[1] PAL became such a success at curving anti-social behavior, that its popularity spread throughout the US.

---

1   California Police Activity Website, 2019, https://californiapal.org/home/about-us/.

Officer Ron Williams was in charge of the PAL program for the Glendale Police Department and Glendale Unified School District. He was mentoring at-risk youth and established a youth boxing program. Many of these athletes became successful boxers as adults. Ron did an amazing job. He was able to acquire two vans with the support of congressional leaders. I spent time with officer Ron learning how the program worked and how it was funded. I spoke to Ron about utilizing some funds to build an after-school sports program so the children in the middle schools could compete and plan for high school and college. It seemed to be a good use of funds and a way to have a larger effect on the city of Glendale. Ron liked the idea and supported me.

It was not long after Ron and I spoke that he was replaced by Officer Renae, who took over as manager of the PAL program. I approached Officer Renae about my ideas, and she was supportive as well. She showed me a contractual agreement between the PAL program, parents, and students. The contract obligated students to maintain a C average, avoid school suspensions, avoid bullying, avoid fights at school, and avoid gang membership and associated activities.

Many of my students had arrest records, suspensions, expulsions from other schools, were living in foster care or motels, and were barely passing school—some were on court probation. I needed a waiver for some Roosevelt children to participate with the agreement that they show improvement each month or be removed from the PAL program. Renae obtained the waivers and the students who needed the waivers were allowed to participate in the program. I met with the Juvenile district attorney's office in Pasadena as well as judges and probation officers about the students who wanted to participate in the program to garner support. They loved the idea and supported me as long as I wrote progress reports for the court.

Now it was time to meet with family and the students to seek their consent and commitment. The parents were so happy that there was a chance for improvement, they signed the agreement forms without question. I met with the teachers and explained what I was about to do. I explained that each student in our PAL program would have to attend after school tutoring for forty-five minutes after class in order to improve their grades before participating in PAL activities. The students were required to participate in class. Any attitude issues from PAL students would place them on the bench during games, and they would be suspended from the program for a week. The teachers were excited to see this program roll out.

I ordered flag football and basketball jerseys from a wholesale outlet. Because of the cost of the uniforms, I had to retain possession of them and do the laundry after game day at the city jail laundry facility. We made the program for eighth graders only. This gave the sixth and seventh graders something to look forward to and work toward for their final middle school year.

THE ROUGH RIDER IDENTITY

Unknown to me at the time, Ron, our counselor, and several teachers had gone to the principal and asked to participate in my program as coaches and referees. The teachers were given permission to help me and receive overtime compensation. The *Glendale News-Press* and *LA Times* had received word of our program and wrote an article on the PAL program.

The games were held on Thursdays after school, so we decided to hold pep rallies during lunch on Thursdays. With permission of the drill team teacher and principal, we recruited some cheerleaders and made it happen.

It was Thursday lunchtime before our first home football game. The drill team teacher arrived with sound equipment and music. People started to gather in the quad area near the entrance to the girls' locker room. My players were all dressed in their uniforms and hiding around the corner waiting to be announced. I was a little nervous as I grabbed the microphone off the music stand. "Okay, Rough Riders. Welcome to our first pep rally ever!" Students began running off the basketball courts and eating areas to see what I was talking about. I repeated what I had just said and this time there was cheering the likes of which I had never seen before. Teachers began joining the festivities. Soon the principals were there as well. As I introduced each of the players, they would turn the corner and run through the cordon of cheerleaders shaking their pom-poms. As each player's name was called, the crowd grew louder. After finishing the introductions, it was time to introduce our students to who they were.

"Give me an R."

"R," the students repeated back.

"Give me an O."

The students repeated the letters until we had spelled out Rough Riders.

"Who are we?" I inquired. This took some work, but before long the entire audience was shouting, "Rough Riders!" It was difficult not to cry. Our students were shouting the school's name and not showing their gang signs. We were the Roosevelt Rough Riders. We found our *Rough Rider* identity.

Our head custodian called for me on the radio. The school district facilities office found out what we were doing and arrived in the late afternoon to mark up the field with yard markers and paint. They had created an official football field! I do not recall how facilities heard about PAL. I never told them. I did not care. This was another miracle.

It was game time, and we played Wilson middle school for our first game. The field was packed with parents and other students and teachers who stayed late to see the game. There was so much excitement about this game, it drew more people than the high school games. Even some high school football players came and commented to me after the game about this difference. We eventually lost the game, but the mood was amazing. No one cared. We all shook hands with the opponents and the other police officers that coached Wilson's team.

We began our football practices in September and the local high school football team came out to help our players. At first, only a few high school players came to our practices, but after a few weeks we had more than ten football players from the freshman team showing up. I called the Glendale High School coach and thanked him for his help. He informed me that he had nothing to do with it. His players found out what we were doing and wanted to help me on their own. His players felt that knowing the kids would be a great way to recruit them for high school. The coach even commented about our larger game crowds.

I contacted the University of Southern California Athletic department and told them about our program. I was interested in taking our football players to a USC football game. I thought it would be a great way to introduce our students to the university system at an early age. USC sent me enough game tickets for my family to attend as well. We met members of the USC football team at the dormitory cafeteria and had breakfast with them. We then went to the athletic department where we met the USC Trojan marching band for a pep rally. We marched with the band to the coliseum where we attended the game and sat near the band. Our players were so excited, many were interested in attending college.

The following Thursday was another football game day and another pep rally. This time our team traveled to Wilson middle school in the PAL vans. We brought the cheerleaders with us. Facilities had arrived and marked up their football field too. The referees were my PE teachers when I attended Wilson Middle School: Mr. Knapp and Mr. Rupp. They were about to retire. It was an amazing reunion. I learned later that they were also part of the group of teachers that had transported students to the middle schools for competition along with the Roosevelt staff in the seventies and eighties.

Parallel to the football field was an alley that runs along the entire length of the field. The press photographers were there awaiting our arrival and the start of the game. Parked along the alley were about twenty cars with parents from our school. The parents from Wilson were on the field. It was a sight to see. There were many fathers of our students who I recognized from our pre-PAL meetings sitting in the back of their construction trucks screaming and cheering. The residents whose backyards were facing the alley came outside because of the cheering. It was something they were not accustomed to hearing. We lost that game, but my players were so happy to see their parents cheering for them that they forgot they had lost the game.

The next game was a home game against Toll Middle School the following week. The players asked me if they could wear their football jerseys on game day. The principal allowed this to happen, and it became a tradition. It was their first win.

WE ALL BLEED RED

Basketball season was upon us, and it was time to bring out the uniforms. The girls did not want to play football, but they were interested in playing basketball. We held basketball practice in the gym. I was not much of a football coach, but I was not a bad basketball coach. I led drills and other techniques to gauge the players' talent and decide on player positions. The team was formed and only one girl wanted to remain on the team.

Like football, Thursdays were game day, and we had the usual pep rally. At the pep rally, to my surprise, I felt a tap on my shoulder. I turned around to see former mayor, city councilman, and retired police officer Rick Reyes. He was Roosevelt's first school resource officer, and he had heard about what we were doing with PAL. He wanted to see for himself. It was truly an honor to have him there to evaluate what I was doing. He was very pleased and encouraged me to keep up the PAL program as long as possible.

I met with the PE teachers earlier in the week, and we were able to locate the old controllers for the basketball scoreboards. There were several bulbs burned out and facilities had to do some repairs to bring the system to a running capacity. Prior to meeting with my team, I walked into the gym. I had the sense that something special was about to happen. I reminisced about what was taking place at our school and how my changed attitude and promise to God was manifesting itself before my eyes. It was quite a humbling walk through our gym. My youngest son was visiting me that day and wanted to see the basketball game. I had him stay with the team until our meeting in one of the classrooms.

I arrived at the classroom. The players were very excited, and my son was participating along with the players in their pre-game cheers. After the anxious players quieted down, we talked about the racist issues we had been dealing with at our school, and how we are a group of mixed-race players. I asked several players to tell me the color of their blood. After working our way around the room, the players agreed that all our blood was red. I then opined that we all are the same, and we are Roosevelt Middle School Rough Riders. I requested that our players sit at team benches at lunch as an example for the student body. Further, I explained that this is our first basketball game as a school, and it is really important for us to set an example by making our visiting school players and fans feel welcome.

It was game time, and the cheerleaders formed the rows of two with a paper poster in front for the players to smash through. The sound system was blasting the pre-game music and the visiting school had arrived. The visiting principal and I met them outside our gym. They lined up and awaited my signal to come in for introductions. Prior to introducing our visitors, I explained to the spectators that we needed to make our visitors feel welcome. I asked them to stand to their feet and scream as Toll entered our gym. As I introduced the Toll Middle School Titans, our fans stood up and cheered. The look on the principal's face as she gleamed with excitement and pride as her Titans entered the gymnasium to a standing ovation was priceless. Their school did not have basketball school uniforms at the time because they had been on backorder and had not arrived at the warehouse. Our team was then introduced, and our fans screamed as our players busted through the paper poster. I could not detect the difference between the cheering for our players verses our competitors. That was our goal.

The game was close most of the time. At halftime our drill team teacher said that she had a surprise for the spectators. She asked us to stay in the gym along with the other players rather than retire to the locker rooms for a team meeting, which we did. We were treated to a drill team halftime show. The drill team was amazing, and the fans really enjoyed the show. At the end of the game, students were shouting the countdown of the play clock in unison, "Five, Four," as one of our players let a half-court shot fly as the buzzer sounded. Into the basket the ball fell with a swoosh. All net! We won by four points. The fans poured out onto the gym floor as if we had won a championship game. It was pure pandemonium. Toll's principal grabbed me by the shoulders and said, "Rich this is amazing. I will be back with something amazing too." I assured her that her school uniforms would arrive soon, and I would bring them to her office. My police supervisor was at the game. He came up to me and shook his head as he said, "Wow! Well done. This is great Rich. Way to go."

THE PANDEMIC IS CONTAGIOUS

The following week, I received the rest of the basketball uniforms for three schools, and the games began. During lunch, the lower classmen were reaching out to the senior PAL players and asking for basketball advice. The race barriers had completely disappeared.

Toll wanted a rematch with our school. We drove to Toll in our PAL vans with the cheerleaders. This time Toll was dressed in their basketball uniforms, and they had a Titan mascot. The same excitement was in the air. The halftime shows featured Toll's drill team and ours. This game was not close. Our team won by a large margin. But the same excitement filled the air. The large crowd of parents and students from both sides participated in the pandemonium. The local news media was present. The *Glendale New-Press* was filled with photos of our PAL activities each Friday after our games. Our students were seen showing off their pictures, and there were pictures posted in the administration office announcement boards each week of all the participating schools. There was such a sense of pride happening at the schools. The yearbook teams were having fun with all the excitement; there was plenty to write about.

A few games into our second season, I began to receive calls from

Rosemount Middle School parents who were interested in transferring their kids to our school because of our sports program. I spoke with the principal and the Los Angeles County sheriff resource officer about our PAL program. Rosemont is within the Glendale Unified School district, but their law enforcement support is within Los Angeles County and not the city of Glendale. This meant that if Rosemont wanted uniforms, they would have to solicit funding from PAL through county leadership. I met with the administrative staff at their school. The SRO said he did not possess the talent to coach basketball or football. The school said they could find some PE teachers to help if I was willing to drive up to their school for games. After seeking permission from my police supervisor and school administration, I was only able to participate in basketball games.

Our first game with Rosemont was just as exciting as any other, and the staff did a good job of promoting the game; many students and parents showed up for the game. Rosemont players were so excited to play us, it carried over to their game and they won. The sports pandemic spread district wide.

One day I received a call from an employee from Jet Propulsion Laboratory in Pasadena who wanted to donate an entire weightlifting system for our PAL program workouts. I met with the principal and told her about the possible donation. I told the principal that the equipment could be used by the PE department too. She granted permission and wrote the acceptance letter for the donation. I accepted the generous offer, and the equipment was placed into a side room used by the PE department. It looked new to me and was a great addition to the school. The donor had said that he had read about the PAL program in the newspaper and wanted to support our program.

OUR CHAMPIONSHIP OPPORTUNITY—STAPLES CENTER

In 2005, after coaching Roosevelt for three years, our Rough Riders had won two basketball championships. It was time to increase our talent. Each Tuesday and Thursdays our team would play an adult team that had been using our gym for their pick-up games for nearly ten years. We started playing them my second year of coaching. We lost every game. I changed my coaching strategy and training techniques. Near the end of my final season, we were still the team to beat on the court, and Wilson gave us the greatest competition, but I thought that if we could beat these adults, we would be a really good team. By May, we actually took the lead in some games with the adult team, but they would eventually win.

That same spring, I had heard that the Staples Center allowed private and public schools to play games at the Center. Each school had to write a letter of intent and why they felt that their school or program was worthy of a shot at the limited dates available to participate. I obtained an entry form from the Staples Center and returned it to the selection board. I explained my story of how PAL changed my school, the lives of the student body, the parents, and me. About three weeks later, I received an email instructing me to call Dave C., a board member. I called him. He wanted to let me know that our program was selected to utilize the Staples Center for an event and that included reduced priced tickets to either a Laker's or Spark's game for all participants and their families. Dave told me that he had been working for the sports organization that hosts different Los Angeles teams (Laker's basketball, Spark's basketball, and King's hockey) for years and had not seen any Police Activity League action since he worked at the Inglewood Forum. He missed seeing the at-risk kids living out their dreams and the police officers helping the kids in the community. He said we had won a slot unanimously. I contacted Officer Renae and told her the news. She obtained funds to cover Dave's announcement team to work the scoreboard and the cost of the reduced-price tickets to attend the evening game.

We were slotted for June 5, 2005. It was decided by all the PAL officer coaches that we take the top two teams, Roosevelt and Wilson middle schools, and have the captains from those teams select players from Toll middle school to be divvied among those two schools. This would assure that all PAL players from all the participating schools had a chance to play at Staples Center. It was the Cops vs. the Robbers. My team, Roosevelt, were the Robbers.

The players were instructed to arrive with their families ninety minutes before tip-off. My children came too. Ron, our counselor, and other teachers who had refereed many of our games arrived in their uniforms. My assistant coach, Dave Duran, was there too. To my surprise, many of the city's gang members arrived at Staples Center with their families and introduced themselves and told me who they came to watch play. They were advised against causing any disturbance, and they assured me that they were there to cheer on their family members. Many of them shook my hand and even gave me hugs. This meant so much to me that words cannot describe how I felt. Rival gang members sitting next to one another and cheering for our players. I looked up in the stands and saw this during the game. Another miracle!

Dave C. met with me at the scoring tables and introduced himself. He put my two boys to work and showed them how to run the shot clocks, scoreboards, sub-buzzer, and all the necessary bells and whistles that accompany a professional game. The *Los Angeles Times* arrived for an interview and photos along with Glendale TV channel 6. Glendale TV broadcasted the game for those who could not attend. I felt like a celebrity with all the photos and interviews.

Even the VIP and communications director interviewed me for the Staples Center News. It was entirely overwhelming but amazing for all the PAL kids. They, too, were interviewed on television and by the press. I was so proud of how each of them handled themselves. Things were set for such a great event! Dave announced me. It was time for introductions. He handed me the microphone, and I walked to the center of the court. Staples Center holds eighteen thousand seats, and we filled about two thousand of them. I quickly glanced at the audience and recognized teachers, principals, parents from my school, and the gang members with their families. I introduced the teams, and we went to our assigned seats at the player benches. We were seated where the professional players and coaches sit. All the players were so excited and nervous. We fell behind quickly for the first quarter and slowly caught up and tied by half time. By the third quarter we pulled away and never trailed again, winning our third championship in a row.

It was about an hour before the Sparks game. We had to exit the Staples Center while Dave and the set-up crew prepared the center for the next event. I met with several of the families from our school. They thanked me for my coaching and for helping their children prepare for high school. More gang members approached and gave me high fives. There was so much excitement in the air.

We re-entered the Staples Center with our game tickets. The seats were only about ten rows from the court. I met with the communications director at her office along with two team captains and two students who made the best overall improvement in the program from all the schools. We were told that we would be introduced along with the WNBA Sparks players during player introductions.

It was time for introductions and this time there were about twelve thousand audience members. Our players were nervous as they were called to center court where they were given a basketball from one of the players after introductions. Dave must have been behind this activity. He never told me he was. This was another miracle!

After returning to our seats, several of my players kept pointing to someone sitting near us. They said his name was LeBron James from the Cleveland Cavaliers NBA team. I had no idea who he was, but I had heard his name from the NBA draft a few years prior. After the Sparks game the PAL players and their family and friends departed Staples Center with a sense of accomplishment and the possibility that dreams can come true.

MY DEPARTURE FROM SCHOOL

After a great week of festivities and another successful season of PAL, it was time to depart the school for the summer. Police management needed training officers because of a large group of graduates from the police academy. I was asked to leave my assignment and return to patrol to meet our training needs. I met with the teachers at their staff meeting with the principal and announced my departure. There was some crying as I expressed my gratitude for their support, friendship, and patience as I learned my job at their school. As I finished speaking, they stood to their feet and applauded. Most of them gave me a hug and shook my hand.

THE UNEXPECTED GIFT

It was August 2005, and I was on patrol when my cell phone rang. It was Jimmy, the head custodian at Roosevelt. He told me that a huge crate was delivered to the facilities maintenance office (FASO) and was addressed to Coach Officer Ulrich at Roosevelt Middle School. Jimmy took delivery of the crate at the school and had the crate placed by the main gym doors. "What do you want me to do with this crate?" he asked. I instructed him to open it. The FASO crew pried the crate open and found a letter addressed to me. The letter read something to the effect of:

Dear Officer Ulrich,

I worked at the Los Angeles Coliseum and now the Staples Center as the manager of all electrical maintenance. Now I sit on the executive board for the Staples Center. When you wrote about your life story, what happened to your school and the effect your PAL program had on the kids, I was inspired. As one of the head members for the International Brotherhood of Electrical Workers of Los Angeles, I shared your story. By unanimous vote, we decided to send you a scoreboard with your school's name and dedicate it in your honor. We will send a crew to install it for you. Thank you for inspiring all of us.

Dave C.

Inside the crate was a brand-new scoring system for the basketball gymnasium. To say I was speechless would be an understatement. I had to pull over my patrol car to compose myself. The FASO crew moved the crate into the gym workout rooms until the IBEW arrived to install the scoreboard. I had been gone from the school for two months and miracles were still following my departure.

A LEGACY NOT FORGOTTEN

By the end of my tour at Roosevelt Middle School, eighteen of our players attended UCLA basketball programs and camps designed to prepare players for high school and college. Several of our PAL basketball players who trained at UCLA camp entered high school and were immediately placed onto the varsity team at Hoover High School. That Hoover team entered the state sectional final playoffs with a few of my players. The school district asked me to consider

Team time out during championship game at Staples Center (*top*). Championship game players 2005. (Author's collection)

coaching high school basketball. One PAL player was drafted to Azusa Pacific as a starting tackle on the varsity football team.

Sadly, my friend, counselor, mentor, and coach trainer, Ron Grace, was killed in the Chatsworth train collision on September 12, 2008. The car he was sitting in was struck by a Union Pacific freight train.[2] His funeral was very moving as many of the PAL kids, staff, teachers, and Ron's family were in attendance. I wrote a letter to Ron's wife explaining what he did for me and how with his help, we turned the school around to a more welcoming place with high academics and amazing athletics. Ron had helped me change my attitude and direction. He will never be forgotten. I am so grateful to you, Ron.

2   http://projects.latimes.com/metrolink-crash/name/ronald-g-grace/

Roosevelt MS counselor and PAL sports referee, Ron Grace. (Author's collection)

The new scoreboard from the IBEW of Lods Angeles for Roosevelt MS. (Author's collection)

LESSONS LEARNED

Why did I include this chapter in this book? First, I learned to submit myself to leadership even when I do not agree with their decision. Could it be that they saw something in me that I could not see in myself? Second, I needed to have a grateful attitude and an expectation that something good can happen despite my lack of vision. What harm is there in believing that something great can come from an unexpected place? Could it be that having an opportunity to coach children in the same school district in which I was denied a chance to play in my youth was a way of restoration for me? Lastly, serving others "fixed" me. Being a *kiddie cop* really fixed myself for a better us. It really was a journey of courage that changed others as well.

5

CANCER AND THE GREATEST GIFT

"When your life is on the line and you no longer know how long you will live or when you will die, it doesn't matter anymore if there is no love in your life to share with others. I now have love in my life for the first time. It was cancer's gift to me."

—ROLFE ULRICH

This chapter is for all those people who have been diagnosed with cancer, those who have beaten their diagnosis and entered a long remission, those who we lost from cancer, and the family and friends supporting those with cancer and everyone who needs to find courage and strength in the worst of times.

DEALING WITH FEAR

Any diagnosis of cancer can be a frightful experience. If we were to be honest with each other, we would admit that when we hear of someone receiving a diagnosis of cancer, we are grateful it is not us. We ponder whether cancer has been in our family history, hold our breath, and then find temporary relief when we do not recall a family history of that diagnosis. People diagnosed with cancer do not suffer alone, but it affects everyone connected to the patient. In my case, when my twenty-three-year-old son Rolfe was diagnosed with cancer, I experienced a fear that attempted to take residency within me.

Most of my life had been filled with frightening moments. I experienced many flashbacks as a military veteran and a retired police officer. To say that I was accustomed to facing fearful moments would be an understatement. But this was different. This was my son. Although every mission in the military or call on the police force had some degree of unpredictability, in my career, I had some control based on my choices. When it came to my son's cancer diagnosis, I was facing the possible death of my son, and there was nothing I could do but pray. I felt helpless. It is during that time that I experienced one of the greatest seasons of personal growth.

SOMETHING IS WRONG

It was early November 2016 when my son Rolfe moved home to bring some sort of stability back into his life. Rolfe is an electrician and installer of solar systems for Tesla Energy (previously Solar City). He is accustomed to the painful, back-breaking work of attaching solar panels to residential roofs and wiring them to the main panels. Hearing Rolfe complain of a sore back and painful joints was par for the course.

From the day Rolfe moved back home, he began to complain of painful headaches that would not subside. After two weeks, he continued to complain of these headaches, but he also was having pain in his back and body tremors (mainly in his hands). By the end of the second week with me, I convinced him that it was time to go to urgent care. Rolfe was given headache medicines, told that he may be suffering from stress, and was sent home with a referral to a neurosurgeon the following week at the Kaiser Permanente medical offices in Panorama City, California.

It was now mid-November 2016 as we arrived for our two o'clock appointment at Kaiser. The medical consultation went smoothly, and the neurosurgeon agreed with us that three weeks of constant headaches was enough to warrant an MRI. I told Rolfe to schedule the MRI for as soon as possible—even see if we could have it while at the facility. To our surprise, someone had just canceled for the afternoon. We waited an hour, and the MRI was completed. We were told that we would receive a follow-up call with the neurosurgeon in the next few days.

It was the last Monday in November, and Rolfe was up with the sunrise and ready for work. I went downstairs to the kitchen and saw that Rolfe was not at work. He was seated at the breakfast bar, and he was suffering with tremors all over his body. I checked him for a fever, and his temperature was 98.7 Fahrenheit. He was still complaining of a severe headache and said that his vision was becoming blurry. He called in sick for the day. He stayed home and rested for two days.

By the middle of the week, he was not well. The body tremors continued. He had a fever, and he complained of pain all over his body. Rolfe's cell phone buzzed, and the neurosurgeon told Rolfe that his brain MRI appeared normal. The doctor prescribed a new headache medicine along with other pain medicine. There was still no relief, and Rolfe's health kept declining. He was able to report to work and handle a few odd construction jobs when his installation team awaited new work orders. This continued for the next three weeks.

With Christmas upon us, Rolfe did his best to appear happy and jovial despite his continued headaches, overall body pains, and tremors. Adding to his discomfort was his labored breathing. Rolfe returned to work for the next two days. I had this feeling that something was going to happen to me or my family. This conviction remained with me for two days and really affected my sleep. I could not shake this immense feeling that overwhelmed me.

THE FINAL STRAW

Thursday, December 29, 2016, I was working out at the gym when I received a call from Rolfe. "Dad. I'm in trouble. My body has completely shut down."

"What do you mean?" I inquired.

"I can barely breathe or walk and every part of my body hurts. I am even going blind in my right eye." I insisted that I pick him up from work, but he was already driving and nearly home.

I dashed home, changed out of my gym clothes, and awaited my son's arrival. I was a little nervous and anxious to see what Rolfe meant. About twenty minutes later, the front door swung open as I was coming down the stairs. Rolfe crossed the threshold of the door with much difficulty. In my police career, I had seen many injured and sick persons. My son's appearance was different from anything else I had seen before. He shuffled inside and closed the door. His right eye was a little droopy. He was pale as a ghost, and his breathing was extremely shallow as he displayed body tremors and suffered from ataxic gait, or irregular foot placement. It looked to me as if he had just had a stroke. His pupils were reactive to light, but he was not looking well. I steered Rolfe to his room to change into some comfortable clothing while I packed his backpack with clothing and assorted toiletries. Rolfe was so weak that I had to dress him. I knew that Rolfe was going to be admitted to the hospital, and I needed to get him there as soon as possible.

I drove Rolfe to the Kaiser hospital in Panorama City since I was familiar with this facility, and it seemed to have the best options for care. I was nervous the entire drive down, and eventually we made it to the emergency department (ED) parking lot. I parked in the handicap area and ran to the ER while Rolfe remained in the car. As I entered the ER, I saw a poster near the triage area that listed the symptoms of a stroke. I told the receptionist that my twenty-three-year-old son was in the car and needed assistance, that he had all the symptoms of someone having a stroke. An orderly followed me back to my car with a wheelchair. We placed Rolfe into it, and the orderly hurried back to the ER.

THE DIAGNOSIS

When parking my car, I had a sense of peace mixed with relief knowing that my son was in the hospital. I parked my car and hurried to the ER. I can't remember if I walked or ran. Whenever I face trauma, emergencies, or other matters of exigency, I switch to rescue mode. It is a mode I have grown accustomed to in the military and police where I remain during the storm until the weather clears and I can debrief or unwind.

When I walked into the ER, I found Rolfe already in the triage section. Within minutes, he was wheeled into the treatment area where several clinicians and nurses met him at the entrance. Rolfe was placed in the hallway since there were no open treatment rooms. The laboratory personnel withdrew his blood, and we remained in the hallway awaiting the results from the laboratory. This was the first time anyone had taken his blood for testing.

Having been in the military and worked at a police department, I had grown accustomed to long waits. This is where the old adage "hurry up and wait" evolved. That was the longest wait in my life. It took about thirty minutes before the charge nurse wheeled us into the diagnosis room. The nurse tried to remain cavalier, but her concerned look was not fooling me. I asked her directly what was going on with Rolfe. She told me the doctor would be in soon to speak with me. I knew what this meant. Something serious was going down or at least they suspected there was something seriously wrong. Rolfe kept inquiring what was happening, and I continued to assure him that I did not know. I am not sure if he believed me or not.

The ER charge physician entered the diagnosis room and introduced himself. From the way the nurse was breathing rapidly and trying to avoid eye contact with me as she typed feverously into the mobile computer, I knew my son was in trouble. The doctor took me out to the hallway and began by telling me that they had only a preliminary assumption of what was wrong and had called in an expert to verify what they were seeing, but, he pontificated, "We collectively believe that your son has the signs of Leukemia. We have a call into an oncologist who has adjusted his schedule to meet us here."

"Why do you assume it's leukemia," I asked.

"When someone's white blood cell count is as high as Rolfe's there is a chance of leukemia," the doctor said. "I'm going to have the oncologist take a sample of your son's bone marrow for immediate testing. Your son will need some blood transfusions to save his life because the blood in his body is too thick for his heart to circulate and his cardiovascular system is having to work twice as hard to keep him alive. I am so glad you brought him in. You saved his life."

With that, the doctor left the room. I peeked down the hallway from behind a service cart and could see nurses huddled around one of the stations and pointing in my direction. They were shaking their heads. I went back into the room and put my right hand on Rolfe's chest and felt that his heart was pounding with tremendous force, and he was scared. I assured him that he was in good hands and that we may now know why he was having headaches and other pains.

The doctor came back in to talk to Rolfe. I told Rolfe that I needed to update the family. As I entered the hallway, I looked around and could see the nurses still huddled around the nurse's station, staring at me. I called my mother immediately and gave her the update. She asked if she should leave work, and I assured her it would be a while before anyone could visit Rolfe. I then called other family and told them the preliminary information. They told me to keep them updated as we received a complete diagnosis. I then began to cry. I could not hold my feelings back any longer. It was too much. After composing myself, I called my sister, Beverly, and more family and friends and told them what was happening and then after composing myself, I headed back into the diagnosis room.

It didn't take long before several nurses and the oncologist and his staff arrived. Usually, when faced with tragedy it seems like eternity before things happen. This was not the case. Within minutes, the oncologist was extracting the marrow from Rolfe's hip. The oncologist asked me to step out into the hallway during extraction. As I entered the hallway, I saw the same group of nurses pointing in our direction, and it was obvious that they knew what was happening. After the extraction was completed, the oncologist, Dr. Chung, met with me in the hallway and explained that his reading of Rolfe's blood work in these cases usually leads to a leukemia diagnosis, and he asked me about the events that led up to today and our arrival at Kaiser. He explained further that there was a good chance that Rolfe would be sent to a pediatric oncology facility and that he believed Rolfe may have ALL (Acute Lymphoblastic Leukemia). He said that the results would be back in a couple of days, but he wanted to get Rolfe into treatment before New Year's Day. I had only heard of leukemia but not ALL or the other types of blood cancers. I was about to be educated.

The oncologist and I walked back into the treatment room where the doctor repeated to Rolfe what he just told me. We remained in the treatment room for about an hour while Rolfe waited to be admitted. We eventually made it to a private room. Several nurses and technicians attached Rolfe to several monitors and then administered blood transfusions. Grandma Dodie arrived and brought some comfort to Rolfe. I eventually had to go home to get some rest. I was exhausted. When I finally made it home, I parked the car and just sat there and cried. I needed to cry. I eventually made it inside and tried to sleep.

I made it out to the hospital several times over the next few days and saw some improvement in Rolfe's health. He began to have more color in his complexion and his white blood cell count stabilized.

New Year's Eve was upon us, and I met my sister and my girlfriend for an evening with Rolfe. There was no way we were going to allow Rolfe to bring in 2017 by himself. With Martinelli's apple cider in hand we toasted, to better health for Rolfe. Two days later, Rolfe was transported by ambulance to the Woodland Hills Pediatric Oncology ward where he was admitted for an aggressive treatment regimen.

PEDIATRIC ONCOLOGY

The purple door leading to the pediatric oncology is etched into

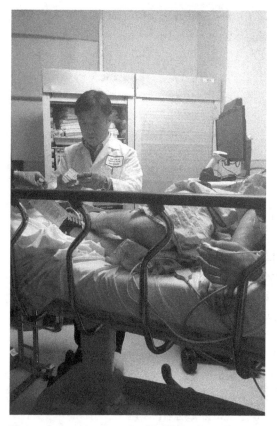

The oncologist taking a sample of Rolfe's hip bone. Kaiser ER treatment room. (Author's collection)

my memory forever. There were so many little children lying in their beds surrounded by parents with worried looks on their faces. Joy was absent in that unit. My son was in room 3309. To my surprise he was sitting up in bed with a smile on his face. I asked him how he was feeling and what he thought of this new place and the staff. He said he was still having pain throughout his body, but the staff was wonderful. He then began to explain his empathy for the children in the ward and how concerned he was for them because they were so young. He was the oldest patient there at the time.

My sister Beverly called me a few days after Rolfe was admitted to the pediatric ward to tell me that she was visiting Rolfe in the oncology unit and had just met with Rolfe's hematologist, Dr. Susan Storch. She was so impressed with her that she had to call me.

Rolfe had so many people visiting him that there were times when it was standing-room only. One day he had seventeen visitors. There were card games, charades, radio-controlled helicopters, flying surgical gloves with painted faces and flying toilet paper coming from inside Rolfe's room on a consistent basis. Rolfe's childhood friends visited, and some were from out of state. Usually when I'd walk down the bleak hallways of the ward, I'd hear laughter pouring out of Rolfe's room. He had a huge flat screen television with an X-Box. There'd be pizza boxes on top of the trash receptacles, and soda cans on all the tables and bed trays. It looked like a college dormitory without the beer.

One time the guys were so loud I went to the nurses' station to apologize for the disturbance. Carole, the

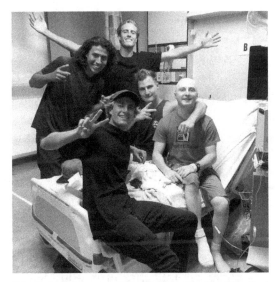

Friends visiting my son at Kaiser Pediatric Oncology, Woodland Hills, CA. (Author's collection)

charge nurse at the time, stopped me before I could finish apologizing and said to me, "Your son has the best attitude we have ever seen in this place and that I have ever seen in all of my years of working here. He brightens up the place. When we know Rolfe is here, we look forward to coming to work. He will beat this cancer before it beats him. The laughter and joy from him are contagious to all of us."

Around this time, I was in my first residency in my master's program. I told Rolfe that I needed to look at stopping my education to be sure that I was able to make all of his required appointments and treatments. Rolfe looked at me and said, "No dad. You need to finish. I do not want to be the reason you did not finish college. If you have to take classes in my hospital room, I won't let you quit!" Being my son's caregiver throughout the process was a great opportunity that stretched my faith and character in many ways. I was so grateful for all the people around Rolfe and that I was able to continue my education.

A short time after Rolfe was admitted to Kaiser of Woodland Hills, two amazing people began visiting him almost every day: Ben and Hannah. They brought him meals, laughter, company, and encouragement. After about three weeks in the hospital, Rolfe was sent to the pediatric oncology and hematology outpatient center for chemotherapy and other cancer treatments while he awaited a blood marrow donor to be found.

THE ONCOLOGY OUTPATIENT CENTER

The Oncology Outpatient Center was located at Kaiser Permanente Woodland Hills Medical Center and was the main office for Dr. Storch. The office manager, Kathy, was a very kind and helpful person who made life easier for Rolfe and me. Rolfe had many spinal taps and small outpatient surgeries at the center. Before one of Rolfe's spinal taps, he had the whole treatment staff laughing along with him while he was under the influence of pre-op medicine. The staff told me later that they loved it when Rolfe came in for procedures just to hear him laugh. One day Dr. Storch spoke to me about Rolfe's health and how much his positive attitude made all the difference in his treatments. She also told me that he never once complained.

Like in the hospital, there were many children at the center. I would hear their name called and see the parents walking them into the treatment area. In the entryway of the oncology center was a wall with one side having painted hand prints with the names of children who survived cancer written inside. On the other side were the names of the children who did not survive. You realize the seriousness and stress for the parents when they look at the walls and contemplate which side their child will land. Rolfe survived, and his handprint was placed onto the survivors' wall. This was gut wrenching to me.

GINGER'S HOSPITAL VISIT

Chemotherapy made my son extremely ill. Nevertheless, it was critical to keep the white blood cell count down, and he needed many transfusions while we waited for a bone marrow match. He had been in and out of the hospital about five times, staying there two weeks at a time. He really missed his Siberian Husky named Ginger. One time I decided to sneak Ginger into the hospital for a visit. I did some surveillance beforehand. I found out from the staff that the time it was least crowded was early afternoon, which meant I'd have to sneak in the pooch in broad daylight. The only people who would stop me on the outside would be the security guards. Over the next couple of days, I monitored their breaks and figured out which ones appeared to be the least observant. Their breaks averaged about twenty minutes where there was no one watching the north and west service doors, where the employees entered. I had never seen any service dogs enter the front, which meant they must have entered through the employee service entrance too.

The day I brought Ginger, I parked in the visitor parking garage and took the stairs. I walked along the outside of the structure to have less contact with people and more opportunities for Ginger to use the bathroom along the way. I had to pass by the drop-off area to get to the employee entrance, but I knew the guard was on break. It took only two minutes for me to access the employee side. I planned it so I'd arrive when environmental services took out the trash, giving me plenty of opportunities to gain access. As one of the workers exited the door with a large cart, I used the cart to block his view of Ginger and headed inside. I headed for the service elevators. To make sure that I would not be seen by other employees, I entered two of the elevators and pushed all the buttons going up. This would occupy the two elevators for a while giving me more of a chance to not be seen by employees. I then pushed the button for the third elevator and waited to be sure no one exited onto our floor. Luck was on my side.

I made it to the third floor where I exited quickly and made it to pediatrics. There is a camera at the main door near the doorbell. I stood off to the side and was able to pull the other exit door open. The nurses were busy with the patients, so I made a dash for Rolfe's room. The nurses never saw Ginger because she was low to the floor and out of sight. I announced to the only nurse at the desk, "Hello. I'm here to visit my son." Her eyes never left the computer as she nodded her

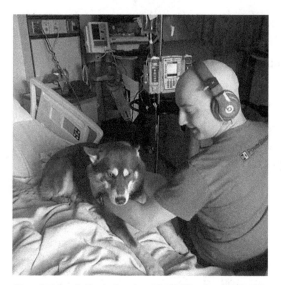

Ginger's visit to Pediatric Oncology Kaiser Woodland Hills, CA.
(Author's collection)

head in affirmation. I took out my camera and filmed the reunion of my boy and his dog. He was so happy. He kept saying to the person he was talking to on his cell phone, "oh my God, Ginger is here! My dad brought Ginger to visit me." Ginger immediately jumped into Rolfe's bed. We visited for about thirty minutes before I realized I needed to get out of there before the nurses or staff came to Rolfe's room. I followed the same route and techniques in reverse and left the hospital without a single person saying a thing to me. Security never saw me. I probably was on camera at least once on the main floor near the baby area, but mission accomplished. I was glad to bring more joy to my son who texted me numerous times with gratitude for how much joy it brought him to see his dog again.

CANCER'S GIFT TO MY SON

It was noon on Monday April 10, 2017, when my son and I arrived at the California State Office for Disability Insurance (SDI) in Van Nuys, California. We were on task to try and determine why the state had not paid my son his disability payments. My son was about to park his car when he looked over to me and said, "Dad. Cancer has given me the greatest gift!"

Stunned. I asked, "What gift is that?"

"Love," he answered. I was really caught off guard. He explained, "When your life is on the line and you no longer know how long you will live or when you will die, it doesn't matter anymore if there is no love in your life to share with others. I now have love in my life for the first time. It was cancer's gift to me."

As we exited the car, I kept pondering what Rolfe had just said to me. My son, who is staring cancer and death in the face with a long road ahead of him, sees cancer as a gift. How is that? I was speechless. Any self-pity within me, just left the building. That was one of those perspective moments in your life when you realize how shallow your thinking or attitude really is. It was another tipping point in my life. We made it upstairs to the state insurance office and, with the assistance of the SDI personnel, were able to resolve the issue.

It was late July 2017 when I received a phone call from the staff at City of Hope telling me that the world-wide search for a donor was completed and a bone marrow match was found in Germany. The match was 95 percent, but the medical staff had to approve the donor and then make the necessary arrangements for us to be admitted to the City of Hope. We were told that the stem cells would be arriving sometime between the tenth or eleventh of August, so we would have to admit one week prior.

A CITY OF HOPE

There is a reason City of Hope is called that. It is the last stop for most patients. If they are going to win their battle with cancer, it is here. The last time I was there, I was visiting one of my training officers who was diagnosed with cancer. He passed away from his disease, but I remembered the beautiful grounds and polite staff.

In the early evening of Sunday, August 6, 2017, we admitted Rolfe into Helford Hospital at the City of Hope, Duarte, California. To say I was nervous was an understatement, but I knew if Rolfe was to have a chance at survival, it was going to be here.

We walked over to Helford Hospital and went to the top floor where Rolfe remained for the first week. The first week was the toughest part of his treatment. Radiation is necessary in preparation for his forthcoming stem cell implant. After the second day of radiation, Rolfe became ill and felt horrible. When in the radiation area, Rolfe met a young man named Casey. He had ALL, too, and was very frightened about the radiation treatment. Rolfe encouraged him and volunteered to be with him during the entire procedure.

One of the proudest moments for me as a parent occurred during Rolfe's radiation and chemo treatments. Rolfe found out that Casey was not responding well to the treatments and stem cell transplant. Rolfe asked me to go out and purchase with his own money a radio-controlled helicopter. Rolfe wrapped up the gift and brought it downstairs to Casey's room while dragging his numerous IV and monitoring machines. That did not slow down Rolfe from bringing joy to someone else. We walked into Casey's room, and he was so excited to see Rolfe. I filmed the encounter on my phone as I fought back the tears and pride in my son for thinking of others despite his own pain and struggles.

A NEW BIRTHDAY

On August 11, 2017, Rolfe's donated stem cells arrived. I had just finished watching a concert with my girlfriend at the Hollywood Bowl, and we were stuck in the parking lot waiting to exit. I Facetimed Rolfe to see if the stem cells had arrived yet. No sooner did I make a connection then I hear a commotion in the hallway near Rolfe's hospital bed. It was his nurses singing happy birthday and arriving with his stem cells. He was literally having a new birthday. We listened intently while crying with joy as they administered a new chance at life for my son. The same attitude that Rolfe had at Kaiser Pediatric Oncology was the same he maintained at the City of Hope.

One of the activities the staff encouraged patients to do was leave their rooms and walk the floors. Each mile (ten laps around the floor) you walked would earn you a charm from the staff. You then placed them onto a necklace that you attached to your IV cart hook. Rolfe was super active and even lifted weights each day. Rolfe accumulated thirty-eight charms during his stay. The staff cheered him on as he did each of his laps. On September 7, 2017, my son came home to recover from the stem cell treatment. Ginger and the family were happy to see him at home. And I was able to earn my master's. My graduation sash is dedicated to my son.

REMISSION, A NEW COMPANY, AND ALOHA

By June 2018, Rolfe had 96 percent of his donor's marrow and no sign of cancer! There were many changes taking place in Rolfe's life. His employer, Solar City, was changed to Tesla Energy. Hannah was moving to Hawaii to go to school, so he decided to send out his resume to a

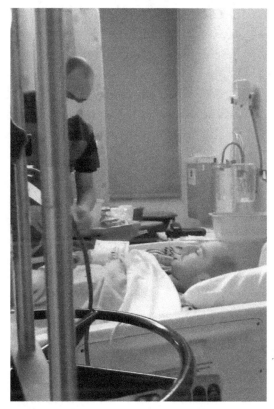

Rolfe's stem cell treatment Aug 11, 2017, City of Hope. (Authors collection)

Tesla facility in Hawaii. Not long after that he was sitting in the Los Angeles International airport waiting to board a flight to Hawaii to visit Hannah when his phone rang. It was the Tesla warehouse manager from Hawaii. The manager was interested in speaking with him about an opening in Hawaii. Rolfe informed the manager that he was on his way to Hawaii in thirty minutes. The manager asked if he could come in for an interview the next day. Rolfe accepted the interview and ended up being offered the job. Within two weeks, Rolfe had moved to Hawaii.

LESSONS LEARNED

My son taught me the true meaning of maintaining a positive attitude despite the worst of circumstances. He lived as an example for all of us. Despite his challenges, he took the time to empathize and serve others. I learned that our children are gifts to be loved and cherished. We are just stewards of their lives for a short time. Can we find love in the worst of circumstances? My son did. Why can't I?

6

RISING FROM INJURY

"Success is not final; failure is not fatal: it is the courage to continue that counts. Success is stumbling from failure to failure with no loss of enthusiasm."

—WINSTON CHURCHILL

It was early Spring of 2001 when my partner and I responded to a call of a suicidal male causing a disturbance in front of the family home. Upon our arrival, the male was still in the front yard yelling at family members who were still inside the home. I was able to successfully handcuff the male. I then sat him onto a small wall that divided the adjoining properties.

My partner, who was in charge of the call, went into the home to interview the family and determine if the male had committed a crime. It was determined that he needed to be transported to a hospital for a seventy-two-hour hold for a mental evaluation.

The male became impatient by the length of time it was taking for my partner to gather the needed information. He kept standing up from the retaining wall, and I would sit him back down. The male eventually refused to remain seated. I grabbed the male by his handcuffs, and he jerked backward. (I was behind him at the time.) The motion snapped my head backwards, and my left hand was smashed between the hand-cuff chain and the subject's back. My hand became numb immediately as if it had been hit with a hammer. I reported what had happened to my supervisor, and he generated an incident report. I did not think much of my injury. I thought my hand must be temporarily numb from the handcuffs compressing my left hand. The numbness never went away.

PAIN AND NUMBNESS

My general practitioner had advised me to ask for an MRI from my brain stem to my tailbone, but it was denied by workers comp. Back then insurance companies frowned on MRI's due to their cost. I eventually hired an attorney to assist me with my injury claims. My lawyer, Laurie M., sent me to a physician who ordered an MRI of my back. By that time I was experiencing pain in my shoulders, right arm, and left leg. They discovered damage in my lumbar area. I was sent for three epidural nerve block injections to provide relief. The first epidural helped me with numbness and pain for a week. The other two epidurals did not work.

The doctor ordered a nerve conduction study, and they determined there were problems with my left foot *and* left hand. I was sent to a surgeon who performed a carpal tunnel syndrome release on my left hand. He believed it might help with the ulnar nerve, but it did not relieve my symptoms. The pain in my left leg radiating down to my left foot was unbearable. On top of that I had pain radiating from my neck and down my shoulder to my back. It was so bad I had to go to the emergency room several times. On each one of those trips, I was given shots of Demerol for the pain and sent home for a few days. I then began experiencing a sensation of not being able to judge where the ground was and ended up limping when I walked. They didn't know what to do for me.

On Christmas night 2002, I was in so much pain I could not sleep. The pain was so severe, I had to keep warm to avoid going into shock. I wrapped myself in a blanket and waited for my wife to wake up, so she could take me to my doctor or the hospital. Morning finally arrived and Maria drove me to my doctor's office. By then, I was not able to use my right arm and had even more trouble walking. My legs were not working. I explained to the doctor what happened to me throughout the night. After examining me, he knew I was in trouble.

EMERGENCY ADMITTANCE

Dr. Anderson immediately had me transported from his office to Providence St. Joseph Medical Center Emergency Department for evaluation. I was administered morphine and wheeled into radiology for an MRI from the base of my skull to the end of my spinal cord. They sent me back to my room where Dr. Anderson was waiting for me. He said that he called in a neurosurgeon, who was on his way to meet with me.

When the neurosurgeon, Dr. John Schnee arrived, he explained that somehow I had fractured my neck and part of the bone structure had splintered and entered into my spinal cord sac. The splinter was compromising my spinal cord. He told me I needed emergency surgery. They would remove the splintered fragments and then stabilize my neck by fusing my C5, C6, and C7 vertebrae together and affix a metal plate to hold the structure in place. Although that was scary enough, he explained that he would take bone from the top of my hip to fuse the compromised areas; it was called an iliac crest graph. He said he would do his best to repair the damage, but he couldn't promise I would ever walk again or return to police work. Dr. Anderson looked at my wife and asked her if she had a career or if she was working. When she told him that she was a stay-at-home mom, he looked at her and said that is about to change.

Dr. Anderson handed me a small stack of consent papers to sign. I had to accept the fact that there were risks associated with the surgery and confirm that I fully understood what was about to happen to me. Dr. Schnee asked me to notify my family before he performed the surgery. I was under the influence of so much pain medicine that I asked Maria to call the family, and I signed the papers without reading them.

The next few days were a blur to me due to the heavy pain medications and steroids to reduce the swelling. Due to the swelling in my throat, I was unable to eat food or drink water for the next couple of days. I spent four days in the hospital and had visits from friends and coworkers from the police department. I never saw my extended family. I did receive a phone call from my sister. *Where was my extended family?* I wondered. *Had Maria failed to notify them?*

ROAD TO RECOVERY

The surgery went well, and I finally made it home. It was hard to sleep while wearing a neck brace. Until a special new bed arrived, I could sleep only in a recliner and only for a few hours at a time, which meant that most of the day I was sleep deprived. This continued for several weeks until the bed showed up. I remember crawling on my hands and knees to move around. Walking without assistance was impossible. I was not able to exercise, so I gained weight.

After my hip area healed, I entered physical therapy. Friends drove me to the rehab appointments. I was met by a team of physical therapists (Kathy and Julie) who met me with a wheelchair. They showed me exercises to strengthen my core and help minimize muscle rigidity and atrophy. After several weeks, I was sent to pool therapy.

Pool therapy was something I looked forward to because of my love for swimming. The pool therapist placed floats on my arms and a floatation vest over my neck and shoulders. Her assistants used a lift that hoisted me into the pool. I was given some round yellow plastic paddles and told to move my arms back and forth. These devices were meant to cause resistance in the water and build strength in my arms. I could barely do that exercise. It was very discouraging. The pool therapist encouraged me, and I pressed forward. I continued the inside therapy and the pool therapy three times per week.

After the second week, we moved into leg exercises. I was instructed to move my legs as if I was riding an imaginary bicycle. After many tries, I was able to pedal forward. It was such a relief. And then I was told to pedal my imaginary bicycle backwards. That was nearly impossible. The therapist explained that I had to re-learn my motor skills and by doing the exercises backwards would help me recover quicker. I was not able to do this for days. I tried circling my arms in a backwards motion, and I struggled with that as well.

I continued the therapies for another month, and I finally was able to pedal backwards and eventually walk on my own, although with a limp. After three months of therapy, I was able to get in and out of the pool without assistance.

I visited Dr. Schnee's office every month as we monitored my healing and improvements. He was amazed at my rapid recovery and couldn't explain my range of movement and how, after only forty-nine physical therapy sessions, I was able to swim laps in the pool and lift weights in the gym. I was given permission to return to work without restrictions.

ANOTHER NECK INJURY

It was spring of 2008 and I had just cleared a residence where there was a complaint of a man wielding a gun. I was coming down the driveway with a rifle when I slipped on gravel on the asphalt and lost my balance. Knowing I was heading to the ground, I turned my body so that my right shoulder would hit the asphalt and would absorb most of the blow. After my shoulder hit the street, my head slammed against the pavement. I did not suffer a concussion because I was wearing my helmet, but I did injure my shoulder, back, and neck. I was sent to urgent care for treatment.

Over the years that followed my fall in the driveway, the pain to my extremities returned, and I was having more difficulties with balance. I started falling at work. I went to a pain management doctor who requested another MRI. The MRI showed I needed another neck surgery. I was removed from duty and sent home. I eventually needed surgery on my C4 vertebrae that was compressing my spinal cord.

RETIREMENT

Your body can only take so much. I knew that the job of a rescuer is a young person's game. My body had taken a beating, and it was time to let go of the job I loved. After meeting with an approved medical examiner, he determined I was permanently disabled and needed to retire from police work.

At the writing of this book, I have had more complications with walking again. According to my neurosurgeon, I have nerve damage from multiple injuries to my spinal cord and several falls only made it worse. I had some epidurals in my spinal cord that helped some, but due to major complications and development of bi-lateral foot drop, I had to have back surgery. I am seeing improvement each day.

FROM THE ASHES

The phoenix is an immortal bird associated with Greek mythology that cyclically regenerates or rises from the ashes of attempted destruction to be born-again from those said ashes. Up to that point in my life, I felt very much like a phoenix.

As I was beginning to heal from my back surgery, another health care trial arose. I began to have a severe headache on the right side of my head that would not subside. Motrin did not provide any relief from the pain. I went to my local urgent care but found out they didn't open for another hour. I leaned the seat back in my car and waited.

There was a knock on my window. I opened my eyes and to my relief it was a male dressed in blue scrubs. When I sat up my headache returned along with some dizziness and slightly blurred vision. My eyesight improved and the dizziness settled after a few minutes. The nurse asked me how he could assist. I explained what had been happening with the headaches. He instructed me to follow him to an employee entrance. I begged the nurse to let me lie down on one of the beds. He took my blood pressure, and it was very high. He took it again and it remained high but lower than first measured. He told me the doctor was on his way and let me stay in bed.

It seemed like eternity, but the doctor finally arrived. I explained to him my symptoms that began the day before. I told him that the only relief was lying down. He told me that I could continue the Motrin but to continually monitor and document my blood pressure and headaches to see if my symptoms worsened or improved.

Over the next two days, I saw no improvement. In fact, I was getting worse. My headache moved into my right eye, and I started to have vertigo. I would lean to the right and nearly fall down. I knew something severe was happening. I just knew I was in trouble!

I had my son Richard drive me to the hospital emergency room. I told Richard to park in the disability parking and to ask for assistance. "Tell the emergency room staff that your father has signs of a stroke and needs help," I instructed him. He ran toward the ER entrance. Within a few minutes, my son and a young man named José burst through the ER doors with a wheelchair. They lifted me out of the car and placed me in the wheelchair. José whisked me off to the ER with my son following close behind. We entered the triage area. I explained to the nurse taking my vitals that I believed I was having a stroke. I begged him to get me to a bed because the pain in my eye and head was excruciating. I told my son to go home because I was sure that I would be admitted, and he had to leave anyway because of COVID-19 protocols. I could see the concern on my son's face as he left. Despite my pleas for a bed, the nurse kept me in the wheelchair and placed me into the waiting room. Why was I being ignored? It was clear to me that he was not listening to me. Wasn't your signature of service, "Thrive?"

I have a very large tolerance for pain. This pain was the worse I had felt in my entire life. I started yelling for help. "Help me! Please. I'm having a stroke." The other patients were becoming disturbed by my loud pleading. Eventually, the male nurse returned to the waiting area where I explained again that I needed to lie down to relieve the pain. He pushed me to a treatment room and assisted me to the bed. As soon as I lied down, the pain subsided.

After about thirty minutes, I heard someone calling my name. No one came to my treatment room, so I assumed that the ER staff had no idea where I was. I sat up, and as I tried to get off the bed the room was spinning. I was able to reach the door without falling. I saw a couple of ER staff who looked surprised that I had opened the door. I told them that I had heard them call my name. They asked who I was. When I told them my name, they said, "Oh, you shouldn't be out of bed."

"Then why did you call me?" I asked with a look of disgust. The blank stare on their faces was priceless.

"Why are you here?" they asked. I told them what I had already told the triage nurse. They walked me to a gurney, laid me down, and took some blood. I was eventually wheeled into radiology where they did a scan of my head. I was then placed into a room inside the ER.

It seemed like an hour before the ER doctor entered my room. He asked me what had been happening to me. I explained everything in detail and added that the vertigo began within the last twenty-four hours. I told him the last time I had vertigo was when I had a sinus and tooth infection at the same time. I told him that I believed I was having a stroke. He assured me that I was not having a stroke but told me he was giving me a shot of morphine and a Z-pack of antibiotics to treat a sinus infection. *A sinus infection!* He shook my hand and said, "Take care, Mr. Ulrich. Follow up with your primary care doctor in a week." He then departed. I was not thriving.

A nurse came back into the room. He gave me a shot of morphine, which quickly relieved my pain. He then asked me if I wanted a COVID vaccine. All I could think at that time was, "Really?" After the nurse left, a nursing assistant came in and helped me into a wheelchair. He wheeled me to the pharmacy and told me that my name would be called. He handed me some discharge instructions and wished me luck. I called my son and told him to come and pick me up near the front entrance of the hospital. I asked the assistant if he was staying to wheel me downstairs to the front where my son was going to pick me up after I acquire my prescription. He told me that I had to wheel myself down and out of the hospital. *Seriously?* Again, I thought to myself, *Is this thriving?* My name was called after a short wait. I took hold of my medicine and tried to wheel myself downstairs. The pain medicine masked the pain but did nothing to stop the vertigo and dizziness. I struggled to use the wheelchair. I had to make it to the elevator and downstairs to the lobby. A nice lady and her daughter saw my struggles and asked if they could help me. I explained where I needed to go. The two of them pushed me to the elevator. They rode down with me and then pushed me into the lobby near the front doors. I thanked them for their kindness.

It wasn't long before my phone rang. My son had made it to the hospital and was trying to find me. He parked near the front and sprinted out of the car and into the lobby. He wheeled me outside. I explained what had happened to me. He was furious. I was hungry, so Richard drove me to In-N-Out. I needed to take my prescription with food. That burger was the highlight of my day. I reclined the seat and slept on the way home.

I followed the prescribed regiment of antibiotics, but the pain in my right eye and head worsened. By the fourth day, I was still experiencing vertigo and now was projectile vomiting. I could not keep any food down and was not able to stand without falling. I was bedridden! The next day, my sister came to visit and agreed that I needed to go to the hospital. The pain in my eye was so bad I was curled up and weeping. My sister called 9-1-1. They had to bring me down the stairs in a folded-up gurney and then blared the siren as we sped away from my home. Within minutes we arrived Henry Mayo Newhall Hospital. I could hear the familiar staff voices and sounds of the emergency department. It wasn't long before my blood was drawn. I explained what had been happening to me.

The ER doctor told me my diabetes was out of control. He said I was suffering from diabetic ketoacidosis. I guess because I was distracted with eye pain and dizziness, I lost track of my blood sugar. The doctor explained that my blood was filled with acids, and I had to be detoxified. He admitted me to the hospital.

Over the next few days, I was fed only by IV. The poisons in my blood caused me to hallucinate. I was not able to sit up without becoming dizzy and the Tylenol they gave me for the eye pain offered little relief. After two days, I was transferred from DOU (one step down from ICU) to a regular floor. The headaches started to subside, but the eye pain remained whenever I sat up in bed.

After several more days, a doctor told me the keto acidosis had run its course. I explained that I was still dizzy and not able to walk without assistance and that when I sat up, my eye and head pain was still ten on scale of one to ten. He assured me things would be back to normal in short order. I was not convinced.

A few minutes later, some physical therapists began visiting me. They questioned my sanity and mental stability. They kept trying to get me to admit that I was depressed. *Really!?* Eventually, another physical therapist came in and said that he wanted to take me in a wheelchair to see how I would tolerate the movements since I would be leaving the hospital the next day. It seemed that the staff needed me out of there because there was nothing more they could do for me. I still felt something was not right. I called my sister and told her everything. Since the eye pain was not related to my diabetes, we were both convinced that something else was happening to me.

I was assisted into the wheelchair and was wheeled down the hallway. It was only seconds until my eye pain was so severe I put my hand over my right eye and screamed for help. I could see that I had caught the attention of the entire staff at the nurses' station, who stopped to see who was screaming for help. The therapist quickly wheeled me back to my room. "That didn't work out well," I commented as he rolled me into my bed. Before I could say thanks, he was gone.

About thirty minutes later a doctor, dressed in navy blue scrubs, entered my room. He introduced himself as the staff neurologist. After explaining my symptoms I had been describing for several weeks, he decided to order a brain MRI to see if I had signs of a stroke. He said he would be back tomorrow to discuss the results. I thanked him for listening to me.

The next morning two medics arrived with a gurney and told me that they would be taking me to an image center on the hospital grounds by ambulance because the hospital did not have their own radiology department. We arrived at the image center, and I was placed into the all-too-familiar MRI machine. It took only ten minutes. Back in my room I was feeling nervous as I waited for the neurologist. I knew in my soul something was wrong with me.

The staff arrived with my lunch. It was not what I had ordered, and the staff treated me a little different. It was subtle, but I could feel that something was wrong and different. *Did they know something I didn't know?* I wondered. I finished my lunch and went to sleep.

I was awakened by a knock on my door. "Come in," I answered. It was the neurologist. He beelined to the bedside computer without making eye contact with me. I knew immediately that he had bad news to share. "I have your results," he said as he pulled up some images on the computer.

Trying to relieve the doctor's obvious angst, I said, "Give it to me between the eyes, Doc. I'm a soldier. It's ok."

"You were right. You had a stroke in the right cerebellum area of your brain. This area is responsible for your muscle movement and balance. It looks like this happened weeks ago." I must admit that despite the bad news, I was relieved that I had been correct the entire time.

My charge nurse came into my room the next day to tell me that I was being transferred back to Kaiser. This was the original hospital who sent me home with sinus medicine and a morphine shot. I think they were embarrassed that they did not catch the stroke the first time. By then, I had been in the hospital for a week without visitors being allowed to see patients. I was lonely.

I spent another week in the hospital. Each day they wheeled me into the MRI to be sure that I had no other strokes. The best part about being at Kaiser was that I could have visitors. The worse part of the adventure was the fact that I was put on a low-sodium diet. What was an already terrible food experience was made worse with no flavor!

My sister spoke to my treating physician and arranged to have me taken to an ophthalmologist during my hospital stay. Even though the ophthalmologist's office was on campus, it was at least a mile away. Since I had to sit in a wheelchair for the transportation and examination, I had to endure serious pain for ninety minutes to find out what was wrong with my eye. It was worth it.

A social worker and a physical therapist came to visit me. They each explained that I needed long-term care at a skilled nursing facility or a hospital that offered acute therapy. I chose the latter, so after another ambulance ride, I arrived at Providence Holy Cross in Mission Hills. This hospital had the best staff ever!

Despite my desire to get into rehabilitation, my body did not want to cooperate. Each time I sat up in bed, I had eye pain. It was expanding to my jaw, teeth, and head. During the stays at three hospitals and visits to two ophthalmologists and eleven doctors, no one could explain the constant pain I was experiencing. I was placed on narcotics that allowed me short times of relief to work with my therapists, but I was still struggling to stand straight up. I leaned and turned right. Eventually, I was discharged, and a home health therapist took over my care. As time went on, I eventually stopped the narcotics because the eye and face pain subsided. The bilateral foot drop remained, but the leaning to the right stopped. I spoke to a neurologist who told me that my trigeminal nerve was affected by my stroke and was the culprit of face and eye pain.

I have recovered from the stroke. I still swim and lift weights. I am still dealing with bilateral foot drop and healing from that too.

LESSONS LEARNED

Through all my health trials, I learned that there are some things we just cannot control. But I also learned that some things can be controlled. We can eat better and exercise. We can take steps to reduce our stress. So, never give up. Exercise. Move as much as you can. Eat healthy. Fight through illness. Push forward. Don't accept defeat. Grab the hand of someone you trust and ask them for help. You are not alone. Walk in faith, literally. As my fellow airman and USAF fighter pilot Lt. Col. Dan Rooney says, "Armed with the power of volition anything is possible." Never give up on your dreams and, if you get hurt, *rise from injury*.

7

PATHWAY TO LEADERSHIP

"The single biggest way to impact an organization is to focus on leadership development. There is almost no limit to the potential of an organization that recruits good people, raises them up as leaders and continually develops them."

—JOHN MAXWELL

A DIFFERENT GROUP OF OFFICERS

It was 1989 and I had begun my work at the police department as a reserve police officer. When you are a new police officer, your goal is to show other officers that you are safe, productive, and an effective member of the team. This includes when you are arresting persons possessing stolen goods or illegal drugs, and and when you are stopping crimes from happening or stopping impaired drivers. Great officer safety tactics and good common sense are important.

Back in the 1980s a lot of people were using cocaine (crack or powder), heroin, methamphetamine, and phencyclidine (PCP or angel dust or elephant tranquilizer"). The users of these drugs were responsible for many violent crimes to support their habits. There was a group of officers in my department who were very effective at arresting many drug user offenders. These arrests solved many property crimes, which kept some of these offenders off the streets and lowered crime rates and recovered stolen property. Public highway safety was improved because impaired drivers were being removed from the roadways by these officers. Who were these officers? These specially trained personnel were known as Drug Recognition Experts (DREs). They were a *different group of officers.*

The DRE officers could determine what categories of drug(s) a user may be under the influence of and if the influence was illegal by statute. They conducted eye exams with pen lights and pupilometers. They carried blood pressure testing kits, stethoscopes, and thermometers and were trained to use them. When I first saw these DRE officers, I thought they were emergency medical technicians (EMTs). They would show up to calls and assist officers with driving under the influence investigations or examine subjects for drug impairment and rule out medical issues. These officers even responded to the emergency rooms of hospitals to assist doctors and nurses with persons who may have taken illegal drugs. The fire department personnel respected these talented officers. I was impressed with the DREs, and after becoming a full-time police officer (1990), I was determined to become a DRE after I completed my regular training and probation (1991).

DRUG ABUSE RECOGNITION

The Glendale California Police Department utilized the training from the DRE program and created the Drug Abuse Recognition program (DAR). This program provided patrol officers some of the DRE training without needing to become a full DRE. I attended the seven-step, "from curbside to courtroom" DAR training at Glendale shortly after graduating from the full-time police academy. Each of the instructors were DRE officers. This was some of the best training I had ever had throughout my career. I used the Glendale DAR system to detain and arrest many individuals for drug influence and other related crimes. In 1996 management recognized my use of the training and eventually placed me in the DRE school with the LAPD.

BECOMING A DRE

The drug recognition program was created by two LAPD officers, Len Leeds and Richard Studdard. These two officers, working with medical professionals, developed the DRE program through the sponsorship from the US Department of Transportation and the National Highway Traffic Safety Administration. The Los Angeles Police Department was the only city agency steering the program in the US. LAPD eventually handed over the reins to the International Association of Chiefs of Police (IACP). California state control of the DRE program was surrendered by the LAPD to the California Highway Patrol (CHP) who inherited the California state police duties.

To become a DRE, an officer had to attend an intense two weeks of courses that included human physiology and anatomy, pharmacology, pharmacopeia, eye exams and comparisons, drugged driving, and psychophysical testing matrix. If students passed the final written exam, they then had to demonstrate with high efficiency the twelve-step process and psychophysical exams proctored by DRE instructors. Once all those exams were taken and passed, the officer must then work in the field and bring actual subjects to the detention centers where they perform the twelve-step process observed by a DRE instructor. After the exam, a sample of blood or urine would be collected from medical facility staff and the samples were taken to a laboratory to verify that the officer's opinion matched the toxicology results. The DRE students must have an average of about 95 percent accuracy on identifying the drug(s) of influence. They must complete sixteen exams proctored by a certified instructor. I was so intrigued by the DRE officers that I followed them to calls and watched them evaluate individuals every chance I could get. I read their reports and learned their observational skills. I began bringing in my own subjects. Many of the subjects were involved in larcenies of all types, and many of them had in their possession stolen goods from their previous crimes or possessed the drugs they had consumed.

DRE SCHOOL

The moment arrived. It was time to attend class. We met in Los Angeles at an old building that once housed a girls' catholic school. The first week was a challenge because it was about human physiology. I struggled with that subject but was determined to pass. It was a lot of hard work, but I passed the written exam and the practical twelve-step process the first time through. Now it was time to work the field.

Patrolling the streets of Los Angeles in a LAPD police car was a crazy experience. There was so much radio traffic and people committing crimes everywhere. The Los Angeles Police dispatch is a non-stop plethora of activity. One side of the street is a robbery while one block away is an assault with a deadly weapon. I felt like a kid in a candy store with the option of choosing anything on the shelf. My LAPD partner and I were assigned Central and Rampart Divisions where officers usually came in contact with impaired persons. If and when we found and detained someone, we were to transport that person to Parker Center for processing. We would then complete the DRE evaluation. My first incident involved a foot pursuit of a male who had just bought cocaine. When he saw us, he ran. We caught him but he swallowed the drugs. He had to be admitted to the hospital for observation, so patrol took over the call for us. I was able to find a total of ten impaired persons over the one-week period. I had to return to my agency to complete the rest of the evaluations.

Officer Tom Lorenz was my DRE instructor and our agency DRE coordinator. Tom was beyond amazing. With his background in narcotics, it was easy to complete the remainder of evaluations. I even found every category of drug influence. I had great success at my own agency because everyone in the department was very encouraging. I finished within two weeks and turned my paperwork into the state coordinator for recommendation for NHTSA certification. I finally received my certification! I was now a DRE.

BECOMING A DRE INSTRUCTOR

Our police department's DAR program had transitioned to the California Narcotic Officers' Association (CNOA) due to their greater footprint over the entire state of California. CNOA was looking for instructors. DRE instructor Tom Lorenz recommended me for instructor status for CNOA. I told him that I appreciated his recommendation, but I felt that I needed more training. Tom placed me into the California State Department of Justice Influence Instructor course in Sacramento, California. It was a sixty-hour course. You are videotaped the moment you arrive until your final presentation is filmed on the last day for your final. Our lead instructor was Professor Amie Ackerman from California State University, Berkeley. She had a profound effect on my public speaking. With this training, I was able to work for CNOA as an instructor for narcotics possession, sales, and influence.

Our department had lost almost all our DREs because their certifications had expired, or they transitioned to assignments that took them out of the field. We still utilized our DAR program through CNOA but needed DREs for special evaluations, poly drug use, complicated drugged driving evaluations, and traffic collision investigations. Seeing this need, I applied for DRE instructor school and LAPD accepted my application and granted me attendance.

The DRE instructor school was a different kind of challenge. We were expected to have mastered every part of the DRE program and prove that we can instruct by teaching in the DRE school on any section of the course. We were responsible for teaching several blocks of instruction that were observed by DRE instructors and then we had to observe DRE students conducting DRE evaluations from real impaired persons brought into the detainment centers. After supervising many evaluations and teaching many blocks, we were recommended to the state coordinator who would certify us for instructor status with the IACP. It eventually happened. I became a DRE instructor.

I traveled the teaching circuit for CNOA with Tom Lorenz for several years. We traveled up and down the State of California at various police agencies, probation departments, and drug courts. I taught at DRE conventions for the IACP and eventually became a consultant for many police agencies.

SIX FLAGS CORPORATION

I had just finished training our reserve police officers in drug influence when one of our reserve police officers, Paul Brubaker, approached me with an idea. He was the security manager for Six Flags Magic Mountain in Valencia, California. He loved the training I had just provided for him and his fellow officers. He asked me if I would be interested in training his security personnel at his park. I realized that there was a need for the corporate world to have drug influence training, but I was not sure where to start.

Paul shared that he wanted his people to stop guests from entering the park after consuming dangerous drugs and that park safety was a concept he wanted to promote beyond established corporate goals. I suggested that he and I put together a training day with his executives to see if there was an interest to roll out a training program park-wide. My suggestion was to train park managers along with the security team to monitor guests and drug abuse within the workplace. Paul agreed and introduced me to the director of human resources, Jo Ann Hagner. Paul and I spent several hours outlining our plan, and she loved our idea. We set a date a few months out. Paul introduced me to Steve Gunning, a long-time employee of the security department at Six Flags. Steve had been through specialized drug enforcement training with the Los Angeles County Sheriff's Department, the Drug Enforcement Agency (DEA) and the Los Angeles District Attorney's office. Steve had been involved with many drug arrests and court trials and was a well-respected employee at the park. Steve joined our team for development.

The day finally arrived. The park president attended with his entire leadership team and the board room was filled with directors and upper management. I was nervous but did my best to share my concerns from ride operator safety, employee abuse of legal and illegal drug use, guest consumption of drugs, and many safety matters that Steve and Paul had brought to my attention. After the corporate meeting and training introduction, I was given permission to create the training curriculum for Six Flags Magic Mountain, Valencia and roll out a safety program after its approval from HR. Six Flags Workplace Drug Recognition was born.

Not long after that initial meeting, the HR director invited me to speak at her annual Professional in Human Resources Association (PIHRA) luncheon as the keynote speaker. My photo and an article about drug influence training I developed for the workplace ended up on the front page of the *Sant Clarita Valley Signal*. My consulting business was launched!

The training program was in high demand and other managers within the park began to ask me to speak beyond the bi-annual training. I was

Keynote speaker at PIHRA luncheon, January 22, 1999, Valencia, CA. (Courtesy of *Santa Clarita Signal*)

introduced to Loss Prevention Manager Rich Pinkerton at the executive board meeting. Rich used to work at the Glendale Galleria Mall at the Nordstrom security department and knew many police officers from my police agency. He had also attended drug influence training from our vice narcotics manager, Don MacNeil (ret.), and saw the similarities in my training. Rich was one of those managers requesting training for his department. Rich thought it would be a great idea to roll out a corporate-wide training program. Corporate leaders heard about what we were doing in California and reached out to me through Rich. The corporation decided to roll out my training nationwide. Rich, Steve, and I flew to Texas for the national rollout that included other training programs. Eventually the program was held each year in Arlington, Texas, where all the department heads came together for a weeklong training program with two of the days dedicated to my training.

MEDTOX SCIENTIFIC

I continued to conduct drug influence training for my police department coworkers, LAPD, Burbank, and other cities. Lieutenant Don MacNeil, who was now retired from the Glendale Police Department and employed with Medtox Scientific, was looking for instructors in the area of drug influence. Tom Lorenz reminded Don about my involvement with drug influence training in the corporate world. Don called me. He and Medtox offered me a job providing training in Drug Abuse Recognition and other related courses to parole, probation, drug courts, the US military, and anyone who uses Medtox on-site drug testing kits. The job evolved into curriculum development.

In addition to the training, we were asked to work the hotline for customers who called for interpretation of testing results from the off-site laboratory. I traveled across the US with Tom Lorenz and on my own. Pharmacists and drug abuse counselors came from Korea to meet with me at one of the Salvation Army Rehabilitation Centers in Southern California. The Tennessee State Department of Corrections assigned a driver who drove me across the entire state of Tennessee to teach drug influence and drug testing to corrections personnel at their state prisons. Medtox utilized my expertise, and I wrote articles in their quarterly newsletters. I eventually left Medtox when the company sold in 2009.

OUR SILENT HERO AND MOTHER OF
IMPAIRED DRIVER DETECTION

After my first neck surgery in 2002, I was forced to remain home for several months. Around that time Dr. Marcelline Burns was looking for testing officers at the Southern California Research Institute (SCRI- UCLA) for a study that involved persons under the influence of controlled substances and alcohol being tested for impaired driving. I was still in physical therapy but my health improved enough for me to venture out—and I was itching to get out of the house and do something productive. I called Dr. Burns and volunteered myself and one of my DRE students, Eric Franke.

Dr. Burns is a *silent hero and the mother of impaired driver detection* to many of us in law enforcement. Here is why:

She earned her PhD from University of California Irving in psychology. She began research on human interaction with drug influence at UCLA. It was not long after that that she established SCRI (1973) and began questioning the means that impaired individuals are evaluated outside the laboratory. This led her to study roadside testing that law enforcement was using to determine if drivers were impaired. She traveled around the country looking at police agency techniques. From that research, she realized that there was no standardized way of testing. No two agencies tested suspected impaired drivers in the same manner. From her search, she gathered about fifteen tests that she thought might work in the field and brought them back to the laboratory for further testing. With the funding and support of the National Highway Traffic Safety Administration (NHTSA), she began her research (1975-1977).

At the conclusion of that research, she reported back that she had found some tests that appeared to be useful for Driving While Impaired (DWI) investigations. These tests were: Romberg (estimating a thirty-second time span while standing erect with your head tilted back and eyes closed), Walk and Turn (walking heel to toe nine steps up and nine back), Finger to Nose, One Leg Stand, Horizontal Gaze Nystagmus (HGN, involuntary jerking of the eyes as they track an object back and forth horizontally), Finger Count, and Paper and Pencil Writing. More research was needed to determine how accurate these tests were. After some refinement and with the help of some police officers it was determined that HGN, Walk and Turn, and One Leg Stand tests were the most accurate. NHTSA agreed with the research and these tests became known as the NHTSA 3 and were used for standardization purposes. Not too long after that were the Romberg and Finger to Nose tests officially added to the battery of Standardized Field Sobriety Tests. These tests were eventually refined to such a point that there was a point system added to the NHTSA 3. This standardization is the only such system recognized by the US Department of Transportation, NHTSA, and the International Association of Chiefs of Police as a valid testing apparatus for determining if an individual is an impaired driver. These are the tests many of you have seen being implemented at roadside.

Dr. Burns dedicated her career and life to helping law enforcement make the right decisions. She has testified in countless historic court cases across the country. When the Department of Transportation wants to find the answer, they call on her. Dr. Burns once told me she wants to be remembered as the lady who made a difference. She certainly made a difference for those of us who knew her. We recognize her as a silent hero.

Officer Franke and I were used to test some theories about the improper use of testing HGN sought by NHTSA at the request of the courts. We tested the distance between the stimulus used and the eye and the speed in which the test was done.

By 2012, I became a testing officer for the National Highway Traffic Safety Administration and the Southern California Research Institute, UCLA. I participated in studies on impaired driving and boating for the US Coast Guard.

CITY OF GLENDALE EMPLOYEE DEVELOPMENT

Shortly after becoming a Drug Recognition Expert Instructor, I was asked by a police manager to take his place as an instructor for a supervisor and manager's course for those who manage and supervise employees who have commercial driver licenses. I teamed up with Health Services Administrator, Monika Fischer, RN. The program has a mandatory drug testing apparatus attached to it. The idea was to teach the managers and supervisors the latest drugs used medicinally as well as the latest drugs used recreationally. We taught some of the signs and symptoms of use and how the administrative policy applies to employees within the scope of these types of investigations. These employees had to have a minimum of two hours of training each year. I taught this program for twelve years. It was truly an honor to help our employees.

DRUG ADDICTS WERE MY GREATEST TEACHERS

As I trained at venues outside of government, such as Salvation Army or addiction specialist companies, I met several students that possessed much more knowledge than myself. Many of them were ex-drug addicts. They had trained and educated themselves to help other drug addicts. They were filled with so much wisdom and knowledge that they became my teachers. I learned that some people take and abuse drugs for rec-reational reasons. Some people use drugs to escape. Many people take drugs to escape physical or mental pain. Prior to meeting these amazing teachers, I had more of a one-sided view of drug abuse. Now with the wisdom of these amazing people, I developed a more well-rounded approach to teaching and training others about drug influence. My eyes were opened wide!

BACK IN THE MILITARY-CIVIL AIR PATROL

In 2008, Captain McCullough was the squadron commander of the 84th composite squadron assigned to Edwards Air Force Base. At the time, my son, Rolfe, was part of the squadron. Captain McCullough had heard about my time in the Air Force and the experience I possessed as a drug expert. She passed this on to the base commander, Colonel Gandy, and I was asked to join the squadron to provide training for active duty and reserve Air Force personnel on a part-time basis. I explained that I was extremely busy with my consulting and full-time police duties, and

Teaching Air Force Sqaudron 84, Edwards AFB, CA (Author's collection)

I did not have the time to serve in the guard as a commissioned officer. Captain McCullough told me I could join the Air Force Auxiliary through Civil Air Patrol and train only when I had time. I agreed to do this for a few years and was sworn in by Colonel Gandy as a 2nd lieutenant senior member to become the Drug Demand Reduction Officer for 84th composite squadron Civil Air Patrol. Our squadron was composed of active-duty members at the base, Air National Guard, active Air Force, and retired military veterans, civilian employees, and parent volunteers. I provided them training, as well as other air bases for several years.

BIOCENCE TECHNOLOGY
While teaching at Edwards AFB, I met the owner of a drug manufacturing company, Allan Lord. Mr. Lord asked me about my medical

training. I told him that it came from the DRE program. He asked me if I would be interested in teaching with his clinical director and Chief Medical Officer, Tim Chapman, MD.

Mr. Lord was the son of Doug and Opal Lord of Texas. Alan's parents were famous because of an orphanage school they attended in the 1930s and 40s. Their story was told in a book titled *Twelve Mighty Orphans* and a film by the same name.

Mr. Lord's father, Doug, had been a huge supporter of the Shriner's Children's Burn Center in Texas where he established a relationship with Dr. Heggers, clinical microbiologist and plastic surgery instructor at the University of Texas Medical School. Mr. Allan Lord was invited to assist Dr. Heggers at the burn center and this led to the testing and study of the BGP complex in a Bio Safety Level 4 (BSL-4) laboratory in Galveston, Texas. The BGP complex was tested against 800 micro-organisms and demonstrated eradication of 95% of these deadly pathogens within 30 seconds. These in-vitro studies were presented to Health and Human Services and the National Institute of Health. BGP was renamed Biocence and eventually granted an NDC (New Drug Code) number for marketing by the FDA in 2014.

I joined Biocence Technology in 2009 to assist Mr. Lord with introducing Biocence to the medical community. At the time I did not hold a master's in business or healthcare, but I did have a desire to help market this product or at least develop the training for its administration at the direction of the chief medical officer. I remained with Biocence for eight years and learned a great deal about the regulatory process when developing pharmaceuticals, the testing process, procurement, and manufacturing. This job was a steep learning process for me and a very large contributing factor in my leadership development.

MY MEDICAL MENTOR & FRIEND

When I joined Biocence, I met Tim Chapman, MD. He was the chief medical officer responsible for partial drug manufacturing processes, testing development apparatus support, co-development of training and medical administration of developed products.

Tim trained me in antimicrobial resistance, cross contamination, vector transmission of disease and illness, and hand hygiene protocols within the healthcare industry. We traveled together and presented to hospitals, BSL-4 laboratory leaders, Department of Defense generals, large medical supply procurement corporations such as 3M, Owens and Minor, Cardinal Health, and

WOCN society convention, Nashville, TN, with Tim Chapman, MD, 2014 (Author's collection)

Medline, nursing conventions, and many healthcare organizations on the proper application of antimicrobials and infection control. In 2014, Dr. Chapman and I were asked by doctors to help with the Ebola crisis in West Africa. Dr. Awino Okech from the ministry of the Congo asked us to create protocols for Biocence administration and an Investigational Review Board (IRB) protocol that would best fit the administration of Biocence for Ebola patients.

Tim also mentored me through my master's in health administration. We spoke weekly. He assisted me in many research topics and edited my prose throughout. Doctor Chapman's mentorship was a huge part of my leadership and medical knowledge growth. He has also become a great friend!

HOSPITAL SERVICE

Now that I possessed a MHA, it was time to put my education to work at a healthcare organization again. I had never worked directly for a hospital but provided healthcare consulting to hospitals and other healthcare arenas. I volunteered to work in administration for the vice president of business affairs at Henry Mayo Newhall Hospital. I was able to implement lean methodologies as well as patient safety in the infectious control sector. When I worked with Biocence, I learned a great deal about anti-microbial resistance and cross-contamination vectors. These are big issues in hospitals and healthcare organizations that cause many of the nosocomial infection issues. I felt that I was able to contribute to our hospital, not only reducing infections, but in saving money as well.

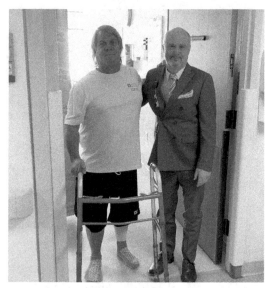

At Henry Mayo Newhall hospital with my high school classmate Kurt Giden, 2019 (Author's collection)

Dr. Chapman and I had many requests to develop protocols regarding infection control and hygiene administration. Together with Dr. Chapman and Kyle Mattner, we developed Anti-Microbial Technology, Inc. Dr. Chapman and I developed the Closed System protocol to control infection and minimize the spread of disease. We are currently working with potential customers to develop new ways of curbing cross contamination in many platforms.

LESSONS LEARNED

I was interested in becoming a Drug Recognition Expert to be more proactive by making more arrests and solving crimes. I believed that many crimes were motivated by those who are drug dependent. As my expertise grew, I realized that there was a need to share the wealth of knowledge I had been accumulating. There was also a need in the public sector with safety and employee management pertaining to drug use in the workplace. Delving further into my expertise, I learned that many drug abusers were seeking treatment from physical and mental issues that were not being addressed properly. I had no idea that what started out as a small self-improvement pursuit became a career pathway to success and leadership.

8

EDUCATIONAL ROAD

"Education is for improving the lives of others and for leaving your community and world better than you found it."

—MARIAN WRIGHT EDELMAN

MY LATE-IN-LIFE EDUCATION

When I was forced to retire in 2013, I had some college credits I had obtained throughout my law enforcement career with continual education requirements to maintain state licensing, and some assorted appearances at different colleges. I had never completed a college degree and there were these nagging questions: "What example am I setting for my children, my friends and potential clients/companies that would like to hire me? Who goes to college in their mid-fifties?" Part of "fixing myself for a better us" meant looking at my education. I knew by now the value of helping others, but how could I link that to my late-in-life education?

A PROMISE REMEMBERED

As you may recall, I began my collegiate quest at the community college level in Glendale. It was a disaster for me because I was not focused, and I was more concerned with joining the military. Before serving my country, as you recall, I promised my mother that I would go to college and obtain my degree if I joined the armed services. It took me thirty-six years to fulfill my promise. This was that journey.

LONG DISTANCE LEARNING

The military said I needed to work on my reading skills to be successful with my military career. This military request came after I had finished my primary job training courses in Texas. My command staff sent me to the Central Base Personnel Office (CBPO) personnel who intro-duced me to one of the first long-distance learning programs offered by a college. The college provided textbooks for purchase, video, and audio tapes for students to take home or come to CBPO for viewing in private rooms. You could attend class anytime you wanted, but you had a certain amount of time to complete the course. This worked well with my military schedule. I took a reading class and a math class. I completed the reading course and was granted college credit from Chapman College (now Chapman University).

LIFE PACIFIC UNIVERSITY

When I left the military, I utilized the GI bill to attend college. I enrolled in a humanities program at Life Pacific University. I attended this col-lege for two years until I had to leave when the school found out about my divorce during my second year. Since this college was a religious school, they frowned upon divorce, so I had to leave.

USC SOL PRICE SCHOOL OF PUBLIC POLICY

When I worked for the University of Southern California, I decided to attend Sol Price School of Public Policy to obtain my bachelor of science in public administration. Unfortunately, I left the university when I was hired full time by the city of Glendale and never obtained my bachelor's degree.

GLENDALE COMMUNITY COLLEGE

In 1995 I returned to Glendale Community College after being hired by the city of Glendale. I realized I would need a degree to compete for promotions. Most supervisors had bachelors or master's degrees. I spent several years attending as many prerequisite classes and administration of justice courses that were offered. My biggest struggle was working the graveyard shift and then going to class after work. I had three young children at the time, which added even more responsibilities. I could barely stay awake. Nevertheless, I was able to make the National Dean's list.

UNIVERSITY OF CALIFORNIA, LONG BEACH

The city of Glendale had an agreement with the University of California, Long Beach, and offered classes at the police department. This was convenient but costly. I began attending the courses with the goal of graduating with my bachelor's degree in the public sector. I attended the university until I could no longer afford the costs and dropped out of the program.

COLLEGE OF THE CANYONS

In 2015, when I was over the loss of my marriage, home, and forced retirement in 2012, I decided to go back to college. I chose to ease back into it by taking an administration of justice course at my local community college. The course was taught by then detective Christopher Casey. Chris was a burglary detective with LAPD. He helped me get back in the saddle, and we talked about me returning to the university level of education. Chris was strict on me and made me really step up my level of performance as the weeks progressed. He groomed me for success by having me assist other students with projects. He also encouraged me to join a master's program at USC.

CHAPMAN UNIVERSITY—BRANDMAN UNIVERSITY

After being convinced by Chris that I needed to attend a university, I went to the University Center at College of the Canyons and spoke to different universities who have classes on the community college campus. Most of the universities had memorandums of understandings with the community college in which certain courses are transferable to the universities for credit and cost savings. I decided to apply for Brandman who managed the long-distance learning program for Chapman University. I chose to pursue a degree in criminal justice. The degree required more classes at the community college while I attended the university.

Mom and I at graduation from Chapman University, Orange, CA, May 2016 (Author's collection)

I chose to take Chris Casey's courses to complete my lower level of education and a speech class. At one time, I had to take sixteen units in one semester. It was exhausting, but I did it. I was able to maintain straight A's throughout. Thanks to the financial adviser, Suzy Mix, for answering many questions I had during the university program.

GRADUATE SCHOOL- USC SOL PRICE
SCHOOL OF PUBLIC POLICY

By 2016, I was serving on the board of Biocence Technology. I had already been with the company for eight years. I needed to learn about lean manufacturing and healthcare from the educational side. The master's in health administration does exactly that for you. There

Post graduate ceremony at USC, Los Angeles, CA, May 2018.
Pictured with my boys (Author's collection)

is a residency built within the program where healthcare leaders mentor you through difficult challenges facing healthcare leadership today. I learned so much from the professors and my fellow students. I graduated in 2018 two years later and was awarded fellowship into the Epsilon Phi Delta society for student honors.

LESSONS LEARNED

I kept my promise to my mother. I was able to obtain two degrees within three and a half years because of my continued education throughout my working career in law enforcement. I learned that although my undergraduate work was based on criminal justice, there was no end to how high I could reach in my education if I was willing to work for it.

There were times that I did not want to get out of bed early, write papers all day, and then go to class at night after my day was done. I was exhausted at times. In the end, it was worth it to me and many of my friends were inspired to go back to college too! Six months later my daughter graduated from college with her bachelor's degree in entertainment business.

Mentoring other students and learning together, and leading home study groups at my home, was part of the servitude and humility costumes of change that were part of fixing myself.

9

FORGIVENESS

"For me, forgiveness is the door you must walk through to an amazing life, while serving others is the key to opening that door."

—RICH ULRICH

THE GREATEST GIFT FOR YOURSELF

Forgiveness is the *greatest gift you can give yourself.* This cannot be overstated. Have you ever felt like you can't forgive someone because you keep replaying an incident that hurt you? Have you ever felt like you can't forgive yourself because of something you did or said? Do you struggle in relationships because you are unable to go beyond certain boundaries because of walls that you have erected for protection, so you will not be hurt again? Have you made an agreement, promise, or self-fulfilling prophesy to yourself: "I will never marry again. I will never let anybody hurt me again. I will never open up my heart to anyone again."? In this chapter, I will explain some areas that created hurt in my life in hopes that this raises awareness in your life, so you can begin the process of forgiveness and healing. These lessons came at great cost.

NOT JUST A FAIRYTALE

The 2015 adaptation of the Disney animated film classic *Cinderella* provides a great example of forgiveness. Prince Charming had just finished fitting the glass slipper onto Cinderella's foot, and the two of them were preparing to leave her childhood home where she was held captive for years as a slave to her evil stepmother. Cinderella stopped at the doorway before leaving her home, turned, looked at her stepmother, who was descending the stairs, and said, "I forgive you." Cinderella was about to leave a life of poverty, want, hurt, and cruelty from others to become a wife, princess, future queen, and leader of her country. She realized the importance and need for forgiveness before moving on to an amazing future. *For me forgiveness is the door you must walk through to an amazing life, while serving others is the key to opening that door.*

THE DISAPPEARANCE AND DEATH OF MY FATHER

My father was stolen from my family. As a child, I tried to pin blame on someone because I did not possess the tools necessary to cope with the disappearance and death of my father. I never sought help through my grieving. There was never a funeral as a means of closure. This left such a hole in my soul. The following details of my father's disappearance and death was provided to me by my mother who lived through some severe personal trials and tribulations as a single mother. She is the hero in this story:

In review, my parents married quite young. My mother was a stay-at-home mom, and she and my father worked together establishing his insurance agency. He ran the business during the day, and she handled the accounting and payroll and worked with him at night when the employees were gone for the day. My mother was in nursing school when tragedy struck. With my father gone, she had to leave nursing school to work full time at my father's agency to try to keep the business running.

Although my father's business was a corporation, it was considered more of an "alter-ego" corporation (all corporate officers were family members). Because of this, the many companies my father represented as a general agent became concerned due to the thousands of dollars in trust funds being held for payment to them. The bank accounts were then all frozen and a check that had been written to the IRS for employee withholding was returned marked "insufficient funds."

The IRS officials arrived at the business and demanded payment. Although it was explained to them the money was in the bank but could not be released, they closed down the business, took possession of all its contents, including checks to be deposited, and padlocked the doors. They even repossessed my mother's car right then as it was registered to the corporation. Because of the abrupt shutdown of the business, thirty-two subsequent lawsuits were filed, naming my mother as the surviving corporate officer.

Needless to say, we lost everything but our home. My mother went back to work as an office manager for another insurance company during the day and also worked at night rating fire policies so we could eat and stay in our home. My mother knew that losing a father and home would be too much for my sister and me. She later secured employment with a prestigious law firm working for the managing partner while continuing her college studies at night.

My mother overcame the many hurdles she faced in life with grace, but it was a long road for her. There were rumors surrounding my father's apparent drowning. His business partner, who was with him on the boat when he disappeared, presented my mother with a holographic will (or hand-written will) turning the business over to him. This is not something the family felt my father would have done. My mother received a phone call from my father's bookkeeper the Monday following his disappearance. He informed her that my father's business partner had come into the office over the weekend and removed numerous client files from the office. Upon receiving this information, my mother fired my father's business partner. He claimed she had no right to do so because the business was now his; however, she had that authority as vice president of the corporation. Because of the business partner's prior association with organized crime, the FBI was called in to investigate. My mother has since told us that the FBI agent was very kind and supportive throughout the entire investigation.

The business partner had started working with my father after my father's best friend was drowned at Yosemite. He insisted they didn't need my mother to handle the accounting as he had purchased an accounting program, which turned out to be very ineffective at first and caused much confusion. Because of the newly discovered circumstances, my mother began her own investigation; however, she was later warned not to go poking around. She was told, "No one is interested in you, but if you persist, your son will be riding his bicycle and will be hit by a car!" She took the warning to heart. She destroyed all her investigative materials and documents. She chose not to share any of the details surrounding his death and merely told us our father had drowned, and we would see him again in heaven. I learned not long ago that my grandfather had warned my father about his ex-cop partner. Grandpa had told my father the man carried a gun, and he believed he had ties to the mob. Several weeks after warning my dad, Grandpa died mysteriously in his sleep from a new diabetic medication. Two weeks later, my father was gone. Hmmm. My grandpa had been an investigative reporter and probably had contacts in Detroit.

The FBI suggested that my mother should wait to see if my father's body was recovered to have a memorial service. She was advised that it could take many weeks before a drowned individual is washed ashore, unless the body has been weighted down, in which case it may never be recovered.

In addition to our business being confiscated by the IRS, they also seized my parents' bank accounts, motor home, and cars, with the exception of an older Ford station wagon that was registered to them. My mother immediately transferred the vehicle to a friend so they would not be able to repossess it. It was our only means of transportation. The IRS even sent individuals to our home who broke into our garage and impounded my father's Ford Thunderbird. All in all, the IRS confiscated five automobiles and subsequently sold them at auction.

Unfortunately, none of the automobiles were paid off, so the finance companies subsequently filed lawsuits against the corporation, naming my mother as a defendant.

My mother filed for Social Security benefits for my sister and me. She was turned down because no death certificate had been issued because, they said, there was no proof of death. That left us with no additional financial support. We had to rely upon only my mother's salary to cover our expenses. She appealed the decision numerous times. She was turned down even after she presented a death certificate and even after the seven-year statute of limitations had run out. According to federal regulations a person is presumed dead if he has been unexplainedly absent from his residence and unheard of for a period of seven years.

My father had an insurance policy with Prudential. It refused to pay the benefit, again, because my father's body was never recovered. The company hired two investigative firms to investigate the circumstances surrounding his death. After two years and many thousands of dollars, they offered my mother a settlement, which was considerably less than the policy amount. She accepted the offer but by the time her attorneys took one-third and she paid off company and personal debts, there was little left.

My mother contacted the attorney representing Prudential. He told her he believed my father was, in fact, deceased, and that his death was a homicide. She asked the attorney if he would be willing to testify on her behalf so we could collect some Social Security benefits. He said he would be glad to offer any help he could. By this time, her appeals had reached the federal courts.

Reading through the appeals docket for benefits addressed to the Bureau of Hearings and Appeals, I learned the following:

- Mr. Ulrich was a family man, a good father and devoted to his children.

- Mr. Ulrich left detail work to others and his partner took advantage of this fact to siphon off money from his insurance service and also write insurance without any company support behind it and pocketed the funds. His partner took approximately $20,000 to $40,000 per month (the IRS noted).

- Mr. Ulrich's partner testified in a deposition that he graduated from the University of Michigan (an investigation showed this to not be true). He was not well liked, had been a police officer with many underworld connections, was dishonest and unscrupulous. He carried a gun frequently and threatened employees of Mr. Ulrich's company among others. His account of the boating accident was not believable:

  » Trolling through kelp, but none was in the area; Boat was noisy—boat found to be quiet because exhaust was muffled by water; Ulrich fell overboard; After the "accident" partner was complacent per Colonel L. of the US Coast Guard; Partner went on search with the Coast Guard but soon became agitated and wanted to be taken back to shore; Partner was calm in reporting event; Mr. Ulrich had bulging briefcase per witnesses, but Ulrich's partner said he had "no briefcase" one time and "it was empty" the other time.

  » Partner convinced Ulrich to draft a holographic will three months before his death leaving the insurance business to the partner with Mrs. Ulrich receiving only $1,300 per month from the profits; Partner had Mafia and/or other underworld connections and they wanted Mr. Ulrich's insurance company (partner admitted to this fact). It was believed by those investigating my father's disappearance (US Coast Guard, FBI, San Diego Police and San Diego county Sheriff Department, two insurance investigators and the Social Security investigator) that he was killed, and his partner was directly involved.

My mother felt assured that finally her children would be able to receive the benefits due to them. However, even after the attorneys for Prudential testified that they believed my father was deceased, the attorneys for the Social Security Administration (SSA) said that they did not have to prove he was alive; she had to prove he was deceased, and without a body, there was no proof. She was turned down once again at her final appeal. Interesting to note, after the case was heard and my mother was outside the courtroom in the hall, the Social Security Administration (SSA) attorneys walked up to her and said they were sorry and felt she should have been awarded the benefits. She asked why they didn't say that in courtroom and their only response was, again, "We're sorry, but we have to do our job."

FIRST RESCUE (MARRIAGE ONE)

I met my first wife, Colleen, while I was in the military. She was a dental hygienist serving in the Air Force. We attended church on a regular basis, and she hung out with me and my friends. Colleen did not have friends when I met her. We had dated about a year when we decided to marry. We attended a pre-marriage counseling program at a church near the base. Prior to our union, many times she would get angry and yell and scream over very minor things. There were plenty of signs that something was wrong, but I ignored them.

I would make excuses to myself: "She'll get better." "She's just having a bad day." "It's hormones." "She's menstruating." And I must confess there were times that I contributed to her response by saying unloving things out of frustration. Despite these signs, I married her. Our marriage lasted one year but was over before it began. We even fought on our honeymoon. It appeared that Colleen suffered from some mental disorder that created in her a violent streak. At the time I never knew what it was.

Colleen was a talented person. She was a good singer and probably could have been a professional. She just needed help for her struggles. She was a very angry person with explosive tendencies. I was hit by many flying objects. In one altercation, she slapped me in the arm and face as she was driving. When she stopped the car for red light, I jumped out to escape. She followed me in the car, driving up onto the sidewalk, trying to convince me to get back into the car. She nearly hit me in the process. I was able to escape when she lost sight of me and drove back home. I eventually returned home, and Colleen did not even recall the incident. One time when I was sleeping, Colleen apparently hit my mother on her head, causing her to lose consciousness. My mother was transported to the hospital where she remained for observation due to a concussion. I never found out the truth of what occurred that day. Colleen denied any wrongdoing and did not recall what had occurred.

Despite my combat training, I never hit Colleen. I was raised that you never strike a woman. At that time, I was not aware of organizations to help men in my situation. I did not know what to do with an abusive woman. I asked Colleen if she would be willing to sit down with a counselor to help improve our marriage. She agreed and offered to set up an appointment. She called a counselor from a church in Pasadena. A few days later, we met with the counselor. He introduced himself and immediately told me that I "needed to be a better husband by supporting my wife and not be so angry and willing to fight at the drop of a hat." I sat there stunned. The pastor asked me several times if I was alright because I just sat there in silence trying to figure out how he would know anything about us or me. I then realized that she had called and scheduled the appointment and had told the pastor lies about our marriage. It was then that I realized there was no way to fix things between us. I moved out of our apartment where we lived with the help of a long-time friend. I waited until she was at work one day to move out. I made sure that I always had a witness with me whenever I needed to have contact with her after our separation.

She begged me to come back and to give us another try. I declined her offers and filed for divorce. Our marriage ended amicably, and we both moved on with our lives.

One mistake I made that had a significant impact upon my future life was not seeking counseling after my failed marriage. This lack of wisdom was one of my many downfalls. According to family sources, Colleen re-married a nice man and has been in therapy over the years. She is now on bi-polar medication and told my sister that she is a "changed person."

SECOND RESCUE (MARRIAGE TWO)

In 1985 I landed a job in the grocery business and worked for Ralphs market in La Canada, California, as a meat wrapper and cutter. I had experience working as a butcher at Tip Top Meats during high school and learned the trade from Wolfe and Joe, some of the best butchers in the business. The two of them had left Tip Top when it moved to Carlsbad, and they transferred to Ralph's in La Canada. While working there, I met a really nice cashier, Janet. She was a lovely gal who was attending Mount Saint Mary's University in Los Angeles. We went on a few dates until I left the grocery business to look for better employment.

I eventually heard that the University of Southern California (USC) was looking for employees in the public safety office and one of the benefits was free college. I applied for the job. They hired me because of my military background. While working at the University of Southern California in the public safety office, I pursued a degree in public administration. It was there that I became good friends with one of my coworkers, Ed.

Janet from Ralph's invited me to her college graduation party, and I invited Ed to join me. I was introduced to Maria and Ed met Janet. Ed liked Janet, and I asked Maria on a date. I took Maria out with my longtime friend Joe. Being a recent divorcee, I needed the support. Meanwhile, Ed and Janet seemed to become acquainted rather quickly. It was not long before the two of them were engaged and then married.

A FOUNDATION BUILT ON A LIE- MY DENIAL OF THE TRUTH

When I first started dating Maria, I learned that she was being treated for bi-polar. Maria told me that she was in treatment and taking tricy-clic medication to ease her anxiety over her mother's desire to control her. I did not think there was any reason that Maria would lie to me, but it did not make sense since she was an adult and able to make her own decisions. I decided to support her by accompanying her to her therapy sessions to learn more about Maria's condition. I was kept in the waiting room. Maria only went about five times before returning one day to tell me that she and her therapist agreed that no further treatments were needed and that she no longer had to take her medication. I never verified this.

ISOLATION OF FAMILY MEMBERS

We continued to date one another for a year before I asked her to marry me. One day, Maria told me that she did not want to have her mother attend our wedding. She suggested that none of her family be there. I told her that I was not pleased with that idea. After many arguments about isolation of family, she was able to convince me that it was our special day. She did not want her mother to ruin it for her.

We decided to have a private ceremony at my mother's house. She chose a specific day when her mother was on vacation in Hawaii to exchange vows. Maria's mother returned from vacation and learned of our nuptials. She was furious. I did not blame her for being disappointed. She was also mad at me and had no idea that I was against the decision to exclude her and fought to have her there. (Her mother never knew the truth). Upset with the both of us, her mother made plans for a wedding reception at a nearby country club where she invited family and friends. It was a nice ceremony, but her mother made it very clear to us of her disdain for our prior decisions. "This ceremony is not for you," she told us. "It is for my friends, family and me."

Shortly after our marriage, Maria became pregnant with our first child. Maria told my best man and friend Joe, "I hope I don't screw up this child like mother did to me." We eventually had two more children.

As time went on, and parenting demands became heavier, I saw Maria struggling with the challenges of child rearing. What most parents regard as typical challenges of children trying to expand their authority, Maria considered to be rebellious and demonic. I thought they were just being kids. This difference in attitude toward raising children became a source of contention between us throughout our marriage.

As a family, we were walking on eggshells, trying to be sensitive to Maria's mental state. We all were looking to escape from her tight grasp, manipulation, and control. We were splintering into subsets rather than remaining a tight close-knit family that adds to society. During one of our dysfunctional and unloving arguments, she was being so judgmental I stopped the car and asked her to meet me outside. I prophesized to her, "If you don't stop judging others and constantly correcting our children for the tiniest infractions, they will grow up and have nothing to do with you." Crickets! It had no effect on her. She showed no emotion or reaction. It was as if she was under the influence of a disassociating drug. Her silence was deafening.

Whenever I confronted Maria about her bad behavior, I was told that I was just retaliating against her. She had to be right in all things no matter the situation or proof to the contrary. If I said the sky was blue, she would argue that it was pink. When some assembly was required, and instructions were needed for assembly, Maria would not read the instructions because they were controlling her in some way or taking away her ability to think for herself. Yet, when it came to our children, they had to be controlled in every way. Her overbearing personality isolated us from those who wanted to love us and spend time with us.

MORE ON ISOLATION & CONTROL

Paul Mason, mental health and addiction care service professional and author of *Stop Walking on Eggshells,* describes the life of a man whose mother had borderline personality disorder (BPD). "My borderline mother claimed that I didn't eat, walk, talk, think, sit, run, urinate, cry, sneeze, cough, laugh, bleed, or hear correctly." Mason went on to say, "Siblings of borderlines spoke of having to fight for their parents' attention and worry that their own children might develop the disorder."[1]

---

1   Paul Mason, *Stop Walking on Eggshells: Taking Your Life Back when Someone You Care about Has Borderline Personality Disorder* (Oakland, CA: New Harbinger Publications, 1998), 4.

Please be forewarned that if you find yourself being controlled by a spouse, lover, friend, or family member to such a point that you have been isolated from other family members, you may be a casualty of a borderline personality disorder. After you grow up and move away from home, you may find yourself competing with your siblings over trivial matters because of living with someone with BPD. Let me explain.

Maria criticized and judged everyone who came into our family. She criticized and controlled our children in every way possible. They could not do anything correctly. Maria would create problems that never existed. This became so annoying to me and the children that we found ways to busy ourselves to avoid participating in her schemes. It became so merciless that as a family, the children and I hated even to go to movies or amusement parks with her. Maria projected her own issues onto us and others. Mason opines that "projection is denying one's own unpleasant traits, behaviors, or feelings by attributing them—often in an accusing way—to someone else."[2]

THE FROG AND THE BOILING POT

Place a frog in a pot of cold water, and it will not try to escape. Ignite a flame underneath, and eventually, as the water heats to a boil, the frog will try to escape, but it will be too late. Likewise, our problems began slowly. First, it was little criticisms of mistakes made by family members. These mistakes would continue as is typical, but before I knew it, each visit with a family member had to be carefully controlled by Maria. At first it seemed as if Maria was just wanting the best for our family. Like the frog in the cool water, the temperature slowly began to rise until it was too hot for comfort. How could my wife and the mother of our children have evil or bad intentions for our well-being?

Our children wanted to visit their extended family, but because Maria was so judgmental and there were so many problems after every visit, the children stopped asking to go. Visits with my extended family

---

2   *Stop Walking on Eggshells*, 54.

became so stressful for my children and I that we avoided family events just to keep the peace. I dreaded the holidays because it meant I'd have to come up with an excuse as to why we couldn't attend. I could no longer deal with the stress of my job and Maria's constant pressure. Our family became even more isolated from others.

After my separation and eventual dissolution of my second marriage, Maria's family and my own began to slowly assimilate back into our lives. This is when I realized how much my children suffered by not having relationships with their grandparents, aunts, uncles, and cousins all those years. I felt a sense of loss too. It was partly my fault. I did not have the tools necessary to properly deal with a family member suffering from a borderline personality disorder. My denial and outside image played a role in the enablement of the dysfunction.

THE PERFECT FAMILY PORTRAIT

What sickens me most about my family life was the beautiful family portrait I painted for others to see. To most outside our family, we were seen as a strong, loving, committed family. The ugly truth was far from beautiful. I truly loved Maria, but her behavior was too destructive. I was constantly being pushed away by her religious overtones and manipulations. It was too much for me to navigate. Despite this feeling of desperation, I felt the need to keep up a façade to my friends, extended family, and coworkers that we were this loving Christian family. Nothing could have been further from the truth. Are there any pretenders out there like me? Sometimes the shame of failure creates a fear to address the issues even though help is out there if you set aside your pride and look.

FAILURE IN COUNSELING AGAIN

I tried counseling at our local church, but the same thing that happened to me with Colleen happened again with Maria. I found myself at the end of judgment before I was even able to explain my view of our marriage and family life. I was so frustrated with the church counselors, that I left the church altogether. Maria eventually left that church too.

SUSPICIOUS RELATIONSHIP

Maria found another church, but I did not attend, neither did our children. It was half a day that we could be free of her. Shortly after Maria changed churches, different men would call our house asking for Maria. When I asked them how they knew Maria, they said from church. Maria would talk to them for a few minutes and that was it. Maria met a married man at her church by the name of Jim. One day when I was out with Maria and the kids, Jim called Maria's cell phone, and she spent nearly half an hour providing marriage counseling. I told Maria to hang up and asked her why she was giving this man or any one marriage advice since she was not a counselor. Secondly, I questioned her why he was calling her and not his pastor or a counselor. She explained that Jim did not trust the pastor. I told her it was not a good idea to provide advice to people, and I asked her to stop taking calls from anyone seeking counsel and to refer them to a therapist. She assured me this would stop.

THE CHURCH TAKEDOWN

Jim had an underlying hatred for the pastor of Maria's new church. He had provided financial start-up funds to plant the church and believed that the pastor had failed to meet his needs as a member of the congregation. Jim's wife was bitter and refused to attend the church because she thought the pastor mishandled congregational matters and Jim's behavior was bizarre. Sound familiar? This was the perfect opportunity for Maria to control someone (Jim) and his church.

I was under the impression that Maria had ceased all calls to the men who reached out to her for advice. One day, she asked if Jim could come to the house and meet with her about some problems regarding their church. She asked me to join their meeting, so I thought the concerns might be genuine. After dinner Maria and Jim talked about their concerns, and there appeared to be some legitimacy to their complaints. The two of them created a business plan that included a new school for the church with Maria as the administrator. It sounded like my wife was going to integrate back into the workplace. This definitely piqued my interest. Everything sounded good until they began to devise a plan that was designed to remove the pastor from the church and take away any rights he would have to the new school. The more this plan unfolded, the more I saw how evil it was. I stood up from the table and proclaimed, "This meeting is over. Jim, you need to go!" After Jim left our home, I explained to Maria that the plan to remove the pastor was not their job but the church council's. The new school adventure sounded great at the beginning, but I could not support the way they were going about it. Of course, I was the bad guy. I made copies of the business plan just in case the two of them decided to proceed without my knowledge.

ESCAPING THE BOILING POT- A TIPPING POINT

As you can see, there were many red flags in my relationship with Maria. The clues were right in front of me, but I ignored them. I would hear sirens or see collisions on the roadway and hope that somehow Maria was dead, so my misery would stop. I was looking for an escape. This frog was desperately trying to escape the boiling pot of water but was unable to tip it over no matter how hard I kicked the sides of the pot.

In February 2012 Jim offered Maria a job in his property management company. I called Jim to find out if it was true, and he said that it was. I told him that I thought it was a good idea and that it would be good for Maria to get out of the home and work. We all wanted her out of the house. She took the job.

A few weeks later our middle son, Rolfe, spent Easter week with my sister and her family. He took a part-time job working at his uncle's furniture business. During his visit, he confided to my sister some of the atrocities he had suffered at the hands of his mother and how she told him to never tell anyone, or they would be taken away from us. Because of these threats he had never told anyone before.

Both my mother and sister were trying to figure out how to break the bad news to me in such a way that I would not do anything harmful to Maria or myself. The abuse had long since stopped, so there was no need for them to intervene.

In mid-May 2012 our youngest son, Richard, was being recruited by colleges and universities regarding baseball prospects. He needed an SAT or ACT exam in order to complete his college applications. On June 9, 2012, I drove him to South Pasadena, California, for an ACT exam. After the exam, I asked him how he thought he did. He said he felt he did well on the test but complained about a headache. I assured him that if I had to take that exam, I would probably have a headache myself. He explained that he was not having a headache from the test but from memories of his mother hitting him in the head when he would not behave or answer test questions the correct way. He continued to explain what his mother had done to him and his siblings during their childhood. He continued to explain how she threatened them not to say anything to me and how they hoped I would catch her in the act and report her to the authorities.

On the drive home, I called my other two children, and they confirmed his story and provided even more details. Rolfe then communicated to me that he had confided in my sister. I was furious at Maria, but if it was true, it was my way out of the horrible marriage—a way of escaping the boiling pot. If you can believe it, even in my despair, I was actually relieved that I had a way of removing Maria from our family. I was also overwhelmed when I thought about what I had to do next. I felt horrible for our children but was glad they now knew I knew and was there to help them. I promised them that if everything they were telling me is accurate, their mother would have to give an account for her actions. They seemed to be relieved. I was so happy to be able to finally rescue them! They had been silenced for so long.

THE CONFRONTATION

The drive home took forever. I had to confront the most judgmental person I knew. When I arrived home, I told Richard to stay out of the house while I spoke to his mother. I found her in the kitchen. I was able to get her attention and told her that I had just spoken to our children over the last hour and learned some pretty awful things she had done to them.

I asked if what they accused her of was true. She did not say anything but gave me the "deer in the headlights" look. I had seen the "Uh, oh, I'm caught" look many times before in my job. I was speechless and in shock.

After gathering myself, I turned to her and said, "I need you to pack your things and move out immediately, or I will have you removed by an emergency court order from the sheriff's office. If any of this is true, I will have you prosecuted!" Our conversation moved to the bedroom where she was lying prostrate on the floor. She looked up at me and asked in a contrite tone, "What must I do to be forgiven?"

"Repair the damage you caused," I answered.

"You're not God," she yelled.

"No. I'm worse. I'm your husband and father of our children," I retorted.

With that, Maria disappeared from our bedroom. I sat on our bed and cried for at least thirty minutes.

I gathered myself again and walked around the house. Maria was nowhere to be found. For about ten minutes I searched our property for her. I could not find her, but I found her cell phone on the kitchen counter of the guesthouse. Looking at the text messages, I saw that she had texted Jim, "Something awful has happened. I will call you." Looking at the call log, I saw a phone call made by her to Jim. The call lasted forty minutes. It seemed strange to me that after confronting her about abusing our children, she called her boss. It was then and there that I became suspicious that Maria and Jim were involved in a relationship beyond work. Maria returned to the main house and packed up a few things and moved into our guesthouse. At first, I wanted her off the property altogether, but the more I thought of things and cooled down, I realized that keeping her next door would allow me to gather some intelligence for the inevitable investigation.

SUSPICIONS CONFIRMED

It was the summer of 2012. Richard and I flew to Montgomery, Alabama, for his walk-on tryouts for Alabama State University baseball.

We had just spent the day at the university ballfield when I received a phone call from the pastor of Maria's church. He called to let me know that Jim's wife's brother had called the church office and left a message saying he was concerned that Maria and Jim were in an inappropriate relationship. Jim's brother-in-law had expressed these concerns to his sister, Jim's wife. The pastor played this message to me over the phone. I took this time to explain to the pastor what Jim and Maria had planned to build a school at his church and remove him from ministry.

I spent the next four days of tryouts in the Southern heat trying to stay focused on my son's amazing opportunities, but the weight of these confirmed suspicions made it more of a challenge. I was anxious to get back home and see what Maria was doing to our home and personal property.

When I returned, I confronted Maria about the affair. I was told that I was a "sick pig" for thinking such a thing. She never denied the affair. Maria did say that Jim's brother-in-law was mentally ill. Then Maria blamed me for insisting that she accept a job from Jim. We lived in a small town, and it didn't take long to find out that other people in our community thought Maria and Jim were more than just coworkers. I wondered if they were all suffering from the same "sick pig" syndrome.

Since I was the administrator of our cell service, I was able to look at the call logs. Maria spent approximately three to four hours per day on the phone with Jim before she ever worked for him. A mutual friend of ours confided in me that she had told Maria she was spending too much time talking with Jim. This friend had admonished Maria about her behavior as a married woman.

A SECOND SURGERY

Late June 2012 I had to undergo my second neck surgery. My longtime friend and mentor, Dr. Tim Chapman, came to the hospital and kept an eye on me. He stayed with me the day of the surgery and the week that followed. Maria never showed up at the hospital but spent the entire day working for Jim and attending meetings. I did not trust Maria at that point. I stayed at my mother's home for a week while I recovered from surgery. I took my firearms to my mother's house until I was well enough mentally and physically. Dr. Chapman stayed with us, so he could monitor my condition and help me in my recovery.

PREPARING HER ESCAPE

After a week at my mother's, I was well enough to return home. Maria was still living in the guesthouse. I learned that Maria opened her own checking account. Even though Maria still withdrew money from our joint account for food and fuel, she was not adding to it. Each morning, Jim would pick her up from the guesthouse, and they would carpool together to his business. Sometimes Maria would work until midnight or travel to places like Palm Springs, California, for "business matters." I also found out that Maria had removed our children as beneficiaries from her personal bank account shortly after I confronted her of child abuse.

One day I told Maria that people in town were talking about her and Jim, saying it appeared as if they were dating. I suggested that she may want to stop seeing Jim or working for him until things cooled down. "He's married like you," I pointed out.

Maria looked up at the ceiling and said in an almost singing voice, "God. Rich doesn't want me to obey you."

"So now you're justifying your inappropriate relationship with Jim by saying God told you to do it," I accused. She did not respond and left our bedroom.

DOMESTIC VIOLENCE

In August 2012, Maria needed to go to the mall to shop for an iPad case and I needed some things from the mall as well. Things had settled down between the two of us, and I offered to take Maria to the mall, which was thirty miles from our home. I had taken some insulin that morning and ate a small meal. When we neared the mall, I felt my blood sugar was dropping below normal. I knew I needed something sweet. I parked the car and stood near the drivers' door to try and gain some composure while I figured what to do next. I was feeling lightheaded and knew I was in trouble. Maria, seeing me standing near the door, asked, "What's wrong?"

"I'm having a diabetic episode—low blood sugar," I answered.

"What do you want me to do?" she asked.

I closed the door and began walking toward the mall entrance. "Call 911," I said.

"I can't believe you are doing this to me," she responded.

When we reached the main entrance door to the mall, I headed toward the food court. Maria did not stay with me. I learned later that she headed to the iPad case kiosks. The last thing I remember was asking the server at Hot Dog on a Stick for a lemonade and telling her I was having a diabetic emergency. I do not recall paying for the drink. I somehow recovered and ended up sitting at one of the tables within the food court. Someone must have stepped in to help me. Maria finally showed up at my table when I was recovering.

"Where were you," I asked.

"I was right over there," she said, pointing toward the kiosks. It was then that I realized we were done as a couple, and she wanted me out of the picture. I knew then I could never trust Maria again even with my life. I had already lost trust regarding our marriage and our children but that incident in the mall let me know she was truly dangerous. She must have really wanted me dead. She knew I had a large insurance policy because of my job. I figured she just wanted to collect upon my passing. This was the beginning stages of *domestic violence* toward me.

After arriving home, I made some changes to my will and removed her as a beneficiary from all my insurance policies and estate planning and added my children as primary.

CONFRONTING ABUSE

One evening when all our children were home, they wanted to confront their mother about a few things that were on their hearts and minds since they were feeling more emboldened. We all walked over to the guesthouse to talk with her. We knocked on the guesthouse door. Maria cracked the door open. I told her that our children wanted to talk with her. She opened the door and went and laid back on the couch with her arms folded across her chest and replied, "Go ahead. I have to work tomorrow morning." It was only 8:30 p.m. The kids kept asking her why she did what she did to them, and she kept blaming everyone except herself. This lasted about forty-five minutes with her never sitting up or taking the issue seriously. "Can we just get on with this? I'm really tired," she complained. Our children left and I remained. I told Maria that I had told my police agency about the abuse. I then retired for the night.

FALSE IMPRISONMENT

Early the next morning my bedroom door slammed open and struck the chest of drawers. This jerked me awake and hurt my neck, which was still in a brace. In came Maria and her Weimaraner dog. They entered the bathroom. I heard the shower running and thought it was seriously weird when I looked in the shower to see Maria and the dog inside. As I laid back down before getting up, the dog came out of the shower, went to the side of my bed, and shook water all over me, the walls, and my bed. I crawled out of bed and went into the shared bathroom off the hallway.

Maria came to the bathroom yelling, "Why did you throw me under the bus?"

"I'm a mandatory reporter. I'm not losing my job because of your bad decisions." I tried to leave the bathroom, but she blocked me inside. I yelled for the kids to wake up and help me. No one came to my aid. I took Maria by the arm, put her into a compliance arm hold and escorted her out of the house. Her dog followed. She and her dog went back to the guesthouse.

After everyone awoke later in the morning, I summoned my daughter's boyfriend to accompany me to the guesthouse. I needed to confront Maria. With my cell phone recording, I knocked on the door. Maria came to the door. I told her to not come back in the main house without knocking first. I also told her that coming over and trying to provoke me to anger was not acceptable. I told her that the abuse of me and the children was to cease immediately, or I would have her arrested and get a restraining order. Maria stayed away for days.

My neighbor Kelly was outside near the front of her house. I knew that she and Maria were friends, so I threw a nugget toward Kelly to see if Maria was talking with Kelly about our family business. Kelly knew Maria and I were having issues because Maria would go over to her house to drink and talk. I told Kelly that because Maria had violated my trust, I was going to divorce her. I parted ways to see if Kelly would say anything to Maria. When I awoke the next morning, there were a dozen or so 8.5 x 11-inch paper printouts scattered about my bedroom floor, inside the refrigerator, the freezer, and the cupboard that read, "I don't want a divorce. I want a husband who will support and love me." Apparently, Kelly relayed the message.

Things quieted down for a week, and I was feeling like working on some projects that I had neglected prior to my surgery. I was working in the garage on a project and needed the whole garage for two days. I asked Maria to park her SUV in the driveway. She would not move the car, so I moved it out of the garage and parked it in front of our home. She was so angry she backed up her SUV diagonally to take up the whole driveway. With white shoe polish she tagged both rear side windows of her car with the word "beloved." After two days of parking her car outside, Maria came to me and asked if I was done with my project and if she could park the SUV back inside the garage. When I asked her why she was so concerned about leaving her car outside for a few days, she said, "The elements are not good for my car." Her car was a three-and-a-half-ton Excursion built upon a Ford F-350 truck chassis with an International diesel motor. It was very heavy and could be outside for a few days. I told her that I would be done in about two more days.

I was in our dining room when I heard Maria revving her SUV engine. It sounded like it was having difficulty moving. I looked out and saw Maria trying to jump the edge of the patio deck to park underneath the wooden patio roof. I shouted for her to stop. "You're going to damage the patio," I said. She ignored my pleas, looked directly at me, and jumped the patio foundation and slammed into the side of the guesthouse. The patio and the side of the house cracked. After she stopped the engine and exited the car, I asked her why she needed to park on the patio, and she said that her car needed to be out of the elements.

"You couldn't wait two more days?" I asked. "Are you aware that you have cracked the patio deck and hit the guesthouse wall?" She ignored me and went into the guesthouse.

THE CRIMINAL INVESTIGATION

As a mandatory reporter, I am required by law to report domestic violence, elder abuse, and child abuse to law enforcement or investigative bodies. Based on the incidents that led up to her alleged child abuse and her response and actions toward me, it was time to notify outside law enforcement to document the history. My agency was notified immediately when I first learned of things in early June. I told them that I was gathering as much evidence as I could while she was on the property and that there was no clear threat or present danger to our only child in the home, who was seventeen years old at that time. My department was very supportive of me and advised me to seek a restraining order if needed and to keep them in the loop as the investigation moved forward. By now, Maria's bizarre behavior was escalating, and the need for a restraining order was approaching quickly.

September 2012 I called the police and filed the first report claiming child abuse, domestic violence that was perpetrated on me the month before, abandonment during a medical emergency, false imprisonment, and reinjuring my neck by startling me from sleep. A patrolman came to our home and took a report. My two adult children did not live with us any longer. The officer took statements from Richard and me and then left. The case was assigned to the special victim's unit and an investigator was assigned to the case, and I notified my police agency.

About a week later, a police detective came to my house. He told me that the officers at the station did not believe that I was not aware of the abuse my children suffered. I told him that I trusted Maria and that when they were very young she had told them never to tell anyone or me about the abuse or they would be taken away from both parents and would regret it. I told the detective that not everyone knows everything that goes on in their own homes when they are gone and that they should not judge me without knowing all the facts. He told me someone called the police station claiming to be Maria's attorney and requested a copy of the police report. They would not leave their name. The report was not released. While the detective was speaking with Richard, Rolfe arrived home from work and was able to speak with the detective. One of the most disturbing parts of the investigation was when the detective walked me into the bathroom the children used. He pointed to the side of the sink next to the toilet. Engraved into the marble was the word *help*. Rolfe had inscribed it years ago in hopes that I would see it and ask who did it and what it meant. I have sat on that toilet so many times over the twelve years that we lived there and never noticed the cry for help. Richard knew about the inscription too. The detective concluded his questions and then told me he would be contacting my daughter too. She was living in Ohio and planning to attend Ohio State University.

The detective met Maria and Jim at a location away from Jim's business. Maria insisted that Jim accompany her during the interview. Maria denied any abuse toward our children, accusing them each of lying. The detective then asked her, "Are you telling me that all three of your children would lie to the police knowing that providing false information to us would constitute a crime and we would arrest and charge them?" She did not reply. Later the detective asked me if Maria was having an affair. He explained that in his many years of detective work, he had never seen anyone bring their employer along when interviewed by the police. "I guess where there is smoke there is fire," he joked.

The detective spoke to our daughter by phone, and she confirmed her brothers' statements. The detective called me and said that a special prosecutor from Los Angeles County would be handling the case. The prosecutor had asked the detective to use a telephone ruse (a lie) to bring forth a confession from Maria. After discussing with our children the process, they each said they were not comfortable with the idea and did not want to be responsible for jailing their mother. They only expressed that they wanted her to receive help. The detective told me later that the prosecutor really respected our children's forgiveness of their mother. I did too.

At the conclusion of the investigation, everyone believed the children. And the fact that each of our children just wanted their mother to receive help played a big part in that. But the statute of limitations on the last incident had passed, so no charges were filed. Maria escaped prosecution. At first, I was disappointed but soon realized that my children were able to finally tell their story. This empowered them.

Three years later, Rolfe saw his mother and Jim drive into a car wash near our home. He followed them into the service area. He jumped out of his car and approached the drivers' door of her car. She opened the car door and Rolfe said, "Hi mom."

"Hi David," she responded.

"My name is Rolfe," he corrected her.

She did not even remember her son's name. The two of them sat down together, while Jim stood away from them. Maria began to blame all our family's problems on me. Rolfe told her to stop and said, "Mom. What you did to us three kids was horrible. You know what you did. I want you to know something. I forgive you."

MY SECOND DIVORCE

From the moment I learned of Maria's criminal conduct toward our children, her romantic involvement with Jim and her domestic violence against me, it was time to file for divorce. It was time to close another chapter of my life.

It is normal to want to avoid a divorce at all costs. Who wants a bad relationship record, and there is always hope that the relationship might improve, right? I knew that at some point, I would have to look at my choices of partners and realize that part of this mess was my responsibility.

It was late October 30, 2012, when my divorce attorney called Maria and told her to be in court the following day. Maria showed up without a lawyer to the first hearing to find out that I had filed for dissolution of marriage. Maria was eventually able to secure an attorney and I filed sole occupancy of our residence and a restraining order. Maria was ordered out of the guesthouse.

At the time of filing for dissolution, our youngest child, Richard, was still a minor. The judge granted me temporary custody of him. Due to the past domestic violence and bizarre behavior, Maria was restrained from contacting me or our youngest son.

CONFESSIONS OF FORGIVENESS

I chose to forgive the people who killed my father or were responsible for his disappearance and the government who refused to provide benefits for our family and the children who made me feel like an outcast without a father.

I forgave Colleen for her assaults on me, not receiving needed help, for lying to a church pastor and friends by telling them that I was not a good husband. I forgive her for not admitting the truth of her violence toward me and my mother. I forgive myself for choosing to marry her when I knew it was not a healthy relationship. I forgive myself for looking to be rescued rather than seeking the help I needed to be a complete and healthy person.

I forgave Maria for abusing our children. I forgave her for betrayal of our marriage vows. I loved her, lifted her up in public, and never said an unkind word against her while she lied about me behind my back. I forgave her for pitting me against her family and mine. I forgave her for telling her family that I was to blame for our isolation when it was her who judged everyone who came into our lives and put us all on an island. I forgave her for leaving me that day to die in the mall when I asked her to summon help. I forgave her for failing to take responsibility for her actions. I forgave her for not valuing our children enough to get the help she needed to have a possible relationship with them in the future. I forgave her for removing our children as beneficiaries of her assets. I forgave her for lying about her mental illness. I forgave myself for enabling her, for not standing against her judgmental ways.

Colleen,

You served our military members in the Air Force. You helped churches lead music and worship. You are a great singer with great possibilities. I am proud of you for taking responsibility for your mental challenges and remaining married to your second husband to this day.

Maria,

I don't blame you entirely for our failed marriage. I want to thank you for the three wonderful children that came from our union. I thank you for providing opportunities for our children to prosper, for coaching our daughter's soccer team when the AYSO was short coaches and for encouraging our daughter to be an entrepreneur. Thank you for becoming a senior member in Civil Air Patrol for Rolfe and Richard, for driving them back and forth the long distance to the airbase. Thank you for serving on the baseball board and creating the leagues' yearbook each year to offset the league fees. Thank you for developing the layouts and graphics for many of my training manuals, which are still some of the greatest curricula ever produced in the field.

Maria, you possess many talents, and it would be unfair of me to disregard them. I wish you all the best with your future and hope that someday you will realize that the greatest treasure of your heart and mine is our three children.

LESSONS LEARNED

Events can be accidents or deliberate acts against you from another person or something you did to someone or yourself. The reason it occurred or how it happened is not as important as what you are going to do about it in order to move forward with your life. I could blame others for my position in life. I could hold onto unforgiveness, regret, grief, and hurt. I could tell myself, "I didn't do anything wrong" or "It was everybody else's fault, not mine."

I failed in two marriages. One marriage that was over before it began and another that lasted twenty-four years. I tried everything not to fail in marriage only to fail substantially. I was an enabler of dysfunction and chose incorrectly. I rescued rather than loved and failed to allow the other person to learn their lessons. Selfishly, I used marriage as a vehicle to find someone who would rescue me.

Time is our friend when entering a relationship. Give yourself enough time to really learn about someone. It is healthy and wise. Spending every day with a person with no time in between removes the chance to step back and look at your relationship from a distance. Loving people unconditionally is a very rewarding practice that frees people to become what they were truly meant to be.

There were a few clues with my first marriage and plenty of clues in my second that I should have caught. Despite the clues, I remained in a dysfunctional situation. As a result, our children suffered. Eventually, the truth will rise to the surface, and one must face the consequences of their choices. For me, the truth surfaced when I realized that you can never love someone enough if they are not willing to be honest with themselves about needing help. In the end, it was me deciding to "fix myself for a better us."

It is my hope that you will learn from my mistakes. This way you can knock over the boiling cauldron before you are scalded. Maybe you will avoid choosing the wrong person because your motives were wrong and selfish as mine were. No matter where you are at the time of this reading, please forgive yourself. It will be the greatest gift you can ever give yourself to move forward.

10

WHY FIX MYSELF?

"We cannot be our best self and do our best for others until we go deep inside and find that unconditional love of self."

—JEANNE ROBINSON

IT STARTS WITH YOU

You may have been fired from your job, or your lover or partner has left you. You may be recently separated or divorced from your spouse. You may have just had an argument or a fight with someone. It is easy to blame the other person. When you share your story with others, maybe you place yourself as the victim caught in the crosshairs of the other person's weapon.

I learned to stop blaming others and fix myself. If you were to be honest with yourself, you would have to admit that it takes two to agree and/or disagree. If you take an honest inventory of yourself, you likely will see that you contributed to the problem in some way. You may not be the instigator or the dominant player in the ruckus, but you may have been the enabler. There may be someone out there who did nothing wrong in a dispute. I just haven't met them yet.

Many people have approached me after separating from their loved ones and tried to convince me that they were the innocent victim in their abusive relationship. I would let them vent for a while as they tried to gather me as an ally. Others have shared their job firings or separation from their family. I would witness as they filed false police reports, lied in declarations and court documents, and even lied under oath in family court to receive better spousal support. Does this ring true with anyone?

When the dust finally settles, if it ever does, I am questioned by some, "What would you do? What do you recommend I do?"

That's when I humbly reply, "I chose to fix myself for a better us. I forgave those who hurt me and forgave myself for my poor choices and bad decisions. Forgiveness is the greatest gift you can give yourself. I carry a mirror wherever I go to remind myself what others see in me. I had to walk away from self-pity to avoid a life where I would be lost at SEA, where I would have no Sympathy, Empathy, or Affection for others."

The older you are, the more exposure you have to life's failures and successes. I had always loved teaching and mentoring others. I traveled around the US teaching drug influence courses and developing curriculum for the corporate world, civil service, and our military.

When I was forced to retire, told that I may never walk again, experienced some family tragedy, and lost my home, I thought my life was over. I had forgotten the love and purpose for my life. I was headed for the body of water called self-pity and depression. In this chapter I am sharing with you some of the lessons I had learned on my journey. It is my hope and prayer that you will garner wisdom from these pearls so you can wear them around your heart the rest of your life.

LOST AT SEA

When bad things happen in our lives, some of us are tempted to feed self-pity. We can remain in a self-consumed posture. We can be so wrought with our demise that we have no Sympathy, Empathy, or Affection for others. Then we are lost at SEA.

Being lost at SEA can be as bad as being lost in an ocean and waiting for a rescue that may never occur. When you are lost at SEA, you lack the basics of relationship importance. Unfortunately, many people struggle in their close relationships. They don't see those around them as human beings, but only as someone to meet their needs. That mentality is a recipe for narcissism. It could be they are incapable of loving others because they are incapable of loving themselves. It could be they have lived their lives in a survival mode for so long that they know no other way. Be forewarned that those who operate this way may have a borderline personality disorder.

We can float on the ocean of narcissism awaiting a rescue that will never come and allow those around us to become invisible, or we can do something astonishing that will positively change our lives and those around us forever. These are some of our choices: focus on ourselves, others, or both. I suggest you focus on improving yourself to avoid the SEA.

One of the examples of a child who had been raised by a mother who was lost at SEA and struggling with border line personality disorder occurred when my son Rolfe penned an adaptation of a Skylar Grey song "Invisible":

Why Do I Feel Invisible?

Even when I'm walking on a wire

Even when I set myself on fire

Every day I try to look my best

Even though inside I'm such a mess

You sit and watch with your judgmental talk

Yet I tried everything to make you see me

Believing in myself will set me free

Here inside my quiet heart

You cannot hear my cries for help

You will not spare time to listen to me

What you see I cannot be

Sometimes when I'm alone I pretend that I'm a king of my own

A world where I control the throne

You cannot hear my cries for help

I am invisible to you, a place I do not condone

I finally came to realize it's not me you despise

It's a world you created and don't realize

A way to hurt others and it's quite despicable

How you hurt others who are invisible

SELF-PRESERVATION

I define self-preservation as protecting oneself at all costs, even if it means harming others because they are invisible to you. Many self-preservationists can become narcissists. We all have self-defenses built into us to protect ourselves and our loved ones in times of extreme danger. However, when self-preservation becomes your standard modus operandi, you can destroy your relationships with others and eventually it can land you on an island. Self-preservation can be a destructive mechanism that empties you into the SEA.

THE KEY TO AMAZINGNESS

A few years ago, while driving with my sister Beverly, in a moment of self-pity, I needed some empathy. "I just want things to go well for me," I complained. "I want love in my life and for things to turn out better for me and my children." Have you ever sought pity and received a pep talk? Well, that's what happened to me. She responded to my solicitation properly. "You're an amazing person," she said. "I see the end for you. You just need to find the key to unlock your amazing life." This did not bode well with me at the time. I wanted sympathy not prophecy.

Teaching and mentoring others was my key to amazingness and success. After returning to college to finish my bachelors and master's degrees, I was placed into many mentoring roles as a fellow student. Those were some of the greatest experiences in my life. My fellow students looked to me for wisdom. Being a mentor distracted me from my failures and pushed me even further into amazingness.

We are all mentors. We are either mentoring someone for good, for bad, or for something in between. Either way we are mentoring others by the example we set. People are watching how we handle adversity and success in our lives.

Don't be the person lost in self-pity. Rather steer your ship toward others and seek that mentor inside of you. You will change your life by serving others in the process.

John C. Maxwell states, "Leadership is not about titles, positions, or flowcharts. It is about one life influencing another. We cannot become what we need by remaining what we are. Change is inevitable. Growth is optional. A man must be big enough to admit his mistakes, smart enough to profit from them, and strong enough to correct them."

Gary John Bishop in his book, *Unfu*k Yourself* (2016), talks about what to do when things happen to you in which you have no control. "You must first accept that while there are things that have happened in your life that you had no say in, you are 100 percent responsible for what you do with your life in the aftermath of those events. Always, every time, no excuses."

Bishop continues by talking about the willingness of change as being in "a state in which we can engage with life and see a situation from a new perspective. It starts with you and ends with you. No one can make you willing, and you cannot move forward until you really are willing to make the next move."

THE PUSH-ME-PULL-YOU BEHAVIOR

At the beginning of this chapter, I mentioned that many people seeking relationship advice from me try to get me to side with them in an attempt to gather as many allies as possible. If this happens to you, you may consider telling them that you take the side of good behavior and, if there are children involved, that you take the side of the children, what's best for them.

Good behavior pulls us together like magnets with opposite charges. Bad behavior pushes us away from each other like magnets with the same charges. Think about this for a moment. Let it sink in. Your good behavior attracts others to you. Your bad behavior pushes others away from you.

The benefit here is that when people do or say things that are hurtful to you, you can confront them about it by addressing their behavior and not them directly. This will help you to lower peoples' self-preservation response because you are addressing their behavior and not them as a person. You are separating the person from their behavior. There are always exceptions to this—and some people are clearly not teachable—but in general this will give you a tool that will enable you to forgive those who have hurt you and love the person who harmed you.

On October 2, 2019, one of the greatest examples of behavior separation and forgiveness occurred in a Dallas courtroom. Brandt Jean's brother, Botham Jean, was killed by Dallas police officer Amber Guyger. According to Guygers' testimony, she had accidently entered Botham's apartment, believing that it was her apartment and shot him, thinking he was an intruder. A jury found her guilty of murder, and she was given a ten-year sentence. During the penalty phase, Brandt gave a victim statement. He told Guyger:

"I don't want to say twice or for the hundredth time how much you have taken from us. I think you know that, but I just… I hope you go to God with all the guilt and all the bad things you have done in the past. Each and every one of us may have done something that we have not supposed to do if you truly are sorry. I know I can speak for myself;

I forgive you. I know if you go to God and ask him, he will forgive you. I don't think anyone can say it. I'm speaking for myself and not even for my family, but I love you just like anyone else. I'm not going to say that I hope you rot and die just like my brother did, but I personally want the best for you. I wasn't going to ever say this in front of my family or anyone, but I don't even want you to go to jail. I want the best for you because I know that's exactly what Botham would want you to do. The best would be for you to give your life to Christ. I think giving your life to Christ would be the best thing that Botham would want you to do. I love you as a person, and I don't wish anything bad for you."[1]

He then asked the judge for permission to hug Guyger. The judge granted the request, and the two of them nearly ran toward one another in a gesture that caused many in the courtroom to weep. The two of them held each other for about a minute as they cried upon one another. The healing that scene brought is an untold story. I look forward to hearing more about the impact this had upon many.

DREAMS

He was born Daniel "Rudy" Ruettiger, one of fourteen children. His dream was to attend the University of Notre Dame and eventually play football for the Fighting Irish. Many people tried to discourage Rudy from his dream. After the loss of his childhood best friend, he left for South Bend, Indiana, to pursue his dream. He started by attending Holy Cross College adjacent to Notre Dame. Rudy continued to apply for Notre Dame while building his educational resumé at Holy Cross. Rudy was rejected admittance many times, but on his last year of eligibility, he was finally accepted to Notre Dame.

Rudy spent all his time serving on the football prep squad in hopes of someday marching out of the tunnel at Notre Dame Stadium. With the last game hanging in the balance as a senior, several members suggested to the coach that Rudy "dress" in their place. The coach allowed

---

1   See: https://www.youtube.com/watch?v=NkoE_GQsbNA.

Rudy to dress for the senior game. Rudy went in for a defensive play and sacked the quarterback with twenty-seven seconds left on the clock as the fans shouted, "RU-DY, RU-DY." The players carried Rudy off the field, and he has since been the only Notre Dame player to have that distinctive honor.

Rudy says, "It starts with a dream. Visualize your dream and make a commitment. Having a dream is what makes life exciting. Never underestimate the power of a dream. It will change your life. A dream gives you the ability to determine your future."[2] Many in Rudy's family were inspired by his success and went on to achieve college degrees.

Tammie Jo Shultz dreamed of being a military pilot and applied the United States Air Force. The Air Force turned her down. She did not give up on her dream and applied for the Navy. She was accepted and began Naval aviation school in Pensacola, Florida. She graduated with the rank of ensign and obtained her military pilot wings. Tammie was not able to fight on the front lines with other military members during the Iraqi conflict, so she was made a flight instructor. She eventually became a commercial pilot. You can read more about this in Linda Maloney's book, *Military Fly Moms: Sharing Memories, Building Legacies, Inspiring Hope.* On April 17, 2018, Southwest Flight 1380 had an engine failure when a blade from the motor broke apart sending debris into the cabin and killing one passenger. Remembering her military training, Tammie Jo safely landed the Boeing 737 aircraft in Philadelphia. Her actions were recognized in a congressional resolution for her heroism. What would have happened to those passengers if Tammie Jo failed to follow her dreams?

"Dreams are like the starting pistol to get things started. They're just the beginning, but you have to have that beginning," Tammie Jo Shultz said on *Jay Leno's Garage* aired October 2, 2019. One day I was speaking to a friend about the importance of dreams. She told me that she can't afford dreams. She must live in reality. I told her that I cannot

---

2   See: https://www.rudyinternational.com/.

afford not to have them. "Dreams are what get me out of bed every day. Dreams are what guide me. Dreams distract me from my physical pain. Helping people is a dream I'm living where I never want to wake up."

HEALTHY BOUNDARIES

You may have members in your family with mental illness or their behavior creates difficulty to have healthy relationships. What do you do? Can boundaries serve as a healthy posture? In Paul Mason's book, *Stop Walking on Eggshells,* says "emotional limits are the invisible boundaries that separate your feelings from those of others. These boundaries not only mark off where your feelings end, and someone else's begin, but also help you protect your feelings when you are feeling vulnerable and provide others with access to your feelings when you are feeling intimate and safe with them. People with healthy emotional limits understand and respect their own thoughts and feelings. In short, they respect themselves and their own uniqueness." Anne Katherine (1993) says, "The right to say 'no' strengthens emotional boundaries. So does the freedom to say 'yes,' respect for feelings, acceptance of differences, and permission for expression."[3] Was it Robert Frost who said, "Good fences make good neighbors?"

VALUE OF OTHERS

As a leader in the military, law enforcement, and the corporate world, I have learned the lesson of gratitude and value for others. Leaders who take the time to recognize others will be respected and admired. In the book *Crucial Accountability: Tools for Resolving Violated Expectations, Broken Commitments, and Bad Behavior,* the authors talk about people feeling "unsafe when they believe one of two things: 1. You don't respect them as human beings (you lack mutual respect). 2. You don't care about their goals (you lack mutual purpose). When others know that

---

3   *Stop Walking on Eggshells, 112.*

you value them as a person and care about their interests, they will give you an amazing amount of leeway."[4]

Sheldon Yellen, CEO of the property and restoration company Belfor Holdings, Inc, understands this concept and takes time each day to hand write birthday cards, get well wishes, and the like to his more than nine thousand employees. When Yellen hears of accomplishments that his employees have done for the company, he takes time to recognize them.[5]

Brian Chesky, co-founder and CEO of Airbnb, wrote the forward of Chip Conley's book *Wisdom @ Work (The Making of a Modern Elder)*. Chesky explains the value of Chip and his contribution in the company as an elder, "He'll show you that wisdom has very little to do with age and everything to do with approach. He'll teach you that when you open your eyes, ears, and heart, you'll find that everybody has a story worth hearing… if you're paying close attention, someday your story could help others write their own."[6]

Everyone has value. Whether you have similar beliefs or values should not be a qualifier of value for others. You may be polar opposites, but if you take the time to listen and look for the value of others, your life will be filled with the greatest treasures, and you can take these treasures with you on your journey and enrich the lives of others.

ASSIMILATING INTO SOCIETY AFTER INCARCERATION
I spent nearly three decades of my career arresting people and many of them were incarcerated as a result. I toured jails and prisons and saw people I knew I had put there. I even arrested classmates from my youth.

---

4   Kerry Patterson, Joseph Grenny, et al., Crucial Accountability: Tools for Resolving Violated Expectations, Broken Commitments, and Bad Behavior (New York: McGraw-Hill, 2013).

5   Allana Akhtar, "A CEO who writes 9,200 employee holiday cards a year explains the value of gratitude," Business Insider, December 24, 2019, https://www.businessinsider.com/ceo-writes-7400-employee-birthday-cards-each-year-2017-6.

6   Chip Conley, *Wisdom at Work: The Making of a Modern Elder* (New York: Currency, 2018).

Do I ignore or discard these people from "fixing themselves" because they have been incarcerated or made bad decisions? Do I treat or look at them differently because they were criminals? Haven't we all erred in our lives? "But Rich, these people committed criminal acts," some will say to me. Yes, they did, and they were convicted too. No, I do not look at them any differently or worse than myself, or you! At some point, these people will be released into society. What then? Do you really believe anyone who doesn't see a positive future in front of them can be rehabilitated?

In the Society for Human Resource Management blog, Teisha Sanders wrote an article about second chances. According to research, there are nearly 70-100 million men and women in the U.S. with criminal records. This may mean that one in three persons struggles with obtaining employment.[7]

According to Second Chance Jobs for Felons, there are now at least 275 companies that hire ex-felons.[8] Providing an opportunity for people to obtain respectful employment can make a difference.

There will always be the exception from those not willing to change, but for those wanting to make a change, fix themselves, there is hope. I commend those willing to try!

Successful musician, artist and music producer, John Legend, created *Free America* in 2014 and teamed with *Unlocked Futures* to provide social entrepreneurs who have been deeply impacted by the criminal justice system the opportunity to reach their potential. Legends's company is working with many social projects to help recently incarcerated individuals assimilate back into society.

---

7   Teisha Sanders, "Second Chance Hiring - How Employment Can Change Someone's Life," The SHRM Blog, April 29, 2019, https://blog.shrm.org/blog/second-chance-hiring-how-employment-can-change-someones-life.

8   See: https://secondchancejobsforfelons.com/

THE MIRROR

King of Pop Michael Jackson sang, "If you want to make the world a better place, take look in the mirror and make that change." Stephen Gower asks the question, "What do people see when they see you coming?" Hold up a mirror and look. What do you see? Do you like what you see? I am not talking about your outer beauty. I am referring to your inner self. You know exactly what I am referring to. Let me provide a real-world example: You are in the breakroom at work having coffee with coworkers and in comes, you know, that person who sucks all the oxygen out of a room. They are the person who always finds a way to turn the attention or conversation upon themselves. You pretend you are done as you say goodbye to your coworkers and then everyone scatters.

I will be willing to bet that if you truly examine yourself, you will find that the very things that annoy you about others are things you struggle with in your own life. One friend told me that "your enemy can be your greatest teacher if you are willing to be teachable."

Imagine you are holding a mirror in front of your face just before you approach others. Think about how you approach others before you arrive and remember that mirror before you speak and act.

THE FEAR OF CHANGE—A LEADERSHIP DILEMMA

You may be asking yourself, "Why are you talking about those in leadership and their dilemma?" Are any of you leaders reading this book? You may be trying to implement change at your place of employment. You may be the leader of your family or friends. True change will begin with you! It did for me!

If you have attended business courses in college, you probably have heard the buzz about the importance of making improvements within an organization. You may be encouraged to become a change agent as Stephen R. Covey refers to it in his book *The 7 Habits of Highly Effective People.* Despite the need for improvement, many leaders have expressed to me that they struggle with change and implementing it.

How many of us embrace change? How many of us sleep on the

same side of the bed each night or drive the same route to and from our place of employment? We are truly creatures of habit, or in other words, belief determines behavior. Could it be we are afraid of breaking the routine, of disrupting the status quo? The common denominator of this fear is *change*. Just the thought of such a disruption in our lives can overwhelm us at times. As leaders, what do you do when your organization or circumstances need to change, or require re-direction, and you are faced with the responsibility of leading your people through the newly adopted change? You become the agent of change. You use your leadership talents and experience and demonstrate a positive attitude with strength and resolve. A positive attitude makes you a protagonist to change and will inspire others to overcome their fears. If we, as effective inspirational leaders, remain in a quagmire of doubt, we generate an atmosphere of uncertainty, which truly becomes a *leadership dilemma*.

THE EMPTY LOVE TANK

In the book *The 5 Love Languages: The Secret to Love That Lasts*, Gary Chapman speaks of a metaphor he had heard several times. "Inside every child," he writes, is an 'emotional tank' waiting to be filled with love. When a child really feels loved, he will develop normally, but when the love tank is empty, the child will misbehave. Much of the misbehavior of the child is motivated by the cravings of an 'empty love tank.'" Chapman cites an example of a minor child who contracted a sexually transmitted disease. Her parents were devastated and blamed the school for teaching her about sex. After speaking with the child, Chapman learned that she was suffering from an empty love tank. Her parents divorced when she was six years old, and the mother re-married when she was ten. Her mother now had someone to love her, but no one loved the child. She met a boy at school who was older than her, and she believed the boy loved her because he treated her well. She was not interested in sex as much as wanting to be loved.

THE BETTER US- AN OVERLAPPING EFFECT

How could fixing myself lead to a better us? In the drug recognition training we learned how influence changes when multiple drugs are taken in combination with one another. Sometimes the effects of the drugs produce no signs in the body, which we say have a null effect. Then there is the additive effect where two drugs enhance the effects. If one drug dilates the pupil and so does the other drug, then the pupils will be dilated. A third reaction is the antagonistic effect where each drug cancels out the other. One drug might cause the pupils to dilate and the other drug causes the pupils to constrict. The outcome is unknown. Then there is the overlapping effect where one drug produces no symptoms, but the other drug does. One drug might cause the pupils to dilate and the other drug does not effect the pupils. In that case, you will see dilated pupils.

Fixing yourself has an overlapping effect on others. People around you are affected by your positive change. They become inspired by your change. They begin to lose grip of self-pity when surrounded by your presence.

SAYING GOODBYE

When someone has left your life for whatever reason, or you may have needed to leave them, it may be a good idea to consider saying goodbye. For me, I never said goodbye to my father. His body was never found. His disappearance left a hole in my soul. Never seeing his body robbed me of closure. A grief seminar a friend of mine and I attended recommended having a funeral for a loved one in their honor and to bring a witness. Both of us really needed to do this.

First, we drove to the cemetery where my friend's father was buried. My friend attended his father's funeral, but he had some unforgiveness that he needed to express toward his father and used this opportunity to vent and forgive. Here we were two guys standing in an open mausoleum weeping, shaking, and dropping prostrate before the marble markers. Our cries echoed off the walls. At that moment, we didn't care. The look of peace and healing on my friend's face encouraged me!

We both ran to my car and sped away toward San Diego. I had no idea where to go. We drove around the fishing boat launches in the bay. As we neared one, I had the strong urge to stop and park. I am not sure if it was the right place, but the sense in my soul was so real that I believed I was where my father left on a boat with his business partner decades ago. I reached into my glovebox and grabbed my father's military dog tags. I stood in front of my car and raised them into the air while I told my father I knew he did not mean to leave me, my sister, and my mother. I told him that he had five amazing grandchildren and one of them looks just like him. I proclaimed that I would make him proud. I reached back and tossed his dog tags into the water. As I shouted goodbye, tears ran down my face. My friend covered his face as he wept alongside me. He put his arm around me and said, "we did it!"

After that day the hole in my soul was filled. The need for affirmation was gone. Saying goodbye made the difference!

LESSONS LEARNED

Are you consumed by self-pity and lost at SEA? There likely is a mentor inside waiting to be discovered. Go and find that mentor and enjoy a life of amazingness that will change other people's lives and especially yours—forever! Live out your dreams and encourage others to follow theirs. Value yourself. Look for the value in others. It is there. It's in all of us. Live a life of love. Love is risky. Love is costly. Run to it. Carry a mirror everywhere you go. Before you judge others, look at that mirror. Look at your reflection and see what might need fixing for a better us.

Fixing Myself for a Better Us required me to change. I was fearful about this needed posture. Why should I fix myself? Was I that bad of a guy? Well, hmm. The real questions for me were, "Why not?" "What can it hurt?" I know. My pride! Do I love myself enough to change? Was that love conditional? To quote a longtime schoolmate and friend, Jeanee Robinson, "We cannot be our best self and do our best for others until we go deep inside and find that unconditional love of self."

ACKNOWLEDGEMENTS

This is the most important chapter of my book. There are so many people to thank for their intervention into my life. Many of you read parts and the whole manuscript to verify its accuracy.

MY CHILDHOOD

My mother, Dolores (or Dodie as she is known by family and friends), is the hero in this story. She was really the first peace officer in the family. She investigated my father's disappearance and death so thoroughly that the mob indirectly threatened my life to get her to stop! My mother completed one and a half years of nursing school before she had to quit to provide for my sister and me. I thank my sister, Beverly, for her love and support.

I also thank my uncle Carl who paid my hospital bill without being asked to when my mother had no ability to cover such expenses.

I'm grateful to Don Drew Esq for his amazing work when he tried to obtain Social Security benefits for my family after the mandatory seven-year period had expired. Thank you to the members of the FBI, San Diego Police Department, US Coast Guard, San Diego Sheriff's Department, Prudential Insurance investigators, Richard Field, attorney representing Prudential Insurance Company, who offered assistance to my mother with her appeals to the Social Security Administration over survivors' benefits and the law firm of Musick Peeler & Garrett for investigating the tragic loss of my father.

Thank you to my childhood friends for our journey together. Some of you took the time to read parts of my manuscript and checked the details of my memory and made improvements of content and accuracy: Tim Casey, Joe Reuter, Beverly Ulrich Powers, Jeanne Oliver, Kyle Mattner, Tim Chapman MD, Brigitte Jung Whitehead (my second sister), Sherri Robirds, and Jeanne Robinson. Thank you to the Pebbleshire Pirate families: Bowes, Persinger, Flett, Eddington, Meiner, Borra, Casey, and the pirates forever in our hearts: Lori and Stacy.

SERVING MY COUNTRY
Thank you, Doug Christ (my DI) for your guidance and discipline. I thank my basic training recruits for our partnership in training, never giving up, pushing ourselves through, knowing we had the weight of the world on our backs. We are grateful for your willingness to lose your lives for the benefits of freedom we all enjoy. Go 3711! Thank you, all my childhood friends, for your lovely cards and care packages you sent me when I was in basic military training. Thank you to my fellow airmen from the 60th Military Airlift Wing: Bill Spieler, Charles Boles, Phyllis Keith Boles, Steve Bassett PhD, and Alton Findlaytor. I thank the 82nd and 101st US Army Airborne units for allowing me the privilege of deploying with you on some of the most sensitive and successful operations. Thank you to my squadron commander, Major C., of the 60th Aerial Port Squadron for trusting me to raise the standards of our troops and allowing me to serve in the Air Force Honor Guard. Thank you to my drill team and honor guard members for the memories we made as we performed in competitions, parades, and burials of our service members. Lastly, thank you to my friend, Joe Reuter. You encouraged me to serve our country and have remained a loyal and trusted friend over these many years.

THE RESCUER

I thank each and every member of the University of Southern California Department of Public Safety for your dedication to the safety of the student body, staff, and alumni. I thank all of the members of the Glendale California Police Department who worked day and night to protect the citizens of Glendale and residents of California, knowing that it could possibly cost you your life. Blessings to the families who stood by all of us.

Thank you to my training officers: James Lowrey, Richard Navarro, and Charles Lazzaretto. Thank you to the following officers for verifying the content and accuracy of the incidents: Annamaria Taylor Lazzaretto (dispatcher), Christine Goebel (dispatcher), Ian Grimes, LeRoy Hite, Tyrone Hunter Jr., Robert Murray, Mario Yagoda, Linda Reynolds, Tom Broadway, James Trudeau, Louie Mazadiego, Don Meredith, Doug Staubs, and Dennis Wilson. Special thanks to LAPD officers Dick Studdard, Tom Paige, and Michael Delgadio for allowing me to attend DRE training and teach your officers in the DRE program. Thank you Glendale Police Chief Ron DePompa who trusted me to train officers in our department, officers across our country and our US military. Thank you to Glendale Fire Department personnel for helping us with the funeral of Charles Lazzaretto.

KIDDIE COP

Thank you to officers Roger Johnstone, Ron Williams, Sue Shine, Renae Kerner, Craig Granados, Ron Insilaco, and Mike Rock. Thank you to the following school officials and teachers: Robert E. (security officer), Anne Gibson, Karen Teal, George Engbrecht, Beatriz Bautista, Ron Grace, David Duran, Pam Zamanis, Richard Sherrick, Kelly Johnson-Moore, Ken Marmie, and Mayor Richard Reyes. Special thanks to Dave Cavelli of the Staples Center executive board. Thank you to the International Brotherhood of Electrical Workers for your generous gift of a new scoring system for Roosevelt Middle School. Thank you to the University of Southern California Athletic Department for your generous support of our football team and game tickets. Thank you to

UCLA basketball coaching staff for the awards for our athletic players to attend basketball camp. Thank you to the Homenetmen Ararat Chapter Basketball coaches for trusting me to train your players.

CANCER AND THE GREATEST GIFT

Another hero in this story is my son Rolfe. He taught me a valuable lesson about love that I will never forget. Despite his own health struggles, he took the time to reach out to others during his treatment. He brought joy to the entire oncology staff when he was in the hospital.

I would like to thank my mother, Dolores (Grandma Dodie) for all the homemade soups and goodies she brought to Rolfe. Thank you to my sister, Beverly, who arranged many visits and kept them staggered so someone was always visiting Rolfe. Thank you, Richard, for willing to be tested as a possible match for your brother. Thank you to my friends Gillian, Brigitte, and Sherri for your emotional support, prayers, meals, and visits to the hospital. Lastly, I thank my fellow students (Adriana, Armen, Amanda, James, Michael, Nick, and Joey) at USC MHA master's program for your amazing encouragement and help in keeping me on track throughout the program while I was caretaking for my son.

Thank you to Hannah Schwartz and Ben Strauss who visited my son nearly every day in the two hospitals. I thank all the men and women who faithfully serve the patients at all Kaiser Permanente hospitals, treatment centers, urgent care facilities, and medical offices. A special thank you to the staff at Kaiser Hospital Pediatric Oncology Department, Woodland Hills, California: (Jessica, Elisa, Carole, Melanie, Cristina, Rossana, Kathy, Dolores, Anitha, Kristie, Mylene, Maya, Brecken, Franklin, Regina, Emilou, Blanca, Tessie, Angie, and Preetha), the staff at the City of Hope in Duarte, California, and to Susan Storch MD—a graduate of Yale University—who dedicated over thirty-seven years of her life to medicine. She is an amazing person who took great care of my son, communicated well with me and my family, and believed in the power of a positive attitude. This is the belief that eventually catapulted my son through the worst of times, through treatment, and on to remission. She retired after she saw my son's treatment and his care transition to the City of Hope. Thank you to Doctors Spielberger and Sahebi and their entire bone marrow transplant team and staff. Thank you to Derek's stem cell donor from Germany. I never met you, but I am grateful to you for volunteering your stem cells for my son's life!

RISING FROM INJURY

Thank you, Dr. Richard Anderson, Dr. Schnee, and Dr. Mark Liker for your miracle surgical skills. Thank you to my physical therapists, Kathy and Julie. Thank you to my attorney, Laurie Marenstein, and the entire staff at Universal Pain Management. Thank you to the staff at Providence St. Medical Center in Burbank, Henry Mayo Newhall Hospital, Providence Holy Cross Medical Center-Mission Hills (Rafael), and StarWorld Home Health (Juan Garcia).

PATHWAY TO LEADERSHIP

Thank you to Fran Judge, Paul Hayashida, and Tom Lorenz for helping me become a DRE. Thank you to Tom Lorenz for your partnership and guidance as we traveled abroad teaching. Thank you, Paul Brubaker, Rich Pinkerton, and Steve Gunning for trusting me with your training of Six Flags Corporation personnel. Thank you, Don MacNeil (Glendale PD ret.), for bringing me into Medtox and trusting me to co-develop curriculum for you and the staff. Thank you, Dr. Marcelline Burns, and Dr. Dary Fiorentino of the Southern California Research Institute for inviting me to be a testing officer. Thank you to president and CEO of Biocence Technology, Allan Lord, for inviting me to serve in your company. Thank you to my friend and mentor, Tim Chapman, MD, for your wise counsel, mentorship, and friendship. Thank you to the "Front-Line Leader" and CEO of Scripps Healthcare, Chris Van Gorder. A retired police officer who made it to healthcare leadership. I learned by your example.

EDUCATIONAL ROAD

Thank you to adjunct faculty member of College of the Canyons, Chris Casey, for steering me in the right direction. Thank you to the faculty and staff at Chapman University and special thank you to Suzy Mix. Thank you, Glendale Police Chief Ron De Pompa, for recommending me to the USC MHA master's program acceptance board. Thank you to the professors at USC Sol Price School of Public Policy. Thank you to my fellow students.

FORGIVENESS

Thank you, Vivian Epperson, for your love and support to my family through difficult times with Maria. You took our family on trips to the lake when we had no money to be sure our family had a summer vacation. You watched from a distance never judging anyone, including Maria. My children think the world of you for your support. Thank you to pastors Linda Lange and Gene Stabe for doing your best to intervene with love and compassion. Thank you for your wise counsel during some very difficult times.

Thank you, Dr. David Jones, PhD, for your wise counseling, therapy and advice as I traveled down my road to healing and forgiveness.

Thank you to members and leaders of Resurrected Life Ministries who taught me that separating a person's behavior from their person, is the easiest way to accept and love people.

WHY FIX MYSELF?

Thank you to all three of my wonderful children. Fixing myself was done as an example for you and to leave the right legacy for you to move forward toward your amazing future! Thank you to my sister, Beverly, for seeing amazingness from a long way off when I could not see it myself. Thank you, Jeanne Robinson for your wise counsel and friendship during the development of this book.

Thank you to my friend Gus. I miss our time together as we shared our success and failures as fathers and patriarchs of our families.

Thank you to my editor, Geoffrey Stone, and graphic artist and cover designer, Mark Karis.

Thank you, James R., You have always been one of my favorite heroes and patriots. Thank you for your guidance and advice.